1000 Years of

ENGLISH
LITERATURE

came a voice from over the
d with great power it
walk in the visions of Joe
Murder on the way
had a mask like Castlerea
smooth he stroked
been brotherhood flowed
will fit it well they
in admirable slight
by one
him human hea

1000 Years of
ENGLISH LITERATURE

Chris Fletcher
with Roger Evans, Sally Brown
and Jamie Andrews

The British Library

First published in 2003, reprinted with additional material in 2012 by
The British Library
96 Euston Road NW1 2DB

All texts by Chris Fletcher except:

By Roger Evans: Launcelot Andrewes. Ben Jonson, John Milton, John Dryden, Thomas Traherne, Introduction to the Eighteenth Century, Jonathan Swift, Alexander Pope, Daniel Defoe, Lady Mary Wortley Montagu, Samuel Richardson, Laurence Sterne, Thomas Gray, Samuel Johnson, Robert Burns, William Cowper, William Wordsworth, Jane Austen, John Keats, P. B. Shelley, Sir Walter Scott, Charles Dickens, Alfred Lord Tennyson, Edward Lear, Christina Rossetti, George Bernard Shaw, Lawrence Durrell, Dylan Thomas and Stevie Smith

By Sally Brown: Emily Brontë, Charlotte Brontë, Anne Brontë, Lewis Carroll, Thomas Hardy, Oscar Wilde, Katherine Mansfield, T. S. Eliot, Virginia Woolf, Sylvia Plath and Harold Pinter

By Jamie Andrews: Revision to General Introduction, Revision to Introduction to the Twentieth Century, John Osborne, B. S. Johnson and Harold Pinter (revision)

By Rachel Foss: Arthur Conan Doyle, Jean Rhys, Beryl Bainbridge and Wendy Cope

By Zoe Wilcox: Mervyn Peake

By Tanya Kirk: Stella Gibbons and Kenneth Grahame

By Kathryn Johnson: Tom Stoppard and Terence Rattigan

By Chris Becket: J. G. Ballard and Graham Swift

By Helen Melody: Ted Hughes (revision) and Angela Carter

By Steve Cleary: John Betjeman and Laurie Lee

By Duncan Heyes: James Joyce

Additional editorial contributions by Jamie Andrews

British Library Cataloguing-in-Publication Data
A catalogue record for this book is available from The British Library

ISBN 978 0 7123 5873 6

Designed and typeset by John Overeem, British Library Design Office
Colour reproduction by Dot Gradations Ltd, UK

Frontispiece: Detail from Percy Bysshe Shelley's manuscript for 'The Mask of Anarchy'. See pp. 114–5
Pages 222–3: Detail from Alexander Pope's translation of the 'Iliad'. See pp. 80–1

Contents

Introduction

What's so fascinating about literary manuscripts? An answer might well be found by looking at three remarkable discoveries made in 1934.

Colonel W. Butler Bowden, frantically searching in a cupboard at his home near Chesterfield for table-tennis equipment, unwittingly turned up (among a pile of old books which he at first vowed to toss on the bonfire 'so we may be able to find Ping Pong balls & bats when we want them') the 'Book of Margery Kempe', the earliest surviving autobiography in the English language and probably the earliest 'literary' work by an English woman. A safe in the bedroom of the warden of Winchester College disclosed, to the astonished scholar W. K. Oakeshott, the only manuscript of Malory's *Le Morte D'Arthur*, hitherto known solely from an edition printed in 1485 by William Caxton, through whose studio the manuscript is thought to have passed. Until the manuscript for Coleridge's verse *Kubla Khan* came to light, the only clear authority for it, and the famous story of its remarkable inspiration, was the author's 'preface' in *Christabel and Other Poems*, where it was first published in 1816. Those familiar with the poem and its evocative associations were intrigued to see not only that the carefully written out 'fair copy' (or finished text) seemed absurdly far removed from a 'fragment' snatched from the flux of drug-induced visions, but also that the attached explanation of its composition painted a far less romantic picture than Coleridge supplied in print. Not even a mention of the infamous 'man from Porlock'.

Such dramatic discoveries do not happen often, let alone grouped together in a single year. Yet any library founded with three extraordinary collections in 1753, to which it has added ever since, might be expected to be able to boast equally important items with which the remarkable class of 1934 could share its shelves. This is indeed the case with the British Library, the custodian of every manuscript featured in the pages that follow. It is a testimony to the breadth and depth of the Library's collections that a well-plotted story of the English literary tradition can be told entirely from its own holdings.

In some cases an embarrassment of riches presented itself in the compiling of this book. Which George Eliot manuscript to choose from the almost complete holdings of her novels? Byron's earliest manuscript drafts, or his very last? Which of the major Oscar Wilde plays? Or his tear-stained 'De Profundis' instead? A draft of which poem from the entire manuscript of William Wordsworth's 1807 *Poems, in Two Volumes*?

There are, of course, omissions. Although it has plenty of his letters, the library holds no significant poetic manuscripts by T. S. Eliot (his draft of *The Waste Land*, covered with Ezra Pound's annotations, is in the New York Public Library); nor, apart from annotated proofs and a number of letters, is there much of note by Yeats. For the earlier period it would be desirable to be able to boast not just the largest number of copies of *The Canterbury Tales*, but the most important among them (the Ellesmere manuscript, in the Henry Huntington Library, California).

Any literary manuscript in the hand of John Donne would find a place on any curator's list of *desiderata*. Yet only three poems actually penned by him are recorded (at the Bodleian, Harvard and in private hands). Even less has come down to us from Marlowe, while of Philip Sidney and Edmund Spenser, the world has precious little. In truth, very few writings survive in autograph (written in the hand of the author) before the Restoration. This fact played a significant part in determining the present selection. For the early and medieval period it was a choice (with one remarkable exception) of drawing upon significant copies or making do with nothing. The ever-so-slow but steady increase of the autograph record after about 1500 allowed for the inclusion of only those manuscripts actually produced by their authors.

Many remarkable individual stories of manuscript survival (such as witnessed in the year 1934) will be told throughout this book, but it is worth sketching out here the general provenance and shape of the collections to which they now belong. The British Library, an integral part of the British Museum until 1972, was effectively established in 1753 with three great collections which had already been accumulated by men of great vision and dedication. The library of the writer and antiquary Sir Robert Cotton (1571–1631), badly damaged in a fire of 1731 in Ashburnham House, Westminster, preserves a wealth of early material, much saved from the monasteries dissolved by King Henry VIII after his split from the religious authority of Rome. Thanks to Cotton we have the unique tenth-century manuscript of 'Beowulf', the longest surviving and most important early literary work in the English language and, among the treasures of the medieval period, the poems 'Sir Gawain and the Green Knight' and 'Pearl'.

The Harleian collection gathered by Robert and Edward Harley, Earls of Oxford, contains a rich vein of literary material. One verse anthology, known as the 'Harley Lyrics', comprises more than half the known secular lyrics to have come down to us from the Middle Ages, while Harley manuscript 7368 contains three pages of Elizabethan secretary hand (a difficult, heavily abbreviated style of writing) thought, almost certainly, to be the only example of Shakespeare at work. Sir Hans Sloane, Lord of the Manor of Chelsea and a wealthy and influential physician, was another important collector of manuscripts. Included are the beautiful and strange prose reflections of fellow physician Sir Thomas Browne, and a volume containing the bawdy song 'I have a gentil Cock', thought to have been variously owned by a professional minstrel and the Benedictine monastery of Bury St Edmunds.

Among other important complete (often referred to as 'closed') single collections acquired by the Library after its foundation was that of the Royal Manuscripts, formed by successive sovereigns of England. Before being given to the nation by the authority of George II in 1757, the collection of some 2000 volumes was stored in an old dormitory in Westminster School. Among them was Jonson's 'The Masque of Queens', composed for the New Year festivities at Whitehall Palace in 1609 and subsequently presented to Henry, Prince of Wales, thus escaping the fire of 1623 which broke out in the author's lodgings, to claim a great many of his papers.

T. J. Wise, bibliographer and, as it turned out, sometime forger of printed documents, was responsible for creating a fine collection of literary manuscripts. The richness, in his Ashley Collection, of the works of major authors of the nineteenth century is witnessed in these pages by drafts of works by Byron, Percy Bysshe Shelley, the Brontës and Christina Rossetti, while his enthusiasm for the manuscripts of living authors is plain to see in the draft dramatization of *The Secret Agent* sold to him by the ever-needy Joseph Conrad. By far the largest collection of manuscripts held at the British Library, however, is the Additional series. As the name suggests, this is a growing (open) collection upon whose shelves might be found for example, Lawrence Durrell's draft of *Justine*, which came to the Library by bequest in 1995.

The earliest work represented in this book is a poem written in an elevated heroic style, in alliterative verse expressed through a West Saxon idiom impossible to understand unless the language has been studied. Among the most recent are the notebooks of poet Wendy Cope, whose slyly humorous language engages with the everyday, even mundane, aspects of human existence. In between these two works (or worlds), separated by 1000 years, we have allegorical poems, didactic poems, verse romances, nonsense verse, secular lyrics, elegies, tales, short stories, novels, prose tracts, 'histories', masques – the list could go on. The term 'work' does not here exclude the genre of the literary letter (as for example, T. S. Eliot's reflections from the Margate seafront or Jonathan Swift's letter to 'Vanessa'), or the diary (such as Dr Johnson's, kept while touring north Wales). Some works exist in the process of creation or, to put it more crudely, 'draft' state, while others represent a perfect 'fair copy', as immaculate and immutable as the printed page.

What then is meant by the 'author' of a work? For at least half of British literary history the very concept of authorship is problematic. 'Beowulf' may have had no one single identifiable master, with the text gradually shaped through the course of an oral tradition until caught for posterity upon vellum by a scribe. The 'Harley Lyrics' are entirely anonymous, no one is certain whether the English poems in the copy of Charles d'Orléans's 'Prison Book' are by Charles or not, and scholars have devoted considerable energy to the task of feeding all the varying copies of *The Canterbury Tales* into a

computer to try to get as close as possible to the text intended by Chaucer. Of course, the problem would be at least partially solved if a copy of the Tales had come down to us in Chaucer's hand but, as has been discussed earlier, in an age of professional scriveners the autograph manuscript was rare indeed. And would the problem of the author's intention necessarily be solved by the scrutiny of a manuscript written in his or her own hand? Of the numerous versions of the same poem in Auden's notebook, which is the most authoritative? The author himself had problems deciding.

If many of the manuscript treasures referenced above came into the national collections through a mixture of calculation and chance, usually many years after their author's death, today's writers are keenly aware of the importance of arranging for their collections to be deposited during their lifetimes. Throughout much of the twentieth century, an impression of British institutional indifference to contemporary literary manuscripts led to a 'migration' (sometimes, unfairly, deemed a 'loss') of British authors' papers to well-funded North American libraries. From Evelyn Waugh to Graham Greene, Julian Barnes to John Osborne, the papers of writers whose texts course through the British literary psyche lie in library vaults many miles from home.

However, recent years have seen a renewed national appetite for collecting, spearheaded by a number of key acquisitions by the British Library. Major collections – often running to several hundred boxes of papers – have been added to the Library's holdings during the first decade of the twenty-first century, many of which are featured in the later pages of this book. The bawdy exuberance of a highly politicised writer such as Angela Carter, or the unapologetically working-class argot of the innovative B. S. Johnson, have expanded the range of voices represented in the nation's literary pantheon; while other new additions have resolved collecting sagas begun many years previously. When over two hundred boxes of manuscripts and diaries belonging to the former Poet Laureate Ted Hughes arrived in the Library in 2008, the acquisition closed the book on a story that had begun in the mid-1960s. At the time, husband and wife Ted Hughes and Sylvia Plath shared not only a single typewriter, but also sheets of paper: manuscript traces of a mutual creative intensity, some of which were bought soon after by the British Library through a scheme championed by fellow poet (and librarian), Philip Larkin. Later, Hughes's massive paper output found different homes in both Britain and in North America, and it was only on the tenth anniversary of his death that his final great collection – including previously unknown drafts of his *Birthday Letters* – joined those earlier scrappy typescripts at the heart of the British Library.

For many living authors, the chance to arrange the disposition of their manuscripts affords the opportunity of choosing their own plot of prime posthumous real-estate, and ensuring genial company in the years to come. Writer Graham Swift was delighted to discover that his literary remains would be stored in perpetuity across the aisle from those of his friend and fishing companion, Ted Hughes, while even old enemies might be tickled to share an archival afterlife on the climate-controlled shelves beneath the bustle of the Euston Road in central London.

But what of the future of writing itself? We hear more and more how today's authors eschew the notepad and the typewriter in favour of the PC, laptop, tablet, or even mobile; of their neglect of the postbox in favour of the email account,

Facebook status update, or tweets. Yet the history of literary transmission, from the grandest of narratives to the slightest of couplets, has always been a history of change, from tales told round the fire, to vellum, to paper, to printing, to the typewriter, telex, telegram, telephone, text, or tweet. The challenges facing the modern curator are not insurmountable. Indeed, the candid nature of much contemporary communication opens up whole new opportunities for researchers to get closer to an author's thoughts and writing techniques.

This process is changing the shape of literary manuscripts, and of the libraries that collect them. When the papers of Wendy Cope were transferred to the Library's site in London in 2011, curators didn't only need to worry about booking the van. They had to also send digital forensic experts to extract the immaterial aspects of Cope's archive: in this case, an enormous collection of over forty thousand emails stored in 'the cloud', and whose survival was, if anything, less certain, than the boxes of poetical notebooks dating back almost half a century . The ephemeral nature of these new digital manuscripts will demand ever greater attention from their creators, who require on-going support if their work is not to disappear into a digital 'black hole'.

What has not altered, however, is the magic of manuscripts. In an age that allows the almost infinite cloning of texts and images, the joy of a privileged peek at a single, unique artefact remains unsurpassed; and the more that new collaborative ways of thinking and working collapse distances and merge identities, the more important it is that the creative spark of the individual talent should be preserved, and celebrated, at the heart of the nation's cultural memory.

Early and Medieval

As twilight fell upon the outreaches of the Roman Empire at the beginning of the fifth century, pagan Germanic tribes began to move into Britain. Was it a dark age that followed? For what has come to be known as English Literature, it represented a dawn. The swift conversion to Christianity of the Anglo-Saxon invaders, and their consequent devotion to the importance of the written (rather than remembered) word, produced a culture in which writings could be formally set down, shared, preserved, passed on and developed; in other words, a culture with its own literary tradition.

Many of the earliest texts which have come down to us are of a religious, administrative or political nature: the first written specimen of Old English (or Anglo-Saxon) is a set of constitutional instructions; King Alfred's great programme of translations from Latin into Old English in the latter part of the ninth century, intended to reassert a sense of cultural cohesion in the face of Viking threats, included Bede's *Ecclesiastical History of the English People*, completed in 731; it was Alfred again who began the Anglo-Saxon Chronicle, a record of events which was continued through to the middle of the twelfth century and represents the first history of a western country in its own language; among the most outstanding sacred texts is the Lindisfarne Gospels, written down in an uncial script in about 715, illuminated to a quality unparalleled in early English art and given, some 250 years later, an interlinear translation in a Northumbrian dialect.

The political and religious significance attached to the written word contributed to the survival of works written as much for enjoyment as for edification. Without Alfred's insistence upon the importance of setting down texts in the vernacular, 'Beowulf', whose origins as a recited (or sung)

text may date back as far as the sixth or seventh centuries, might never have been captured for posterity in the West Saxon dialect by a scribe around the year 1000.

Most would agree that 'Beowulf' is the most important extant Old English literary text and it can justly take pride of place at the beginning of this book. Wulfstan's 'Sermon to the English' cannot, perhaps, be described as a literary text in the strict sense of the word, yet its strong theme, vivid language and rhetorical skill mark it out as a carefully considered, powerful piece of writing. Perhaps more than this it is represented here because, whereas the vast majority of manuscripts from the period are scribal copies which may have no immediate geographical or even temporal connection with their original authors, this remarkable document, dating from 1014, bears annotations by Wulfstan himself – surely one of the earliest examples of drafting in the vernacular.

Over half the known English secular lyrics which survive from the period between the Norman Conquest in 1066 and Chaucer's death in 1400 are to be found in just one anthology compiled by an assiduous scribe (the 'Harley Lyrics' or Harley 2253). This quite astonishing fact reflects both the predominance of religious writing in the period – the apotheosis of which might well be represented by William Langland's 'Piers the Plowman' – and the abandonment of the vernacular for some considerable time after the conquest, in favour of Latin or Anglo-Norman. When the language started to return to literary use, as for example with the verse chronicle 'Brut', written by Layamon around 1200, it did so in a way which partly carried forward the alliterative force of Anglo Saxon lines (revived again even later by the 'Gawain Poet' and William Langland), but also introduced new idioms (particularly from the French) and techniques such as the syllabic rhymed verse. By 1390 English was sufficiently re-established as a literary language for the court poet and friend of Chaucer, John Gower, to choose it over and above French or Latin, in which he was equally gifted, for his most successful work 'Confessio Amantis'.

In addition to its new forms, what has come to be known as 'Middle English' differs markedly in theme from the older Anglo-Saxon tradition. Less elevated, solemn and altogether on a more domestic scale, its loss of an earlier heroic grandeur was compensated for in a new psychological and emotional intensity. Nowhere is this better exemplified than in the candid, confessional 'Book of Margery Kempe', the first truly autobiographical piece of writing in the English literary tradition. Even in complicated allegorical works, intended to instruct the reader on the finer points of theology, a human heart beats. This is the case with the anonymous 'Gawain Poet', whose long poem 'Pearl' would seem to suggest the author's trying to come to terms with a loss actually experienced in its detailed, wrought, questioning account of the death of an infant daughter.

The Romance was undoubtedly the most popular form in the medieval period, from the early, anonymous, 'Sir Orfeo', a jaunty reworking of the classical myth, complete with Celtic setting and happy ending, to Sir Thomas Malory's late great compendium of Arthurian tales, *Le Morte D'Arthur*. The rumbustious tradition, with its tales of courtly love, fighting knights, the supernatural and numerous challenges (to keep an audience gripped), derived from an earlier and generally much more refined body of French literature – an irony not missed by those with a shrewd sense of the follies of the age and a taste for wit, such as Charles d'Orléans and Geoffrey Chaucer.

Chaucer, according to his friend, pupil and fellow poet, Thomas Hoccleve, was 'the first finder of our fair language'. Certainly the regional dialect of the British Midlands in which he wrote is more recognizable to a modern reader than that of, for example, Langland's west England idiom or that of the 'Gawain' poet, from the north-west. But Hoccleve's opinion is perhaps true in a broader sense. Chaucer's technical brilliance, the scope and humanity of his vision and the sheer ambition of his literary effort (*The Canterbury Tales* remained unfinished at his death), led many to claim him as the first poetic genius of the English language. The survival of some eighty-eight manuscripts of *The Canterbury Tales* testifies to Chaucer's great importance, popularity and influence. It also illustrates the increasing demand throughout the period for professionally produced copies of literary works – a demand leading William Caxton to issue the first English printed books (which, to the untrained eye, might be mistaken for the professionally inscribed and decorated manuscripts whose form they at first imitated). One such early book was Malory's *Le Morte D'Arthur* (1485), which stood as the authoritative text until the discovery in 1934 of the unique manuscript which, as scholars more recently established, almost certainly passed through Caxton's own printing studio in Westminster.

'Beowulf'

The origins of the work which stands at the very beginning of the English literary tradition remain shrouded in mystery. It has been conjectured that 'Beowulf' emerged from an oral tradition as early as the seventh century and that it was most probably composed in the eighth, but it is known to us only from the miraculous survival of a vellum manuscript written out in Old English by an anonymous scribe around the year 1000. The long alliterative poem, written in a West Saxon dialect and possibly intended for recitation to the accompaniment of a harp, tells the story of Beowulf, a fifth- or sixth-century Scandinavian warrior hero, who rids the Danish kingdom of a terrible monster, Grendel, and his vengeful mother. His prowess is rewarded with a gift of lands, which he rules in peace for fifty years. A dragon, revenging the theft of a goblet from its hoard, attacks Beowulf's people and he once again goes into battle, a much older man. Although the dragon is killed, with the help of a loyal subject, Beowulf is mortally wounded. His funeral pyre and a prophecy of disaster for the kingdom provides a magnificent conclusion to a poem which, besides offering a compelling narrative, provides a richly allegorical exploration of the emergence of the new Christian faith set against the deeply rooted paganism of the past.

If other copies of 'Beowulf' were ever made, none has come to light. This manuscript, showing the opening of the poem, narrowly escaped destruction in 1731 when the library of its owner, Sir Robert Cotton, caught fire at Ashburnham House in Westminster. The damage is clearly visible around the ragged edges of the vellum pages, which were subsequently set into a modern mount and binding. In 1753 Sir Robert Cotton's library, together with those of Robert and Edward Harley, Earls of Oxford, and Sir Hans Sloane, formed the foundation collections of the British Library (then the British Museum Library), where the manuscript became available for study. It is hard to imagine, given the poem's pre-eminence today, that it was not until 1815, when it was published in Copenhagen by Grimur Jonsson Thorkelin, that it became known at all. An Oxford Professor of Anglo-Saxon, John Josias Conybeare, next turned his attention to the poem between 1817–20, collating Thorkelin's work with the manuscript and preparing the ground for the various subsequent editions and translations which have helped to make it justly famous.

Left: The 'Beowulf' manuscript was copied by two scribes. The changeover between the two can be seen at the end of the first three lines of f. 175v.

Opposite: The manuscript containing 'Beowulf' is known to this day as Cotton Vitellius A XV, a vestige of Robert Cotton's cataloguing system, in which his precious volumes were stored in book cases surmounted by the busts of Roman Emperors; thus the 'Beowulf' manuscript was the fifteenth volume to be found on shelf A in the bookcase supporting the head of Vitellius. The script is known as English minuscule (or lower case) and would have been written out with a quill pen – an instrument which only started to lose favour from the second quarter of the nineteenth century, with the development of the steel nib. Shown opposite is the opening of the poem.

HPÆT PE GARDE[na]

na ingear dagum. þeod cyninga
þrym ge frunon huða æþelingas elle[n]
fremedon. oft scyld sceþing sceaþe[na]
þreatum monegū mægþum meodo setl[a]
of teah egsode eorl syddan ærest pe[arð]
fea sceaft funden he þæs frofre geba[d]
peox under polcnum peorð myndum þah
oð þ him æghþylc þara ymb sittendra
ofer hron rade hyran scolde gomban
gyldan þþæs god cyning. ðæm eafera pæs
æfter cenned geong ingeardum þone god
sende folce tofrofre fyren ðearfe on
geat þ hie ær drugon aldor ... ase lange
hpile him þæs lif frea puldres peal dend
porold are for geaf. beapulf pæs bren ...
blæd pide sprang scyldes eafera sceda
landum in ... Spa sceal ... ... ma godū
ge pyrcean fromum feoh ... gyf tum on ...

Wulfstan
d. 1023

Wulfstan, or 'The Wolf' as he was known in his writings, was brought into the world in the late tenth century after a difficult birth which resulted in the death of his mother. Of his younger years very little is known, although he probably entered holy orders at the important religious centre of Ely in Cambridgeshire. He was appointed Bishop of London from 996 to 1002, when he was advanced to the Archbishopric of York and also given care of the see of Worcester. The veneration in which he was held is indicated by the fact that he came to be regarded as a saint at Ely, in which Cathedral he was buried at his own request.

Wulfstan's political importance is clear from his role as a prominent royal counsellor, responsible among other things for drawing up legislation on behalf of Kings Ethelred II and Canute. These sacred and secular skills are both seamlessly and subtly joined in the most famous of Wulfstan's many writings, 'Sermo Lupi ad Anglos' (The Sermon of the Wolf to the English), which he first delivered in 1014. In attributing various unwelcome affairs of state to divine retribution, Wulfstan is able to launch a cleverly camouflaged critique of unjust laws, burdensome taxes and other political issues of the day.

Below left: In this volume of Anglo-Saxon documents, King Cnut (or Canute) and his Queen, Aelfgyu, are shown presenting a cross upon the alter of Newminster and Hyde Abbey, Winchester, *c.* 1020.

Opposite: The text of Wulfstan's sermon is found in just five manuscripts. That which is in the British Library is particularly significant in that the scribal text includes what are thought to be Wulfstan's own annotations, allowing us to make an extremely rare direct association between a document of this age and its original author.

A translation of the opening of Wulfstan's Sermon as shown opposite. The introductory passage is in Latin:

The sermon of the Wolf to the English, when the Danes were greatly persecuting them, which was in the year 1014 after the Incarnation of our Lord Jesus Christ:
Beloved men, know that which is true: this world is in haste and it nears the end. And therefore things in this world go ever the longer the worse, and so it must needs be that things quickly worsen, on account of people's sinning from day to day, before the coming of Antichrist. And indeed it will then be awful and grim widely throughout the world. Understand also well that the Devil has now led this nation astray for very many years, and that little loyalty has remained among men, though they spoke well. And too many crimes reigned in the land, and there were never many of men who deliberated about the remedy as eagerly as one should, but daily they piled one evil upon another, and committed injustices and many violations of law all too widely throughout this entire land.

SERMO LUPI AD ANGLOS · QUANDO DANI
MAXIME · PSECUTI SUNT EOS QUOD FUIT
AÑ · ÄLO · XIIII · AB INCARNATIONE DÑI
NRI IHV XPI :~

Leofan men gecnawað þ soð is· Deos worold
is on ofste· 7 hit nealæcð þā ende· 7 þy hit is
on worolde aa swa leng swa wyrse· 7 swa hit sceal
nyde· for folces synnan· ær Antecristes tocyme·
yfelian swyþe· 7 huru hit wyrð þōnne
egeslic 7 grimlic· wide on worolde· Understandað
eac georne· þ deofol þas þeode nu fela geara·
dwelode to swyþe· 7 þ lytle getreowþa wæran
mid mannū· þeahhy wel spæcan· 7 unrihta
to fela ricsode on lande· 7 næs a fela manna
þe ymbe þa bote· smeade 7 swa georne
swa man scolde· ac dæghwamlice man ihte
yfel æftr oðrū· 7 unriht rærde· 7 un
laga manege· ealles to wide· gynd ealle
þas þeode· 7 we eac forþā habbað fela byrsta
7 bysmara gebiden· 7 gif we ænige bote gebidan
sceolan· þōn mote we þæt to gode earnian· bet
þōn we ær þyssan dydan· 7 forþā mid miclan
earnungan· þ yrre we us betwux· þa yrmða þeah
onstead· 7 mid swyþe micelan earnun
gan þ bote moton æt gode geræcan·

The 'Harley Lyrics'

Although songs of love and high living were undoubtedly popular in the Middle Ages, the vast majority of surviving manuscripts from the period address theological matters. This reflects, perhaps, not only the concerns of a more sacred age but the fact that the transmission and preservation of the written word fell mainly to the religious houses. We must therefore celebrate the fact that over half the known secular lyrics which have come down to us from before 1400 survive in this one manuscript, known as the 'Harley Lyrics' (after its owner Sir Robert Harley). Despite its great literary significance, the vellum volume is fairly unexceptional in appearance and contains, in addition to its remarkable collection of non-didactic material, a diverse range of often very conventional prose and verse writings. The lyrics are written in a hand of around 1330, suggested to be that of a professional Shropshire scribe (another, earlier, scribe being responsible for an initial sequence of Anglo-Norman religious pieces). The original compiler of the manuscript, as is predictably the case with such early texts, should not be identified as the author of the verses; indeed, the identification of different dialects suggests that neither should the verses be attributed to any one poet.

Opposite: Perhaps the most famous among the thirty-two 'Harley Lyrics' is 'Spring'. Its ebullient images of the world re-awakening after winter contrast with the doleful mood of the disappointed lover, who threatens to forego the season's 'bright wealth' of joys and hide himself away in the forests. In the first verse, transcribed below, new love is associated with spring's perpetual return.

Lenten ys come with love to toune
With blosmen and with briddes roune, (blossom, bird song)
That all this blisse bringeth.
Dayeseyes in this dales, (Daisies)
Notes swete of nyghtegales,
Ech fowel hire song singeth.
The threstelcock him threteth oo, (thrush chides on)
Away is here wynter wo
When woderove springeth (woodrush)
This foules singen ferly fele, (vast numbers of birds)
And wlyten on here wynne wele, (warble in their great joy)
That al the wode ringeth

An engraving of Robert Harley, 1st Earl of Oxford, after a painting by Sir Godfrey Keller, 1714.

At chirche ate shomb chepyng ase dogge y am dyue
sit me were leuere of hue ben to fare hue
to eke of al my kynne
atte constorie heo tenneþ vs eke
ant chisscheþ vs enele e boyse to sare
a pruest proud ase a po
seþþe weddeþ vs bo
Op de heo wortheþ vs bo
sor wymmene ane

Lenten ys come wiþ loue to toune
Wiþ blosmen e wiþ briddes roune
þt al þis blisse bryngeþ
Dayes eyes in þis dales
notes suete of nyhtegales
vch foul song singeþ
þe þrestelac him þreteþ oo
Away is huere wynter wo
When woderoue springeþ
þis foules singeþ ferly fele
Ant wlyteþ on huere wynne wele
þat al þe wode ryngeþ
þe rose rayleþ hire rode
þe leues on þe lyhte wode
Waxen al wiþ wille
þe mone mandeþ hire bleo
þe lilie is lossom to seo
þe fenyl e þe fille
Wowes þis wilde drakes
Miles murgeþ huere makes
Ase strem þt striketh stille
Mody meneþ so doþ mo
Ichot ych am on of þo
For loue þt likes ille
þe mone mandeþ hire lyht
So doþ þe semly sonne bryht
When briddes singeþ breme
Deawes donkeþ þe dounes
Deores wiþ huere derne rounes
Domes forte deme
Wormes woweþ vnder cloude
Wymmen waxeþ wounder proude
So wel hit wol hem seme
ȝef me shal wonte wille of on
þis wynne weole y wole forgon
Ant wyht in wode be fleme

In may hit murgeþ when hit dawes
In dounes wiþ þis dueres plawes
ant lef is lyht on lynde
Blosmes bredeþ on þe bowes
al þis wylde wyhtes wowes
So wel þeh onder fynde
ynot non so freoly flour
ase ledies þt beþ bryht in bour
Wiþ loue who mihte hem bynde
So worly wymmen are by west
one of hem ich herie best
from yrlond in to ynde
Wymmen were þe beste þing
þt shup oure heuene kyng
ȝef feole false nere
Heo beoþ to rad vpon huere red
to loue þer me hem lastes bed
When heo shule fenge fere
Lut in londe are to leue
þah me hem trewe troube ȝeue
for tricherie to ȝere
When trichour haþ is troube yplyht
Byswyken he haþ þt suete wyht
þah he hire obes swere
Wymmen war þe wiþ þe swyke
þt feir ant freoly ys to fyke
þt fere is o to fonde
So wyde in world ys huere won
in vch a toune vntrowe is on
from Lystresþe to Londe
Of treuþe nis þe trichour noht
Bote he habbe is wille ywroht
at steuenyng vmbe stonde
ah fool is þt lieuis hem on
to late comeþ þe ȝeyn char
When loue on haþ ybounde

'Sir Orfeo'

The genre of the Breton Lay (or song) can be traced to the French poet, Marie de France (fl.1160–90), who composed twelve lyrics dedicated to Henry II of England. The tradition probably stretches much further back, however, into the ancient days of Celtic minstrelsy. Although such an early provenance is thought unlikely in the case of 'Sir Orfeo', it is perhaps the most famous example of the form in Middle English, with its familiar theme of love set in the mysterious 'otherworld' of fairyland. The poem, probably written in the early fourteenth century, takes its inspiration from the well-known classical legend of Orpheus but neatly transforms the sad ending of disobedience and loss of the earlier narrative into a happy vision of fidelity and order. Just below the middle of the page displayed, Sir Orfeo declares that he would rather lose his life 'than to lese the quene my wyfe'. On realising that his queen has indeed been lost – to a fairy king, no less – he visits the 'otherworld' in disguise. He charms the king with his musical skills, wins back his wife, and returns home to prove the loyalty of his subjects.

Just three copies of the poem survive. This one is written out in an early fifteenth-century hand, with a sixteenth-century note suggesting an association with a curate of Baddesley Clinton in Warwickshire.

The text differs in many respects from the other extant sources (in the National Library of Scotland and the Bodleian Library, Oxford). This suggests a wide oral transmission of the poem by minstrels, resulting in much variation when the texts came to be set down.

Below left: The fear of strange abductions evidently extended a powerful influence upon the medieval imagination. This illustration from the magnificent Taymouth Hours of 1325–35 depicts the 'wild man' seizing and ravishing a lady out walking in the woods.

Opposite: In the following slightly modernised transcription, the queen describes to Orfeo the terrifying appointment she is obliged to keep, under threat of death, with the fairy king. The text begins on the second line down in the manuscript:

And then he brought [me] again home
Into our owne orcharde,
& sayde to me this afterwarde,
"Loke to-morew that thou be
Here under this ympe-tre;
& yif thou makest ony lette,
Wher-euer thou be, thou shalt be fet, [fetched]
& to-tor thy lymes alle, [torn apart]
That nothing thee help schalle;
& though thou be ever so torn
Yet shall thou away be born."
When the Kyng herd this case,
'Out!' he seyde, & Alase!
Me wer leuer to lese my lyfe
Than to lese the quene my wyfe!'
He axed consel of many a man,
But non of hem help hym can.
On the morewe, when tyme came,
The kyng his armes, forsoth, he name,
& two hundred knytes with hym,
Wele y-armed, stout and grym;
With the quene went he
Into the orchard, under the tre.
Ther made they watche on every syde,
& cast them there fir ti byde
& suffre deth every-chon,
Er sche schulde from hem gon;

And þis forest ouȝtoke onoy
& say þe þeaute droū home
in to onyr olde oþayde
& fende to me pro aftyde
tofe to mofelle þ you be
heye þudey put ympe þe
& ȝif þ makeþ þin lotte
Whor on þ be þ schalt before
& to toȝe þy þymes alle
þ no puȝ þo holp schalle
& pann þ be fo to toȝe
þis schalt þ a þoy be boȝt
Why þo þe þyng þ þyþe pio caþt
out þe forde & Alaſe
me Laoyr lord to loſe my lyfe
pū to loſe þe quene my þrfe
he ayed counfel of many & men
but no of þe hole heū ran
on þe mofoþe & þe tyme came
þe þyng þo þymes foþooþ he wanue
& toþe hudþeþ þurpeþ & þy
þyele pymeþ þowt a gyne
þet þe quene þeþt þe
unto no oþþayd þudey þe þo
þ made por þatþe or oū fede
& caſt þo þe for to biþe
& fuffeþ doþþ oþþ eþon
þy þeþe þþulde pþ þe þou

William Langland
fl. 1360–1387

William Langland was born in the West Midlands around 1332, was well educated, took minor orders and most likely lived a life of modest means in London with his wife and daughter. Little else is known of him – other than that he wrote one of the masterpieces of medieval literature. 'Piers Plowman' opens 'in a somer seson' on the Malvern Hills and proceeds to portray the corruption rife in contemporary society, famously represented by a 'Fair Feeld ful of Folk'. The poem's narrative, which slips between dreaming and waking states, is shared by a character referred to as 'Long Will', who is often associated with Langland himself, and an honest ploughman, Piers, who displays Christ-like attributes. Although the long poem is a complicated allegorical work, intended first and foremost for the edification of its readers, its sheer imaginative power and poetic brilliance raise it far beyond the level of theological dogma.

About fifty manuscripts of the poem survive, in various locations. There are three versions, the earliest of which, the 'A-text', has been dated to around 1362. It is quite probable that Langland himself spent at least the last twenty years of his life trying to perfect the work, with each new version embodying his own additions and revisions. Another theory suggests a number of different authors may have had a hand in the poem's development.

Below left: This fine-printing of the title poem, published in New York in 1901, portrays the 'lovli lady'.

Opposite: Shown here is the latest version of the poem, the 'C'-text, in a manuscript volume written out by a scribe probably just before the end of the fourteenth century. The poet describes a 'loveli ladi' who explains three truly necessary things: meat, clothes ('vesture') and drink. A stern warning is issued about the last, and a later owner of the manuscript has marked a passage relating to the Biblical story of Lot, noting in the margin that 'thorow dronkkynnis all myschf ys wrott' (through drunkenness all mischief is wrought).

he wolde þat ʒe wrouʒten · as his wille were
ffor he is fader of faith · and formere of alle
To be faithful to him · he gaf ʒow fiue wittis
To worschepe him þer wiþ · while ʒe liuen here

Wher fore he het þe elementes · helpe ʒow alle times
and bringe forþ ʒoure biliue · boþe linnen and willen
In mesure þauh hit muche were · to make ʒow at ease

The comaunded of his curtasie · in comune þree þinges
ben none so nedful as þo · and nemene hem i peude
and ʒiuene hem bi ʒelke · ʒeuerse hem wher þe likeþ

þe furste of hem is fode · and uesture þe secounde
and ʒriuke · þat do þe good · but do hit nouʒt out of tune

Loke hou loth in his lijf · poru likeʒoure ʒrinke
wickedli he wrouʒte · and wreyed god almiʒti
In his ʒronkenesse a day · his douʒtren he dizte
and lai bi hem boþe · as þe bok telleþ

In his glotenie he gat · guyles þat we cheyses
and al he witte hit þe wyn · his wickede dede

Inebriemus eū uino ⁊ dormiamus cū eo ut seruaʒ possimꝰ

poru and poru wommau · was loth þer encombred
ffor wiþ oreʒ delitable ʒrinke · boþe daies and nyʒtes
uesure is medicine · poru pou michel uilue
al is nouʒt good to þe goste · þat þe gut asket
Ne lisflose to þe likame · þat lef is to þe soule

loue nouʒt þi likame · for a laere him techeþ
þat is þis wyecheode world · wolee þe bi gile
ffor þe feud and þi flech · foleben to siðeze
and þat sley þi soule · and poru sette hem in þin heyte
I wisse þe þat þou be iwar · leste þei þe differne

A madame meyci quod i · me likeþ wel ʒoure wordes
But þe monere on þis molde · þat men so faste biholden
Telleþ me nou to wham · þat tresour apendeþ

So to þe gospel quod sche · and seo what god seide
Whan þe peple aposede him · of a peni in þe temple
and ye askede of hem whose was þe coigne
Cesares þei seiden · soþliche we knolwen
Reddite cesari · quod god · þat to cesar bi longeþ
Et que sunt dei deo · or elles ʒe don ille

For riʒtful resou schulde · ʒelbele ʒow alle
and kyndelich · be waʒdeþ ʒoure soules to kepe
and titmy of ʒoure tresouʒ · to take hit at ʒoure nece

The 'Gawain Poet'
fl. *c.* 1380

The 'Gawain Poet' remains one of the most mysterious figures in English literature. We know almost nothing about him, other than that he was associated with a noble house in the late fourteenth century, and that he wrote the four untitled poems which survive in just one manuscript and have come to be known as 'Pearl', 'Sir Gawain and the Green Knight', 'Patience' and 'Cleanness'. The poet was a contemporary of Chaucer, but as J.R.R Tolkien has pointed out, the two could hardly have written in more different styles. Whereas Chaucer's works are often characterised by their immediacy and use of an increasingly dominant southern idiom, his anonymous counterpart, from the more sparsely populated West Midlands, created a didactic and richly complex body of work composed, not in the language of the everyday, but in the powerful alliterative forms of the earliest Anglo-Saxon poets. His polished use of this highly literary and elevated style places the poet at the forefront of what has been termed the alliterative revival of the late fourteenth century.

Of the four poems, 'Sir Gawain' and 'Pearl' are the most celebrated. The latter may well reflect the author's own experiences in its moving depiction of a father's anger, sorrow and incomprehension at the death of his infant daughter, or 'Pearl'. Dreaming upon her grave, he sees her on the other side of a river, grown up and radiantly dressed. She reproaches him for his sorrow but, overcome with longing, he plunges in to join her. Although he immediately awakes, still a grieving man in the mortal world, he is able to find some consolation in the thought that his daughter is now a 'queen of heaven'. 'Sir Gawain' has an enduring folkloric quality and the story is familiar to many who have never read the original poem. During a great New Year's Feast at Camelot, a mighty horseman attired all in green offers his neck to the sword of anyone who will promise to yield his own in return, one year hence. Gawain accepts the challenge, embarking upon an adventure in which his fidelity and courage are tested to the full. The poem achieves a great thematic richness from its fluent, instructive and entertaining assimilation of pagan, romance and Christian elements.

Left: This homely illustration from the manuscript shows the father's amazed reaction on finding his lost 'Pearl'.

Opposite: This small and naively decorated vellum manuscript of around 1400, written in the tight, angular hand of a copyist, escaped destruction in the Cotton fire of 1731. It remained largely hidden from the world until the palaeographer and Keeper of Manuscripts, Sir Frederic Madden, published it in 1839. It provides the unique source for the four known poems of the 'Gawain Poet'. Shown here is the opening of 'Pearl'.

John Gower
1330–1408

'Confessio Amantis', John Gower's long poem of about 1390, is one of the most skilled treatments of love in the English language. The poet, of an educated and landed background, refers in his text to both Richard II, who commissioned the work, and, in an early version, at least, to his friend Geoffrey Chaucer, who is encouraged to proceed with his own 'testament of love', 'Troilus and Criseyde'. The narrative, written in Middle-English in deft octosyllabic couplets, relates a dialogue between a priest and his 'confessor', who is encouraged to consider how the seven deadly sins have frustrated his chances of love. In return for his honesty, the priest draws upon a great store of 'goodly' tales, each chosen to teach the man how to overcome sin and find true love. In the beautiful and moving conclusion of the poem, however, the confessor gives up his quest – not only because the priest reminds him of higher truths (symbolised by a gift of black beads) but because he is by now an old man. It is likely that Gower, who possibly practised law, composed his poem in the priory of St Mary Overie, Southwark, where he had lodgings in the latter years of his life. He lies magnificently memorialised in the church there, known today as Southwark Cathedral.

The effigy of John Gower on his tomb in Southwark Cathedral. Representations of three of his most famous works cradle his head.

Opposite: Shown here is the beginning of the fourth book (of eight) which features sloth. 'Lachesse', as the confessor reveals, has in the past cunningly prevented him from wooing 'the swete May'. Some of the proverbial phrases in the following passage are still in current use.

Upon the vices to procede
After the cause of mannes dede,
The ferste point of Slouthe I calle
Lachesse, and is the chief of alle,
And hath this propreliche of kinde,
To leven alle thing behinde.
Of that he mihte do now hiere
He tarieth al the longe yere,
And everemore he seith, Tomorwe;
And so he wol his time borwe,
And wissheth after God me sende,
That whan he weneth have an ende,
Thanne is he ferthest to beginne.
Thus bringeth he many a mischief inne
Unwar, til that he be mischieved,
And may nouht thanne ben relieved.
And riht so nouther mor ne lasse
It stant of love and of lachesse:
Som tyme he sloutheth in a day
That he nevere after gete may.
Now, Sone, as of this ilke thing,
If thou have eny knouleching,
That thou to love hast don er this,
Tell on.
My gode fader yis.
As of lachesse I am beknowe
That I may stonde upon his rowe,
As I that am clad of his suite:
For whanne I thoghte my pursuite
To make, and therto sette a day
To speke unto the swete May,
Lachesse bad abide yit,
And bar on hond it was no wit
Ne time forto speke as tho.
Thus with his tales to and fro
My time in tarieng he drouth:
Whan ther was time good ynouh,
He seide, "An other time is bettre;
Thou schalt mowe senden hire a lettre,
And per cas wryte more plein
Than thou be Mouthe derst sein."
Thus have I lete my time slyde
For Slouthe, and kepte nouht my tide,
So that lachesse with his vice
Fulofte hath mad my wit so nyce,
That what I thoghte speke or do
With tarieng he hield me so,
Til whanne I wolde and I might nouht.

This lavishly decorated manuscript is an early issue (sometimes referred to as a 'publication') of the poem, written out by a professional scribe around the time of the poet's death in 1408. Forty-nine manuscripts of the poem are known. The marginal rubrication (words in red) indicates whether the confessor or the priest speaks and is also used for Latin summaries and notes.

Geoffrey Chaucer

c. 1343–1400

Geoffrey Chaucer was born some time between 1339 and 1346, probably in Thames Street to a 'citizen and vintner of London', and is likely to have studied either at Oxford or Cambridge University. By 1357 he appears to have been a page in the household of Edward III's son, Lionel, Duke of Clarence and in 1359 he 'bore arms' against the French, who captured and successfully ransomed him. His father died in 1366 and shortly afterwards he found himself in the King's service, campaigning again in France. He married, probably by 1366, Philippa, a lady in the Queen's household. This no doubt helped his advancement at court, although it has been suggested, from his literary treatment of matrimony, that the union was not a happy one.

Business took Chaucer to Italy in 1372–1373, where he visited Florence and Genoa and possibly saw the great poets Petrarch and Boccaccio, in whose works he found inspiration. On his return to London, he found continuing favour, being granted a daily pitcher of wine – which later became a 'tun', to be delivered by the King's chief butler, one Thomas Chaucer, probably the poet's son – and taking up a senior position as a customs official.

Living comfortably in Aldgate, in the city of London, Chaucer embarked on occasional secret diplomatic missions abroad, to France, Italy and Flanders. By 1386, however, his professional fortunes had taken a downward turn, with his replacement at court possibly the result of political machinations. It was during this period of hardship, most likely in April 1388, a year after his wife's death, that Chaucer undertook the famous pilgrimage to Canterbury which formed the subject of his late, great and unfinished work, *The Canterbury Tales*.

In 1389 he was appointed Clerk of the King's Works, a worthy post which, nevertheless, failed to compensate for the loss of his earlier positions and was, in any case, short-lived. Further occupation was found for him as a 'forester', with his meagre salary supplemented in 1394 by a pension from King Richard II. Chaucer's financial worries (he appears to have been somewhat profligate) were finally alleviated on the accession of Henry IV, who doubled his previous income and allowed him in 1399 to lease a house in the grounds of the Lady Chapel, Westminster. According to the inscription on his (later) tomb, Chaucer died on 25 October 1400. He is buried in Poet's Corner, in Westminster Abbey.

Left: Chaucer is one of the earliest English writers to have been accurately represented in portraits.

Opposite: This early copy of The Canterbury Tales, dating from the period shortly after the poet's death, shows the prologue. The provenance of the vellum manuscript has been traced back, with a reasonable degree of certainty, to its original owners. By 1800 it had passed into the hands of William Petty, Marquess of Lansdowne, whose collection of manuscripts was acquired by the Library in 1807.

han þat Aprill wyþe his schoures sote
þe þroughte of march haþe pced to þe rote
And baþed eueꝛy veyne in suche lycoure
Of whiche vtue engendꝛed is þe floure
whan zephirus eke wᵗ his swete breþe
Inspyꝛed haþe in euy holte & heþþe
The tendꝛe croppes & þe ȝonge sunne
Haþe in þe rame his half cours ꝛunne
And smal foules maken melodye
þat slepen alnyȝt wiþ open ẏhe

So pꝛikley hem nature in þeꝛ corages
Than longen folke to gone one pilgrimages
And palmeres for to seke strraungere strondes
To ferne haloldes cowþe in sundꝛy londes
And specialy from euy schyꝛes ende
Of Ingelond to Canterburi þeẏ wende
The holy blisful martur for to seke
That hem haþ holpen whan þeẏ were seke
It befil þan in þat sesone vpon a daie
In Suthewerke att þe tabard as I laie
Redi to wende on my pilgremage
To Canterburie wiþ ful deuotte corage
At nyȝte was come in to þat hostellerie
wel nyne and twente in a companye
Of sundꝛy folke þy auenture ẏfalle
In felaushipe & pilgrimes were þeẏ alle
To warde Canterburi þit wolde ride
The chambꝛes & stables weren wyde
And wele werin esede att þe beste
An shortly whan þe son was to ꝛeste
So had I spoken wᵗ hem euythone
þat I was of heꝛ felaushipe anone
And made forward eꝛly for to rise
To take oure waie þaꝛe as I ȝowe deuise
Bot napeles while I haue time & space
Er þat I ferþer in þis tale pace
Me þenkeþ it accordant to ꝛisone
To tell ȝowe all þe condicioun
Of iche of hem so as it semed me
And whiche þeẏ were & of whate degꝛe
And eke in whatte arraie þat þeẏ were inne
And att a knyȝte þan wolt I furst be ginne

Chaucer, according to his friend, pupil and fellow poet, Thomas Hoccleve, was 'the first finder of our fair language'. At a time when most important poetry was written in Anglo-Norman or Latin, his use of English played a central role in establishing the literary language we recognise today. Although he composed several major works throughout his life, *The Canterbury Tales* has long been regarded as his comic masterpiece. Probably conceived around 1387 and remaining unfinished at his death, *The Canterbury Tales* introduces readers to a series of memorable characters on the pilgrimage from The Tabard Inn in Southwark, London, to Canterbury. Each provides in their own distinctive voice a rich, often hilarious, and always telling insight into the human condition.

Some eighty-eight manuscript copies of *The Canterbury Tales* survive, attesting to the popularity of the poet's work. None is thought to be in Chaucer's own hand. Indeed, even among the large number of official documents connected with his professional career, it is impossible to establish which, if any, bear his own writing.

Above: An older Chaucer is represented here in an early fifteenth-century manuscript of 'The Regement of Princes', a long poem by his friend and pupil, Thomas Hoccleve. Chaucer points to a verse in which Hoccleve explains that those who, unlike him, have forgotten the master poet, 'By his peynture may ageyn him fynde'.

Opposite: This important edition of the works of Chaucer was published in 1896 at William Morris's Kelmscott Press in Hammersmith. The illustrations were designed by Sir Edward Burne-Jones.

HERE BEGINNETH THE TALES OF CANTERBURY AND FIRST THE PROLOGUE THEREOF

WHAN THAT Aprille with his shoures soote
The droghte of March hath perced to the roote,
And bathed every veyne in swich licour,
Of which vertu engendred is the flour;
Whan Zephirus eek with his swete breeth
Inspired hath in every holt and heeth

The tendre croppes, and the yonge sonne
Hath in the Ram his halfe cours yronne,
And smale foweles maken melodye,
That slepen al the nyght with open eye,
So priketh hem nature in hir corages;
Thanne longen folk to goon on pilgrimages,
And palmeres for to seken straunge strondes,
To ferne halwes, kowthe in sondry londes;
And specially, from every shires ende
Of Engelond, to Caunterbury they wende,
The hooly blisful martir for to seke,
That hem hath holpen whan that they were
    seeke.

BIFIL that in that seson on a day,
In Southwerk at the Tabard as
I lay,
Redy to wenden on my pilgrym-
    age
To Caunterbury with ful devout
    corage,
At nyght were come into that hostelrye
Wel nyne and twenty in a compaignye,
Of sondry folk, by aventure yfalle
In felaweshipe, and pilgrimes were they alle,
That toward Caunterbury wolden ryde.

The 'Sloane Lyrics'

c. 1400

It has been suggested that this song (illustrated opposite) might refer to an elaborate and much prized piece of jewellery. Although that may be the case on one level, its real jollity lies in its bawdy puns and sly sexual allusions:

> I have a gentil cock – crowyt me day
> he doth me rysyn erly – my matynis for to say
> I have a gentil cock – comyn he is of gret
> his comb is of reed corel – his tayil is of get
> I have gentyl cock – comyn he is of kynde
> his comb is of red scorel – his tayl is of inde
> his leggs ben of asor – so gentil & so smale
> his spors arn of sylver qwyt – in to the wortewale
> his eynyn arn of cristal – lokyn al in aumbyr
> & every nygt he perchit hym – in myn ladyis
> chambyr

Might this richly suggestive jewel of a lyric have come down to us in a more familiar form? Anyone who has taught, or been taught, one of the jauntiest of Mother Goose's nursery rhymes might well think so:

> Goosey Goosey Gander!
> Whither shall I wander?
> Up stairs, down stairs,
> In my lady's chamber!

The anonymous medieval poet's bright and clear imagery strongly evokes Chaucer's description of the cock Chauntecleer in The Nun's Priest's Tale, which also has a red coral comb, azure legs, white spurs, jet black colourings and the quality of 'gentilness'. This fact helps us to date it to about the beginning of the fifteenth century. The manuscript volume in which it appears contains some fifty-seven English carols and seventeen other songs, often referred to collectively as the 'Sloane Lyrics', after Sir Hans Sloane who owned the manuscript. It is thought that the modest book resided, at some earlier stage, on the library shelves of the Benedictine monastery at Bury St Edmunds in East Anglia and that, despite its lack of musical notation, it may originally have belonged to a wandering minstrel.

Sir Hans Sloane, who lends his name to the 'Sloane Lyrics', the manuscript of which formed his great library.

Left and opposite: 'I have a gentle Cock' appears in an important manuscript volume, sometimes known as the 'Sloane Lyrics', containing fifty-seven English carols (a song with a uniform verse structure and repeating burden) and seventeen other lyrics in English and Latin. The manuscript's hybrid composition reflects the gradual replacement of parchment by paper during the medieval period.

I syng of a myde · þ is makeles
kyng of alle kynges · to here sone che ches

he cã also styllo · þer his modr was
as dew in apyrllo · þt fallyt on þe gras

he cam also stylle · to his modris bовr
as dew in aprylle · þt fallyt on þe flor

he cam also stylle · þer his modr lay
as dew in aprylle · þt fallyt on þe spray

modr & maydyn · was non но but che
wel may swych a lady · goddis modr be

I have a gentil cook · crowyt me day
he doþ me rysyn erly · my matyns for to say

I have a gentil cook · comyn he is of gret
his comb is of red corol · his tayl is of get

I have a gentyl cook · comyn he is of kynde
his comb is of red scorol · his tayl is of іnde

his leggs ben of asor · so gentil & so smalе
his spors arn of syluer qwyt · in to þe wortewale

his eynyn arn of cristal · lokyn al in aumbyr
& euy nyзt he perchit hy · in my ladyis chaumbyr

Omnes gentes plaudite
I sawe myny bryddis setyn on a tre

he tokyn here flyзt & flowyn away
wt ego dixi have goоd day

many qwyte federis hat þe pye
man hoо mor synggy my lyppyn arn so drye

Margery Kempe
c. 1373–*c.* 1439

In 1934 the earliest surviving autobiography written in the English language was discovered in wonderfully eccentric circumstances. According to family legend, Colonel W. Butler Bowden, searching in a cupboard at his home near Chesterfield for a ping pong ball, became frustrated at the piles of old books which hampered his efforts, expostulating to a friend: 'I am going to put this whole lot on the bonfire tomorrow and then we may be able to find Ping Pong balls & bats when we want them.' The friend besought him to allow an expert to check the books first. Shortly afterwards, the medieval scholar Emily Hope Allen identified an undistinguished looking manuscript as the 'Book of Margery Kempe', a vivid confessional work dictated in 1436. Before this discovery, all anyone knew of the work were the seven pages of extracts printed by Wynkyn de Worde in 1501.

As she could neither read nor write, Kempe dictated the final version of her book to a priest in her home town of Lynn in Norfolk, with the present manuscript being copied down shortly afterwards by a scribe named Salthows, possibly under her direction. In a work much more intimate and revealing than other writings in the medieval visionary tradition, Kempe relates her severe mental anguish after the birth of the first of her fourteen children, her vision of Christ and spiritual conversion, her three years of sexual temptation, her pilgrimages to Italy and the Holy Land, her vow of chastity in 1413 (evidently accepted by her husband, John, whom she later nursed through six years of illness), her stormy relationship with the church authorities, her meeting with another highly influential woman, the mystic Julian of Norwich, and her later years of prayer and charitable works. There are no records of Margery's death, although we know that her husband and eldest son died around 1431 and that she was still alive in 1439.

Opposite: The provenance of this manuscript is still by no means clear, although an inscription in the volume indicates that it belonged at an early stage to the Carthusian Monastery of Mount Grace, Yorkshire. After a certain amount of prefatory text, Margery's confessional autobiography (written in the third person) begins towards the foot of the page.

Whan this creatur was twenty yer of age or sumdele mor, sche was maryed to a worschepful burgeys and was wyth chylde wythin schort tyme, as kynde wolde. And aftyr that sche had conceyved, sche was labowrd wyth grett accessys tyl the child was born, and than, what for labowr sche had in chyldyng and for sekenesse goyng beforn, sche dyspered of hyr lyfe, wenyng sche mygth not levyn. And than sche sent for hyr gostly fadyr, for sche had a thyng in conscyens whech sche had nevyr schewyd beforn that tyme in alle hyr lyfe. For sche was evyr lettyd be hyr enmy, the devel, evyrmor seyng to hyr whyl sche was in good heele hir nedyd no confessyon but don penawns be hirself aloone and all schuld be forgovyn, for God is mercyful inow ...

In the absence of any likeness of Margery Kempe we must make do with generic contemporary portrayals of women. Shown here is a woman, with rosary beads, engaged in devotional reading.

A Schort tretys of a creature sett in grett pompe &
pride of ye world whech sythen was drawyn to owr
lord be gret poverte & sekenes & schanne & gret repref
in many dyuers contre & places of whech tribulacyons sum
schal ben schewed aftyr not in ordyr as it fellyn. but as
ye creatur cowd han mend of hem whan it were wretyn
for it was xx. zer & mor fro tym ye creatur had for
sake ye world. and besyly clef on to owr lord or ye boke
was wretyn. not wythstondyng ye creatur had gret
cownsel for to don wryten hyr tribulacyons & hyr felin
gys. And a whyte frer proferyd hyr to wryte frely yf sche
wold. And sche was warnyd in hyr spyryt yt sche xuld
not wryte so sone. And many zerys aft sche was bodyn
in hyr spyryt for to wrytyn. And yus zet it was wretyn
fyrst be a man whech cowd neythyr wel wryten englysch
ne duch. so it was vn able for to be red but only be
specyal grace. for it was so euel obloquie & sclawndyr
of ys creatur. yt yer wold selde men beleue ye creatur.
And so at ye last a preste was soi mevyd for to wrytyn
ys tretys & he cowd not wel redyn it of a iiij. zere
to gedyr & sythen be ye reqst of ye creatur & compel
lyng of hys owyn consciens he asayd a gayn for to
rede it & it was mech mor esy. yan it was a for tyme
And so he gan to wrytyn in ye zer of owr lord a. m.
CCCC. xxxvj. on ye day next aft mary maudelyn
aft ye informacyon of ys creatur. ⁘ Caplm 1

When ys creatur was xx. zer of age or sum dele
mor sche was maryed to a worschepful burgeys of lynn
and was wth chylde wt in schort tyme as kynde
wolde. And aft yat sche had conceyued sche was labowrid
wyth grett accessys tyl ye chyld was born & yan what
for labor sche had in chyldyng & for sekenesse goyng be
forn sche dyspered of hyr lyfe. wenyng sche mygth not
leuyn. And yan sche sent for hyr gostly fadyr. for sche

Charles d'Orléans
1394–1465

Charles d'Orléans was born in Paris into a world of considerable wealth and aristocratic privilege – as might be expected of a nephew of King Charles VI of France. Aged eleven, he married Isabelle, the sixteen-year-old widow of England's King Richard II. In 1407 he endured the first great sorrow of his life, when his father, Louis, was assassinated by Burgundian enemies. Just a year later his mother Valentina died, leaving him both his inheritance and title. Charles married for the second time in the summer of 1410 (his first wife having died in childbirth) and went to battle at Agincourt in 1415. Reputedly pulled from under a mound of corpses, he was held by his English captors for twenty-five years. During his incarceration he would have enjoyed a life of reasonable comfort and privilege, in accordance with his aristocratic status; certainly he moved between various important noble houses, forging strong friendships and putting his considerable intellect and political skill to good use as a mediator in negotiations between England and France.

At some stage, perhaps during his years in England, Charles began a series of lyrics later arranged into a sequence representing the story of the 'lover-prisoner'. The degree to which his narrative is autobiographical has been much debated; although the poems conform to courtly conventions, certain personal details ring true. At some stage between his return to France and his death in 1465 at the old age of seventy, the indefatigable Charles arranged his poems in a manuscript which is known as his 'Livre de Prison'. The original 'Prison Book', which contains both English and French verse, is preserved in the Bibliothèque Nationale in Paris but of the several subsequent manuscripts inspired by the sequence, that featured here is among the most important. Many of the English poems, although not literal translations from the French, clearly derive from the originals and at least one commentator has suggested their author to be none other than Charles himself.

Opposite: The song illustrated here (still awaiting completion by its illuminator) takes the form of a punning confession made to a priest by a lover who has 'stolen a kiss of great sweetness'. Playing upon the religious and linguistic conventions of the time, the lover vows to 'restore' (or revoke) the sin, leaving us – and, presumably, his 'ghostly father' – wondering whether he truly means to repent or has every intention of returning the kiss to his sweetheart.

My Gostly fader y me confesse (My holy father)
First to god and then to yow

That at a wyndow, wot ye how, (you understand how)
I stale a cosse of gret swetnes
Which done was out avisynes (without premeditation)
But hit is doon, not undoon, now

My Gostly father y me confesse
First to god and then to yow

But y restore it shall dowtless (without doubt)
Ageyn if so be that y mow
And that god y make a vow
And elles y axe foryefnes

My Gostly father y me confesse
First to god and then to yow

Another copy of the lyrics dating from the late fifteenth century, includes a famous picture of the Tower of London, where Charles was held for a period during his long captivity in England.

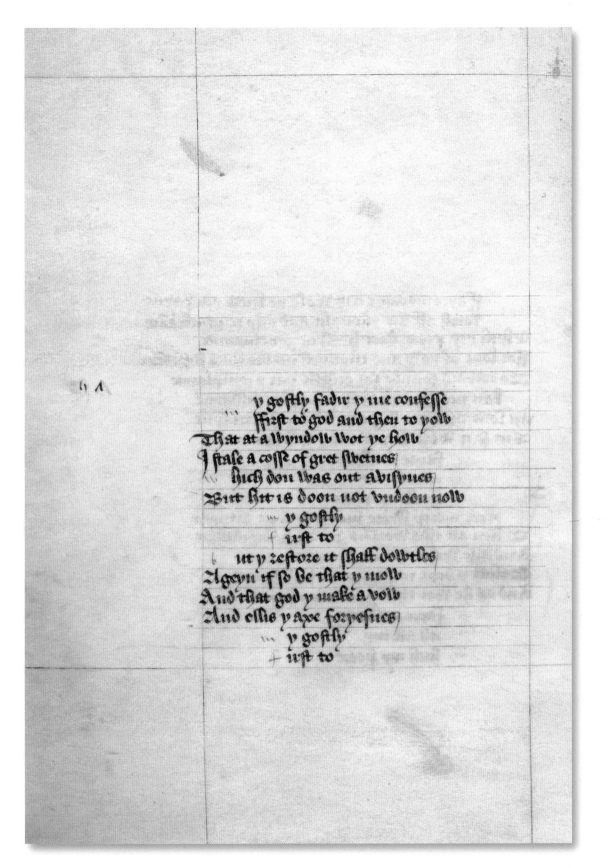

y goftly fadir y me confeſſe
ffirſt to god and then to yow
That at a wyndow wot ye how
I ſtaſe a coſſe of gret ſwetnes
which don was out aviſynes
But hit is doon not vndoon now
    y goftly
    irſt to
   ut y reſtore it ſhall dowtles
Ageyn if ſo be that y mow
And that god y make a vow
And ellis y axe foryefnes
    y goftly
    irſt to

Sir Thomas Malory

c. 1416–1471

Le Morte D'Arthur was composed, at least in part, between 1468 and 1470 while Malory endured one of his many stints in prison. Charged in 1451 and 1452 with attempted murder, extortion, robbery (of Combe Abbey), and rape, the man who was three times a member of Parliament and a knight by 1441, was jailed at least eight times in his life and managed to escape from prison twice. Whether Malory – whose name derives from an ancient Norman word meaning 'unlucky' – was just plain bad or the victim of political intrigue is uncertain. Indeed, until recently virtually nothing was known of him beyond what could be deduced from authorial and editorial references given in his vast prose interpretation of the legend of King Arthur. It is now accepted that Malory was born at some time between 1414 and 1418 to influential parents and can be identified in the records as the knight of Newbold Revel, Warwickshire. Before his parliamentary representations of Warwickshire, Bedwin in Wiltshire and Waresham in Dorset, it is quite possible that he fought in France; it seems probable, later on, that he became heavily embroiled in the civil strife raging between the Lancastrian and Yorkshire nobility, switching allegiances at least once. Despite his extravagant propensity for trouble, it has been suggested that Malory achieved a degree of prosperity in the latter part of his life, as is witnessed by his burial in the affluent Greyfriars church in the city of London.

In 1485 William Caxton, England's first printer, wrote in the preface to his edition of *Le Morte D'Arthur* (of which only one complete copy survives, in the Pierpont Morgan Library, New York) that he was 'enprised to imprint a book of the noble histories of the said King Arthur and of certain of his knights after a copy unto me delivered, which copy Sir Thomas Malory did take out of certain book of French, and reduced it into English.' The only known manuscript source for the work, written out by two scribes and attributed to 'a knyght presoner sir Thomas Malleorre', was discovered at Winchester College in 1934. Although not necessarily the 'copy' text referred to by Caxton (whose edition contains numerous variants from the manuscript), scholars have demonstrated that it almost certainly passed through his Westminster premises during the period 1480–1483. Crucial to their arguments is the presence, on four of its pages, of offset markings from type used by Caxton. Spun into a rich and lengthy whole mainly from numerous tales belonging to the French romance tradition, the work was evidently a commercial success from the outset, being twice reprinted by Caxton's one-time assistant, Wynkyn de Worde. Although of undoubted importance and influence – witness its appeal to the gothic imagination of the late nineteenth century and, in turn, the popular interpretations of Hollywood – there is a tradition of critical scepticism which can be traced back hundreds of years. In 1568 Robert Ascham noted that the 'whole pleasure of [the] book standeth in two special points, in open manslaughter and bold bawdry: In which booke those be counted the noblest knights that do kill men without any quarrel, and commit foulest adultery by subtlest shifts.'

Opposite: The work of two scribes can be seen here in the unique manuscript of *Le Morte D'Arthur*, with the first eight lines penned in a hand different from that which follows.

In the begynnyng of Arthure .ffor he was chosyn kynge
by adventure and by grace for the moste pty of the barouns knewe nat he was
Uther pendragon son But as merlyon made hit oppynly knowyn But
yet many kynges and lordis helde hym grete werre for that cause But well
Arthur on com hem aff the moste pty dayes of hys lyff he was ruled by y counceile
of merlyon So hit felle on a tyme kyng Arthur seyde vnto merlyon my ba
rounes woll let me have no reste but nedis I muste take a wyff & I wolde none
take but by thy councile and advice hit ys well done seyde merlyon that
ye take a wyff ffor a man of youre bounte and noblees scholde
not be wyt oute a wyff Now is y ony seyde Marlyon that
ye love more than a nop ye seyde kyng Arthure I love Gwe
nyvere the kynge doughtir of lodegrean of p londe off Camelerde the whyche holdyth In his house the table rounde that ye
tolde me he had hit off my fadir Vther And this damesell is the
moste valyaunte and fayryst that I know lyvyng or yet that evir
I coude fynde Sertis seyde marlyon as off her beaute and fayre
nesse she is one of the fayrest on lyve. But and ye loved her not
so well as ye do I scholde fynde you a damesell off beaute and
of goodnesse that scholde lyke you and please you and youre
herte were nat sette. But there as mannes herte is sette
he woll be loth to returne. that is trouthe seyde kyng Arthur
But merlyon warned the kyng covertly that Gwenyver was nat
holsom for hym to take to wyff ffor he warned hym that Laun
celot scholde love her and she hym agayne. and so he turned his
tale to the adventures off the Sankegreal. Then he desyred off
the kyng for to have men wt hym y scholde enquere of Gwenny
and so the kyng graunted hym and so Merlyon wente forthe
vnto kyng lodegean off Camylerde and tolde hym off the desire
of the kyng y he wolde have vnto his wyff Gwenyn his doujt
That is to me seyde kyng lodegreans the beste tydyng that
evir I herde. that so worthy a kyng off probesse & noblesse wol wedde
my doughtt And as for my londis I wolde geff hyt hym yf I wyste

Robert Henryson
c. 1439–1506

Robert Henryson is often referred to as a Scottish Chaucerian, a term applied to a group of poets working in late medieval Scotland whose characteristic style echoes the humanism, wit and narrative tone of, as Henryson himself put it, 'the worthie Chaucer'. Although there is some sense in this classification, commentators have increasingly come to view and respect Henryson as an important and original poet in his own right. Retrieving his poetry from Chaucer's far-reaching shadow has, however, proved easier than bringing the man himself into the light. History offers us precious few references to Henryson. Around 1506, the Scottish poet William Dunbar in his elegy 'The Lament for the Makaris', says of death that:

In Dunfermelyne he hes done roune
With Maister Robert Henrisoun.

Another reference can be found in a seventeenth-century manuscript containing a Latin version of Henryson's poem 'The Testament of Cresseid' (a sequel to Chaucer's 'Troilus and Criseyde') which notes that it was 'made & written by one Mr Robert Henderson sometimes cheife schoole master in Dunfermling'. Otherwise, no convincing record can be found of Henryson's attendance at the Scottish universities of the time, Glasgow and St Andrews, and it has been suggested that he may have graduated abroad before taking up a teaching position at the school associated with Dunfermline Abbey.

In addition to his 'Testament of Cresseid', a number of poems can be ascribed to Henryson, among them 'The Tale of Orpheus and Erudices his Quene.' Although his 'Morall Fabillis of Esope' also take a famous source from antiquity as their starting point, their style is unmistakably rooted in the poet's Scottish background.

Below left: The second, third and fourth verses of Henryson's 'Tail of the Cok and the Jasp'. `

Opposite: This charming manuscript of Henryson's 'Fables', written out in an anonymous hand, was produced one year after the first printed edition of 1570.

The first verse of his 'Tail of the Cok and the Jasp' describes how the brisk, bold, and self-satisfied Cock discovers a jewel accidentally swept out of a house:

Ane Cok, sum tyme, with feddram fresch and gay,
Richt cant and crous, albeit he was bot pure,
Fleu furth upon ane dung hill sone be day:
To get his dennar set was al his cure.
Scraipand amang the as, be aventure
He fand ane Jolie Jasp, richt precious,
Wes castin furth be sweping of the hous

The taill of the Cok and the Jasp

Ane cok sum tyme with feddrum fresch & gay
Richt cant and crous albeit he was bot pure
FleW furth vpoun ane dung hill sone be day
To get his Denner set was all his cure
Scrapand amang the as be auenture
He fand ane Joly Jasp richt pretious
Was castin furth be sweping of the hous

Renaissance and Restoration

The arrival of the printing press in Britain at the end of the fifteenth century far from spelt the end of the manuscript as a means of distributing literary texts. As late as the 1660s Katherine Philips seems to have positively mistrusted print (in a turbulent political age where discretion was all), while John Donne saw no collection set in type during his life and was known to his admiring contemporaries almost exclusively through circulated manuscripts. George Peele's 'Anglorum Feriae' of 1595 – written for no less a personage than Queen Elizabeth I herself – evidently had to wait until 1830 before it was published.

Given the proliferation of Donne's verse in manuscript anthologies, it seems surprising that only three poems appear to have survived in his own hand. Yet as for the preceding generations of writers, rarely was any importance attached to an author's own manuscript *per se*. It is entirely possible that handwritten texts by Shakespeare (of which only one highly disputed example exists) and Marlowe (in whose hand we have nothing at all), once no longer required, ended up lining pie dishes or were put to even less dignified use in the Elizabethan 'jacques', as the 'saucy poet' John Harington might have put it. The fact that all the examples here are, indeed, written at least partly in the hand of their authors makes them, therefore, extremely rare among the considerable number of sixteenth- and seventeenth-century manuscripts which have descended to us.

In many cases the existence of autograph manuscripts can be owed to sheer good fortune, such as Thomas Traherne's 'Commentaries of Heaven' which, flitting in and out of London sale-rooms in 1844 and in 1854 (unidentified) was eventually rescued from a Lancashire rubbish-tip in 1967. 'Believe as you List', a play written in Philip Massinger's own hand and marked up as a prompt copy, was rediscovered 'among a mass of rubbish' in 1844. Harington's poetical manuscript, covered in ink smudges and compositors' instructions, is the only known Elizabethan example to have somehow escaped from the printer's workshop once set in type. The album of verse, kept close by Thomas Wyatt through the thick and thin of missions abroad, imprisonment and the fever to which he eventually succumbed, seems to have narrowly avoided destruction at the hands of its subsequent owners, who casually treated it as scrap paper for their doodlings, sums and commonplace musings. We should rather celebrate the rare survival of one half of the 'loose Papers' bequeathed by Samuel Butler to his friend William Longueville than mourn the loss of the other.

Occasionally, enough importance was attached to an author's manuscript at the time of its creation to secure its preservation. 'The Masque of Queens' was composed for the New Year festivities at Whitehall Palace in 1609 and written out by Ben Jonson, in his elegant secretary hand, for presentation to Henry Prince of Wales, thus entering the royal library. In other cases posterity has later collectors to thank. Sir Thomas Browne's notebooks caught the eye of Sir Hans Sloane, another physician with literary tastes, and were it not for William Petty, 1st Marquess of Lansdowne, whose collection was acquired for the nation in 1807, by far the most significant autograph manuscript by John Dryden would be lost to us. The fact that Dryden's poem remained unidentified until 1966 raises the exciting prospect of other important autographs quietly waiting to be discovered, possibly beneath our very noses. Just one sonnet in draft by Shakespeare would cause an academic hysteria well worth seeing. But perhaps, after all, this increasingly secular age was the least suited for the long-term preservation of literary manuscripts. Gone were the didactic texts inscribed on vellum, bound between boards of oak and designed to last. With playwrights competing against one another to satisfy the rapacious appetite for popular entertainment, poets chasing wildly unpredictable preferment and patronage at Elizabeth's court, and everyone subject to the continual vicissitudes of strife at home or abroad, who – apart, of course, from Sir Thomas Browne – would spare a thought for posterity?

Sir Thomas Wyatt
1503–1542

Sir Thomas Wyatt was born at Allington Castle, Kent, in 1503. Educated at Cambridge University, he was twice imprisoned by Henry VIII: first in 1536 for his close association with Anne Boleyn and secondly (and more seriously), in 1541, for his support of Thomas Cromwell, whom the King executed in 1540. Egerton Manuscript 2711 was acquired by the British Museum Library in 1889. Its 136 surviving leaves contain 107 of Wyatt's poems, his penitential psalms, two letters and three other poems, one by Henry Howard, the Earl of Surrey.

During this period one would expect such a collection, even if compiled during the author's lifetime, to comprise copies rather than original autographs. But in this case, several of the poems are indeed written in Wyatt's own hand with many of the remaining scribal copies bearing his own corrections and revisions. The album, which establishes the Wyatt canon, was kept from 1537 until his death in 1542 of a fever, contracted at Sherborne, Dorset (where he lies buried), after an exhausting ride towards Falmouth on a diplomatic mission. As such, it probably accompanied him abroad before his second spell in prison, while he served his king as Ambassador to Charles V.

Certainly his departure from Spain in June 1539 is recorded in his handwritten epigram 'Tagus farewell'. The volume later came into the possession of the Harington family, whose various members carelessly employed it for doodlings, mathematical equations, miscellaneous prose musings and scribbles.

Opposite: The complexity of Wyatt's working methods are much in evidence in this autograph draft of a poem preoccupied with the torments of 'wrathfull love'.

Transcription of the poem illustrated opposite:

What rage is this? What furour of what kynd?
What powre, what plage doth wery thus my mynd?
With in my bons to rancle is assind
         What poyson, plesant swet?

Lo se myn iyes swell with contynuall terys
The body still away sleples it weris:
My fode [n]othing my faintyng strength reperis,
         Nor doth my lyms sustayne.

In diepe wid wound the dedly stroke doth torne
To curid skarre yt neu shalle retorne.
Go to, tryvmph, reioyse thy goodly torne,
         Thi frend thow dost opresse.

Opresse thou dost and hast off hym no cure
Nor yett my plaint no pitie can procure
Fiers tygre fell, hard rok with owt recure
         Cruell rebell to love!

Ons may thou love neu belovffd agayne
So love thou still & not thi love obttayne
So wrathfull love, with spite of lust disdayne
         May thret thy cruellty hert.

A portrait of Sir Thomas Wyatt after Hans Holbein.

ł cuf

Surrey
fo. 41

What rage is this ł what furour of what kynd
what power what plage thus doth my mynd ?
with in the tomb to rauke ł it offend
what poyson plesaunt swete

Lost my rygh swell in contynuall teyll
the body styll sleples away it weris
my foode nothing ' my faintyng strenght reperis
nor doth my tyme sustayne .

In siepe the dedly strok doth torne
to cruel starre ynew shall retorne /
Go to ł try vmph ł reioyse thy gladly torne
thi frend thou dost opresse .

Opresse ỹ dost / and hast off hym no cure
nor yett my no pitie can procure
fierb tygre fell / hard rok it owt reme
cruell rebell vnkynd to love !

may ꝰ love new beloffd agayne
my to slave not to love obtayne .
my wratchfull love so sone this doth disdayne
may thott thy cruelgar to peat .

Launcelot Andrewes
1555–1626

The 1611 revision of the Bible, made for King James I and known as the 'Authorized Version', is one of the great glories of English prose. Regrettably the manuscript of it is lost. It was last heard of as having been sold, together with the copyright, to the King's Printer, Robert Barker, who died in 1645. The work of revision was entrusted to about fifty distinguished scholars who took the Bishops' Bible of 1568 as a basis but nevertheless had the Hebrew and Greek texts before them as they proceeded. Work began in 1607.

First on the list of divines appointed to the task was Launcelot Andrewes, then Bishop of Chichester. He was born in Barking, Essex, and educated at Pembroke Hall, Cambridge. In the early stages of his career he was chaplain to Queen Elizabeth I and Dean of Westminster. In 1609 he became Bishop of Ely and in 1618 Bishop of Winchester.

Andrewes's reputation for great scholarship – he is said to have mastered six ancient languages – ensured his work on the Book of Joshua and the books following it as far as Chronicles, as well as on the five Books of Moses. He was an immensely respected church leader whose very presence awed the often lewd King James into decency. T. S. Eliot considered Andrewes's sermons among the finest written but of even greater beauty are his prayers, Preces Privatae, published in 1648. The saintliness of his nature is touched on in the exhortation to be found near his tomb in Southwark Cathedral: '…stay, it will be worth thy tarrying to know how great a man is here…'.

An engraving of Bishop Launcelot Andrewes by Wenceslaus Hollar, 1643.

Opposite: This letter was written, early in Andrewes's career, on 24 May 1589, to Sir Francis Walsingham, one of Queen Elizabeth's privy councillors. Walsingham was instrumental in Andrewes's obtaining the living of St Giles, Cripplegate, and in his becoming a prebend of St Paul's Cathedral. The hand is beautifully measured and fluent.

I doe, in humble maner, crave pardon of yo Honor, in yt I
have not my self attended, in ye redeliverie of th'enclosed;
to render to yr H. my bownden dutie of thanke, for the
cotents therof.   Being, besides myn excercise to Morrow,
on Monday morning bt ye Feast of my Fathers Company
to pch at Deptford: I promised my self fro yo Honor,
a favorable dispensation, for yr forbearing of my presence till th:
What tyme, I shall waite on yo Honor, to present unto
yr same, my professed humble thankes, o not my thankes
only, but my service o my self to, to be ordered o employed
by yr H. every way.   The same of verie right o dutie
belonging to yr H: as well, in regard, of yor Honors great
bountie to me these yeares past: (Wch while I live I am
bownd to acknowledg.) as now, for ye instant procurment
of these 2 prebends, the one of them no sooner indeed,
but yr other streight begoon.   They are to me, both
sufficient witnesses of yr Honors care for my well doing,
o mindfulnes of me upon any occasion: my prayer to God
is, yt I may not live, unworthy these so honorable dealings
but yt in some sort, (as his holy wisdome shall appoin.
I may prove serviceable to yr Honor, o to, yor Honors
deere care, this church of or's.   What yr H
hath, or shall, further vouchsafe to promise, in my name, in
this, or ought else by me to be done: shalbe I trust so
satisfied, as shall stand to yo Honors lyking, every way.
So recommending, to yo H. yr perfiting of yo Honors owne
benefite,   wt my verie humble dutie, I end.
The L. Jesus, of his great goodnes, graunt unto this Realme
long to enioy yo Honor.   Amen.   Maij 24.

                                        Yor Honors in all humble dutie
                                        o service   so most bownd.

                                        L.   Andrewes

Sir John Harington
c. 1561–1612

'When thou doste feel creeping tyme at thye gate, these fooleries will please thee less.' One piece of foolery may have been on her mind more than most when Queen Elizabeth I uttered these sobering words in 1603 in the closing weeks of her life to her godson, the 'saucy poet' Sir John Harington. Some seven years earlier, in 1596, he had published *A New Discourse of a Stale Subject, called the Metamorphosis of Ajax*, a work whose title teasingly hints at its surprising contents. A 'jacques', or what is still sometimes called a 'john', was Elizabethan slang for a privy or toilet. Harington's carefully illustrated satire, which perhaps predictably failed to secure him the royal praise for which he hoped, proposed a detailed prototype of what is instantly recognisable today as a flushing lavatory – a convenience which, as it turned out, failed to find ready employment until the nineteenth century.

A more serious but less celebrated work is Harington's translation of *Orlando Furioso*, originally written by the Italian Ludovico Ariosto and published in 1532. Harington was reputedly banished from court by Elizabeth for corrupting her ladies with translations plucked from the 'less seemly' parts of the text and charged not to return until he had completed a full English version. He took up his task with gusto and it appeared in 1591.

The elaborate title page of this first printing of *Orlando Furioso* includes a portrit of the handsome author and his distinguished-looking dog, Bungy.

After a spell in Ireland with the ill-fated Earl of Essex and many subsequent years negotiating the vagaries of the royal court (upon which he commented with great flair in the letters and miscellaneous writings published in 1769 under the title *Nugae Antiquae*), Harington died at his home of Kelston, near Bath, on 20 November 1612. His entry in the British *Dictionary of National Biography* describes him as a man 'entirely destitute of restraint'.

Opposite: This manuscript, written out at least in part by Harington himself, is thought to be the only surviving Elizabethan poetical manuscript known to have been the copy text for a contemporary printer. Although the manuscript, which comprises only part of Harington's translation of *Orlando Furioso*, is essentially a fair copy, it does contain last minute revisions and additions. Thus in the second stanza shown here, the word 'prices' is replaced by 'soverayns'. The manuscript bears smudges of ink from the workshop and various instructions for setting the type. The author uses different hands for his marginal annotations and the introductory 'arguments' which preface each of the poem's books.

N. 3
145

N. 4
146

The Argument of the 19. booke.

Angellyca doth heale, and wed Medore :
Marfysa, with that other worthy crew,
Landes (after travell long) vppon the shore
of Amazons; whear when the lawe they knew,
Guydon, that thither come but late before,
fforght with Marfysa, who his myght men shew;
but when the combat ceast, for want of lyght,
Guydon intreats them both with him that nyght.

None can deem ryght [1] who faythfull frendes do rest,
whyle they bear sway, and rule in great degree,
for then both fast and fayned frendes are prest,
whose faythes seem both of on effect to bee;
but then reuolts the faynt and fayned guest,
when welth is wronged, and fortune seems to flee.
but hee that lovd indeed remayneth fast,
and lovs and serues, when lost and all ys past. /

Of all mens thoughtes weare wrytten in theyr fart, [2]
some one that now the rest doth ouerto̅pp,
some other cake that wantes hys grace,
when at theyr prime theyr inward thoughtes should know,
the meaner man should take the betters place,
the greater man myght stoop, and sit belowe
but tell we now how poor Medoro sped,
that lovd hys master both alyve and ded.

In vayn he sowght to yet him to the wood, [3]
by blynde and narrow pathes to him vnknown,
theyr swyftes, and hys slow pase the same withstood,
forst by the burden that he bare alone.
but now, when Clorydano vnderstood
Medoroes rast, he made for him great mone,
and curst him selfe, and was full yll apayd
that he had left hys frend devoyd off ayd.

Medoro all about

19

Divers haue written to thie
effect off the fickellnes off frendes
but specially, Ovid.
Donec eris fœlix multos
numerabis amicos
Tempora si fuerint nubila
solus eris.

Horace. vulgus infidum
vt meretrix retro per
iura cedit.

George Peele
1558–1597

George Peele, born a Londoner, undertook his schooling as free scholar at Christ's Hospital, of which his father was clerk, and subsequently at Oxford University, where he gained a reputation as a skilled poet and translator. He was a student first at Broadgates Hall (now Pembroke College), and later at Christ Church, graduating as a 'Master of arte' in 1579. Peele's adult life in London was characterised by literary effort and dissipation in equal measure. No sooner had he left Oxford than the governors of Christ's Hospital, who had helped to fund his studies, commanded his father to 'discharge his house' of him. By 1585, Peele had married into a certain amount of wealth, which he set about squandering. He had also helped to produce two plays in Oxford, seen his first work, *The Arraignment of Paris*, acted on the stage, and had created his first pageant. There is evidence to suggest that he was in all likelihood an actor as well as a playwright, an occupation which doubtless enhanced his opportunity for exuberant behaviour. One friend described him as 'the chief supporter of pleasance now living'. He died in about 1597 of (according to one source) 'a loathsome disease'.

November 17 marked a special occasion for the Elizabethans, this being the day, in 1558, that the young Queen ascended to the throne. By 1595 the annual celebrations had grown into perhaps the most important and lavish festival in the English calendar. One spectator evidently impressed by the pageantry that year was George Peele. His last known work 'Anglorum Feriae' (shown opposite), a poem written in the blank verse for which he is celebrated, gives a lively account of the day's jousting. Whether it was printed at the time is not known, but Peele, once commissioned by Lord Burghley to compose verses to the Queen, no doubt hoped to win high favour with his patriotic piece.

Right: The first known printing of Peele's 'Anglorum Feriae' was issued privately in 1830. The title page is shown here and reveals that the publication was presented to a Reverend Joseph Hunter.

Opposite: Peele's autograph poem 'Anglorum Feriae' of 1595 has descended to us in this manuscript alone, an important survival from the Elizabethan age – albeit one badly damaged by unknown corrosive substances in the nineteenth century.

To wounde ~~... what ... ne ...~~
that any ~~... in hir ... aues.~~
~~...mon... Starrmge ompany of ...~~
~~... the ... in faire abiliments~~
...showe ... Renowned umberland
Knights ... the crowne in gilded armour dight
mouted at ... Elizabethes approache
enflamed with honors fire, & Lefte his Horse
kept by a dragon laden with faire spoiles:
& there his duetie donne & Large deuice
made (by his Page) knowne to hir Maiestie,
whose gracious eie reflectinge on this Earle
was Lyke Prometheus Life-infuzinge fire,
beholde he standes impacient of delaie
awaytinge there his freindly foes approche
Daringe he standes, True Knighte & challenger
& hardly brookes the tyme of their address
                              That shortly

William Shakespeare
1564–1616

'He was not of an age, but for all time'. Ben Jonson's verse tribute in the first collected edition of Shakespeare's plays (the posthumously published 'First Folio' of 1623, prepared by his fellow actors) is perhaps English literature's most prescient. The young love of Romeo and Juliet, the mature love of Antony and Cleopatra, the jealousy of Othello, the ambition of Lady Macbeth, the anguish of Hamlet and the foolishness of Falstaff strike us with the enduring force of truth.

William Shakespeare was born to a prosperous, middle-class merchant in Stratford-upon-Avon, where he attended school and met the older Anne Hathaway, whom he married in 1582 and with whom he had three children. By 1589, possibly after working as a humble provincial schoolmaster, he had established himself as a dramatist in London and he soon became a leading member of the Lord Chamberlain's Men. His long and evidently very profitable association with this theatrical company as both actor (he played the ghost, for example, in *Hamlet*) and playwright, saw him working at the Globe Theatre, in which he held a share, from 1599, and the Blackfriars Theatre, of which he was a leaseholder, from 1608.

Among Shakespeare's earliest work may be counted two long poems (perhaps written when London's theatres closed due to plague in the early 1590s),

his mysterious, musical, richly dark sonnet sequence and the violent play *Titus Andronicus*. Over the next two decades he would bring a steady stream of plays to the stage, including histories, comedies, tragedies, tragicomedies and the so-called 'problem plays' which defy traditional classification. Shakespeare's most haunting work, *The Tempest*, was performed for King James I in 1611 before his retirement to Stratford-upon-Avon and is often seen as his swansong. He died on 23 April 1616 and lies buried in Holy Trinity Church, Stratford-upon-Avon.

The extreme rarity of manuscript sources by or relating to Shakespeare has long served to heighten the intense speculation surrounding his identity. Indeed, some have gone so far as to argue that no such person existed, being but a convenient front for other writers. However, this lacuna in the record is perhaps not as surprising as it seems. After all, little else has come down to us from his numerous contemporaries, many of whom were at the time equally well regarded and successful. Indeed, scripts of only 18 of his 37 plays appeared in print in his lifetime. Of these, the 'good quartos' probably derived from original manuscript sources or official playhouse copies, while the 'bad quartos' comprised unofficial texts remembered, or partially remembered, by audiences or actors ('quarto' meaning a book made from sheets of paper folded

Shakespeare's celebrated portrait from the title page of the first folio of 1623. The work of Martin Droeshout, it was confirmed as a likeness by the playwright's friend and colleague, Ben Jonson.

Opposite: Shakespeare's three-page contribution to 'The Book of Sir Thomas More' comprises a new beginning for the sixth scene in the play, in which More, with his formidable powers of speech, quells a riot against the Lombard and French aliens in London. The hand is a typical secretary type of the time, but does bear certain idiosyncratic characteristics which have helped scholars to attribute it to Shakespeare – most notably a recurrent 'spur' on the character 'a'.

nay certainly you ar
for to the king god hath his office lent
oft dread oft Justyce, power and comaund
hath bid him rule, and willd you to obay
and to add ampler matie to this
he hath not only lent the king his figure
his throne and sword, but gyven him his owne name
calls him a god on earth, what do you then
rysing gainst him that god himsealf instauls
but ryse gainst god, what do you to yor sowles
in doing this o desperat as you are.
wash your foule mynds wt teares and those same hands
that you lyke rebells lyft against the peace
lift vp for peace, and your vnreverent knees
make them your feet to kneele to be forgyven

~~is safer warrs then ever you can make~~
~~whose discipline is ryot; ~~why even yor ~~hurly~~
cannot proceed but by obedience what rebell captaine

as mutynes ar incydent, by his name
can still the rout who will obay a traytor
or how can well that proclamation sounde
when ther is no adicion but a rebell
to quallify a rebell, youle put downe straingers
kill them cutt their throts possesse their howses
and leade the matie of lawe in lyom
to slipp him lyke a hound; ~~and that you sytt~~ say nowe the king
as he is clement, yf thoffendor mourne
shoold so much com to short of your great trespas
as but to banish you, whether woold you go.
what country by the nature of yor error
shoold gyve yow harber go yow to ffraunc or flanders
to any Iarman province, to spane or portigall
nay any where ~~why you~~ that not adheres to Inglande
why you must needs be straingers, woold yow be pleasd
to find a nation of such barbarous temper
that breaking out in hiddious violence
woold not afoord yow, an abode on earth
whett their detested knyves against yor throtes
spurne yow lyke dogges, and lyke as yf that god
owed not nor made not yow, nor that the elaments
wer not all appropriat to yor comforts.
but Chartered vnto them, what would yow thinck
to be thus vsd, this is the straingers case
and this yor montanish inhumanyty

faith a saies trewe, lets vs do as we may be doon by

weele be rewld by yow master moor yf youle stand our
freind to procure our pardon

Submyt yow to theise noble gentlemen
entreate their mediation to the kinge
gyve vp yor sealf to forme obay the magistrate
and theres no doubt but mercy may be found yf yow so seek

four times, as opposed to 'folio' in which the paper is folded once). Comparison between often widely differing quarto and posthumous folio texts has kept scholars engaged for generations in trying to establish Shakespeare's original words – words which may well have met an ignoble fate lining pie dishes or, worse still, serving as the Elizabethan equivalent of lavatory paper.

Six signatures of Shakespeare survive, although doubts have been raised as to whether some or all of these were actually signed by him, or by legal functionaries. Three are on his will, one on a legal document in the Public Record Office and two on documents relating to the purchase of a property (one in the Guildhall Library, London, and the other, shown here, in the British Library). The mortgage deed, discovered in 1768 and once belonging to the celebrated Shakespearean actor David Garrick, bears the abbreviated signature 'Wm. Shakspe'. It is dated 11 March 1613 and evidently completes the purchase by him, with the help of three trustees, of a gate-house in the precinct of 'the late black ffryers, London'.

There is only one literary manuscript which would appear to bear proof of Shakespeare's pen. The collaborative play 'The Book of Sir Thomas More' is mostly in the hand of Anthony Munday, but three pages (one illustrated on the previous page), with extensive corrections, are generally attributed to Shakespeare himself. The imagery, style and spelling have led commentators to this conclusion, together with a comparison with the six surviving signatures. The play, which involved the efforts of some five dramatists around the mid-1590s, was probably never performed, although Thomas Goodal, whose name later appears in the margin of the manuscript, was an actor with the company known in 1592 as Lord Strange's Men, for whom Shakespeare was then writing.

Opposite above: This panoramic view by William Smith dating from 1588 shows London as it was during Shakespeare's first year of residence there. The Rose Theatre, in which he performed, would open on the South Bank in 1592, to be followed, in 1599, by the Globe Theatre. They lay close to the two circular bull and bear baiting enclosures, clearly visible here, and would be reached by playgoers from Westminster and the City by ferry or London Bridge.

Opposite below: The house secured by Shakespeare's signature on the first tag of this deed lay beside and partly over what had once been the lodging of the Prior of Blackfriars. It appears to have been associated with Catholic intrigue (particularly the hiding of priests and papists). One description from about 1586 notes that 'it hath sundry back-dores and bye-wayes, and many secret vaults and corners', while another commented on its 'many places of secret conveyance' communicating with 'secret passages' leading to the Thames.

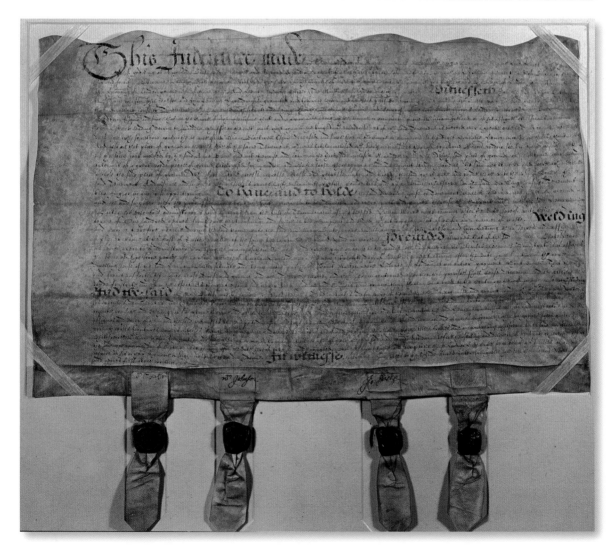

Sir Walter Ralegh
c. 1552–1618

From 1603 to 1616, Sir Walter Ralegh, courtier, coloniser, historian, soldier, poet and first importer to England of tobacco and potatoes – one might say the very model of the Renaissance man – was imprisoned in the Tower of London. He had, in fact, been there before, in 1593, when he infuriated his doting Queen by planning to marry a maid of honour. On that occasion he was quickly released and back in royal favour by 1597, having searched for gold in South America to swell Elizabeth's coffers and sacked Cadiz. Elizabeth's successor, however, was not so easily impressed. Almost as soon as he acceded to the throne, James I accused the flamboyant Ralegh of conspiracy to treason and locked him away.

It was during this long incarceration that Ralegh embarked upon his *History of the World*, dedicated to 'Her, whom I must still honor in the dust.' A notebook kept by Ralegh while in the Tower (illustrated left and opposite) reveals that his time there was hardly that of the desperate prisoner; extensive lists record the contents of his excellent library, while the presence of other hands in the volume points to his use of assistants as he conducted his research. The carefully drawn, annotated and coloured maps charting ancient Biblical lands were, however, all his own work, as was the fairly copied poem on its final page which forms part of (perhaps the conclusion to) a series of poems inspired by his fluctuating relationship with Elizabeth, or 'Cynthia'.

Ralegh's *History*, which started with the Creation but only reached 130bc, appeared in an impressive folio volume in 1614 and, despite a sour reception by the King, was widely admired. Two years later, longing for freedom and adventure, he secured his release from the Tower by volunteering to hunt for gold in South America. The mission was a tragic failure; his son was murdered and on his empty-handed return suspicion mounted that he had invented his story of a gold mine promising untold riches (his 1596 *Discoverie of Guiana* included a description of 'Eldorado'). The old charge of treason was revisited upon his head, which he lost to the executioner on 29 October 1618. He was said to have faced his death bravely, responding to one in the crowd who objected to his head not facing east: 'what matter how the head lie, so the heart be right?'. His body was buried in the chancel of St Margaret's church, Westminster; his head was embalmed by his wife, Elizabeth Throgmorton, the very maid who had inspired Elizabeth's jealousy. If the story is to believed, she carried it with her at all times for the rest of her life in a red leather bag.

An engraved portrait of Sir Walter Ralegh from a 1652 edition of his *The History of the World*.

Opposite: It is thought that Ralegh composed these verses possibly between 1597 and 1601, perhaps to be read at a specific occasion before the Queen herself. Why he should have so carefully copied the verses into a notebook largely devoted to his *History*, quite some time after Elizabeth's death, remains unclear. Two suggestions are that he may have been intending to dedicate the *History* to Elizabeth or that he actually started to keep the notebook from an earlier date than that commonly supposed.

Now we have present made
To Cynthia, Phœbe, Flora.
Diana, and Aurora.
Bewty that cannot vade.

A flower of lores oun plantinge
A patern kept by nature
for bewty, forme, & stature
when shee would frame a darlinge.

shee as the valley of Peru
whose sumer ever lastethe
tyme conqueringe all shee masterethe
by beinge allwayes new.

As elementall fier //
whose food & flame consumes not
or as the passion ends not
of vertues new desire.

so her celestiall frame
and quintessence all minds
bearers togetsoo byndes
shall ever be the same.

Then to her servonts leue her
Lore, nature, & affection
princes of worlds affection
or grayses butt derobe her.

As lore could find a quill
drawn from an angells winge
or did the muses singe
yat pretty wantons will.

yet sawra her could indyt
to pleas all other sence
butt lore & woe expen
sorrow can only write

Ben Jonson
1572/73–1637

'O rare Ben Jonson' reads the memorial slab on his grave in Westminster Abbey and his standing today is such that, in any other language, he would be honoured by many as the national playwright. Jonson, an imposing and powerful man, the son of a clergyman of Borders descent, was educated at Westminster School and became in turns a bricklayer, a soldier in the Netherlands, an actor and finally a playwright. He was imprisoned in 1597, following an appearance in Thomas Nashe's 'The Isle of Dogs' which gravely offended the authorities, and a year later he killed a fellow actor, Gabriel Spencer, in a duel, narrowly escaping execution. Jonson became a devoted friend, admirer and theatrical colleague of Shakespeare, tutored Sir Walter Ralegh's son, travelled through Europe, held court at the Mermaid and Devil taverns before John Donne, George Chapman, Francis Beaumont and John Fletcher, and was lauded by James I, who made him in effect Poet Laureate.

Jonson's major plays, written for the London stage, belong to the period before 1616 when he published a folio collection of his *Works* – the first attempt to elevate the art of the stage play. From 1605, however, he increasingly turned to the composition of masques for the court, prompted by the wishes of James's consort, Anne of Denmark.

The court masque, an entertainment combining drama, poetry, music and dance in lavish settings, enjoyed an enormous vogue with English monarchs from Elizabeth I to Charles I. The one illustrated here, 'The Masque of Queens', was composed for the New Year festivities at Whitehall Palace in 1609, though in the event it was not performed until Candelmas (2 February). The parts were taken by noble ladies of the court, and the sets and costumes were designed by Inigo Jones. The sketches for these still survive in the collection of the Duke of Devonshire.

'The Masque of Queens' came to the Library, by the authority of George II, in 1757 among the collection of Royal Manuscripts formed by successive sovereigns of England. That collection of nearly 2000 volumes had been stored in an old dormitory in Westminster School. The manuscript's having gone into the Royal collection spared it the fate of many of Jonson's papers which were sadly destroyed with the rest of his library in a fire in his lodgings in 1623.

This imposing portrait of Jonson is taken from a set of his *Works* published in 1640.

Opposite: The autograph manuscript of 'The Masque of Queens' comprises twenty folios of Jonson's late-English mixed hand (showing both italic and secretary characteristics). It was written out for presentation to Henry, Prince of Wales, who was to die prematurely in 1612. Here we have the preliminary address to the prince. The underlined words are given extra stress by being written in a pronounced Italic hand.

Humanitye, is not the least honor of yᵉ Wreath. For,
if once the Worthy Profeſſors of theſe learnings ſhall
come (as heretofore they were) to be the care of
Princes, the Crownes theyᵈ Soueraignes weare will
not more adorne theyᵈ Temples; nor theyᵈ ſtamps
liue longer in theyᵈ Medalls, than in ſuch ſubiects
labors. Poetry, my Lord, is not borne wᵗʰ euery man;
nor euery day: And, in her generall right, it is now
my minute to thanke yᵈ Highneſſe, who not only
do honor her wᵗʰ yᵉ care, but are curious to examine her wᵗʰ yᵉ eye, & inquire into her beauties,
and ſtrengths. Where, though it hath prou'd a Worke
of ſome difficulty to mee to retriue the particular
authorities (according to yᵉ gracious command, and a
deſire borne: out of iudgment) to thoſe things, wᵗʰ
J writt out of fulneſſe, and memory of my former
readings; yet, now J haue ouercome it, the reward
that meetes mee is double to one act: wᵗʰ is, that
thereby, yᵉ excellent vnderſtanding will not only iuſte-
fine mee to yᵉ owne knowledge, but decline the
ſtiffneſſe of others originall Ignorance, already
arm'd to cenſure. For wᵗʰ ſingular bounty, if my
Fate (moſt excellent Prince, and only Delicacy of
mankind) ſhall reſerue mee to the Age of yᵉ Actions,
whether in the Campe, or the Councell Chamber, ſt
J may write, at nights, the Deedes of yᵈ Dayes; J
will then labor to bring forth ſome Workes as Worthy of yᵉ fame, as my Ambition therein is of yᵉ
pardon.

By the moſt trew admirer of yᵉ Highneſſe Vertues,

And moſt hearty Celebrater of them.

Ben: Jonſon.

Sir Fulke Greville
1554–1628

Born in 1554 into a noble Warwickshire family, Fulke Greville attended Shrewsbury School where he met Sir Philip Sidney, establishing a close friendship which would endure through their adventures in the literary world of the Elizabethan court. Greville, who helped to bear Sidney's coffin at St Paul's in 1586, played an important part in preserving and publishing the works of his friend. *The Life of Sir Philip Sidney*, which he started around 1610, helped to establish a literary reputation which has long since eclipsed his own, when it finally appeared in 1652.

In 1621 Greville became first Baron Brooke after a successful career as a much favoured, if occasionally chastised, subject of Elizabeth I (a figure above all others revered and mythologised by poets and playwrights of the age), and subsequently James I, who granted him the magnificent gifts of Warwick Castle and Knowle Park. His distinguished and colourful life came to a violent end in 1628 at his London house in Holborn at the hands of Ralph Haywood, an old servant who felt slighted after discovering his exclusion from his master's will. Haywood killed himself immediately after stabbing Greville who struggled on in agony for a month.

The man who met his death through perceived parsimony used his final strength to bequeath large sums of money to the surgeons and attendants who ministered to him. Described by C. S. Lewis as a writer of 'genuinely didactic verse…utterly unadorned and dependent for interest almost exclusively on its intellectual content', the inscription of his own devising, which can still be seen on his tomb in St Mary's Church, Warwick, reads simply, 'servant to Queen Elizabeth, councillor to King James, and friend to Sir Philip Sidney'.

In 1968 the British Library acquired six vellum-bound manuscripts containing the poems, plays and one prose piece by Greville. Sometimes known as the Warwick manuscripts, after their former home, they comprise the work of a known scribe charged with the task of compiling fair copies of Greville's works. The great importance of these copies lies not only in the fact that they were compiled under the direction of their author, but that they include extensive revisions in his own hand, a fact leading one scholar to note that they represent 'the most substantial, authorized manuscript text that has come down to us of any distinguished Elizabethan or Jacobean poet'.

An engraved portrait of Sir Fulke Greville from Edward Lodge's four-volume work *Portraits of illustrious personages of Great Britain, engraved from authentic pictures in the Galleries of the Nobility, and the public collections of the country...*, 1821–34.

Opposite: Shown here is the opening of Sonnet 76 from the sequence *Cælica*, probably written out in the year 1619. The neat scribal copy contrasts vividly with Greville's revisions.

56

The heathen Gods, finite in power, will, birth,

yet worshipp't for their worth, and love to men,

At first kept stations between heaven and earth,

A like wish to the Castle and the Den.

Creation, Meritt, nature dulie weigh'd,

And yet in power, no rule, but will obey'd.

Till tyme and selfenesse wch turned worth, to arts,

Love into complements, and thinges to thought,

Found new pintles to enthrall mens harts,

By lawes, wherein while thrones seeme over-wrought.

Power finely surpriz'd this faith, of man,

And tax't his freedome at more then it can.

For to the Scepters while power doth reserve,

As well the practique; as expownding sense

Of lawes, from wch not flesh can paynlesse swerue,

They being Engines of ommipotence.

With equall power, is not equall man,

Then finely, tax't at more then it can.

Robert Herrick
1591–1674

Robert Herrick was little over a year old when his father, a goldsmith, fell to his death from the window of his London house. The strong suspicion of suicide may have played its part in his son's failure to visit his place of burial, at St Vedast's Church (which still stands, albeit rebuilt, in the shadow of St Paul's Cathedral) for thirty-five years. In his poem 'To the Reverend shade of his religious Father', he asks forgiveness:

> That for seven lusters I did never come
> To do the rites to thy religious tomb;
> That neither hair was cut, or true tears shed
> By me, o'er thee, as justments to the dead,
> Forgive, forgive me; since I did not know
> Whether thy bones had here their rest or no.

Along with his six siblings, Herrick came under the guardianship of his wealthy uncle, to whom he was apprenticed as a goldsmith. He gave up his craft, however, when he decided to enter St John's College, Cambridge in 1613, as a 'fellow-commoner'. He moved to Trinity Hall in 1616 to pursue legal studies and graduated in 1620, by which time he had begun to establish himself as an accomplished poet. Subsequent lively years spent in London among a group of poets devoted to the charismatic Ben Jonson – at, as he recalled, 'the Sun, the Dog, the Triple Tun' – helped to consolidate his literary credentials (and, perhaps, nurture what became

A portrait bust of Herrick from his *Hesperides*, 1648.

a lifelong aversion to the idea of marriage). The direction of his professional life was affirmed with his ordination, in 1623, as an episcopal minister.

Six years later, Herrick entered into an ambiguous period of existence. Appointed in 1629 as vicar of Dean Prior, Devonshire, his rural life, shared with a devoted servant 'Prew', whom he immortalised in verse, a spaniel called Tracie ('no eye shall ever see/For shape and service, Spaniell like to thee'), possibly a tame pig with a taste for beer, and numerous other animals, provided ample opportunity to compose, by his own admission, some of his finest work. It also, however, brought him into contact with locals whom he at times regarded 'rude almost as rudest savages' and inspired in him a frustrated longing for the sophisticated and exciting city life which he had left behind.

It was Herrick's political convictions which finally saw him back in his beloved London. A staunch Royalist, he was ejected from his living by the forces of the Commonwealth in 1646. Whatever he may have thought of the style of his dismissal, Herrick was delighted to be leaving his 'long and dreary banishment', vowing never to return until 'rocks turn to rivers, rivers turn to men'. He settled in Westminster where, although having little of his own money, he was able to rely upon his wide and wealthy circle of friends and family. His return to the centre of literary life (at the expense, it would seem, of his devotional obligations) must have played its part in inspiring him to bring to press his first and only collection of verse, *Hesperides*, in 1648. Herrick was eventually restored to his rural living in 1662 and, despite his earlier protests about village life, there he appears to have remained for the rest of his days. An entry in the church register records that 'Robert Herrick, vicker, was buried ye 15th day of October 1674'.

Chorus

Is, is there nothing can withstand
    The hand
Of Time: but that it must
Be shaken into dust?
Then poore, poore Israelites are wee
    now free
But cannot shunn the Graues captivitie.

        S   S
Alas Good Browne! that Nature hath
        No bath
Or vertuous herbes to stray me
To boyle thee yong againe:
Yet could she (kinde) but back command
        Thy breath
Her self would else ere thou shouldst be inurnd.

        S   2
But (ah) the golden Ewer by stroke
        Is broke.
And now the Almond Tree
With teares, with teares we see
Doth bowde lye and with ill fall
        Do all
The daughters dye, that once were musicall.

        2   S
Thus if weake builded man cann faye
        & Day
He liues tis alls, for why
He's sure at night to dye.
For fading man in fleshly home
        Doth rome
Till he his graue find, His eternall home.

        2   S
Then farewell, farwell man of wee
        Till when
For as the mourners meet
Pale visagd in the street
To speake of this our brittle birth
        In earth)
We meet with thee triumphant in our mirth.

                    Trinitall halls
                    Exequios.

Philip Massinger
1583–1639

'March 10, 1639, buried Philip Massinger, a stranger'. These words, written in the parish register of St Saviour's Church in London (now Southwark Cathedral) record the passing of a man who has been described as one of the most serious professional dramatists of the post-Shakespearian period. Although 'stranger' here simply means that Massinger was not of that particular parish, its use seems ironic given his long and close association with one of its most significant landmarks, the Globe Theatre.

Massinger was born in Salisbury, the son of a gentleman employed at Wilton House by the Herbert family, the Earls of Pembroke. He attended Oxford University, sponsored by the Earl, but left without a degree, having 'applied his mind more to poetry and romances for about four years or more than to logic and philosophy'. He arrived in London in 1606 and soon established a reputation as a playwright, albeit one in a state of constant impoverishment. As was typical of the age, Massinger collaborated on many plays, his associates including Thomas Middleton, William Rowley and Thomas Dekker. His greatest collaborator and friend, John Fletcher, died in 1625, from which point Massinger wrote almost exclusively for the King's Men which only a few years previously had employed Shakespeare as its leading dramatist.

Of the fifty-five plays in which Massinger was known to be involved, twenty-two are lost. Among those that survive, fifteen are thought to be his work alone. One of the most important of these is *Believe as you List*, a tragedy which he had been forced to rewrite after it was rejected a licence on 11 January 1630 by the Master of the Revels, on the grounds that 'it did contain dangerous matter, as the deposing of Sebastian, King of Portugal, by Philip II, and there being a peace sworn betwixt the kings of England and Spain'. The play survives in a manuscript copy, shown here, written out by Massinger himself. Adding to its rarity and interest is the fact that the document is marked up as a prompt copy and includes the names of the King's Men who performed the play on 7 May 1631, together with an endorsement by the Master of the Revels permitting its performance.

An engraved portrait of Phillip Massinger, from an eighteenth-century edition of his works.

Opposite: The autograph manuscript of Massinger's *Believe as you List* was rediscovered 'among a mass of rubbish' in 1844. After it was edited and published in 1849 the manuscript passed through the hands of a number of collectors before being purchased for the nation at auction in 1900. Shown in the margins are various notes written for the benefit of the prompt.

on this or this in vaine, I must contende
the Romane conqueste how am I grinnde
for rrage, and dide in their opinion that
I am deemde an Impostor—
will not the losse of my life quitt the cost?
o rare fingulitie! will they force mee to
bee mine owne hangman—I beare slaue this guilte
of crimes next to bee noemde retrannes surfs favour
by the iudges doome, and is my innocence
so opprssde innocence of a feare crosde binge
holds more contemptible. my better angell
howes wantinge power to alter fate discoverst
their hellish purposes. yes, yes, tis for
my sodest death will not suffice, they ainde at
my soules perdition, and thirst I to him
a fewe howers more of miserie betray for?
noe shee is fret still, & shall see returnd
from whence it came, & in her purenesse triumph
their tyrannie refunde, and fetterd.

<table>
</table>

Flaminius: o she dises!
                  & you art weake this will not doe.

Metellus: marche how Heslo stand

Ent: Taylor   the seconde charge.
(with bread & water)
Sempronius: the honor is wieard eurst my friende
                  for the quittinge cruelst brought my life out.

Taylor: Here's Late this though comes it will kill hunger
                  it is your dayte pittance, yet whon you please
                  your comons may bee mended.

Antiochus: showe mee the way
Taylor: confeste your selfe to bee a counsinge knaue
                  the matter's feasible. but yf you will bee
                  still kinge of the crickets feede on this, & liue
                  you shall not say wee starue you.   Exit Taylor.

Antiochus: stay I beseech thee
                  and take this cruell pittie backe againe.
                  to him that sent it. this is a tyranne
                  that doth exurpende all presidents. my soule
                  but when now this lumpe of clay for prison
                  of it selfe in the want of nourishe ment openinge,
                  god pleasd of her like fetters, and preparde
                  for selfe to make a noble flight as set
                  at libertie, and now this reparation
                  againe mindes. you for whose curious palate
                  the elements are ransacde looke vpon
                  this bill of fare by my princious steward
                  Gecepitie, sent to a famishde kinge
                  and warnde by my exemple, when your tables
                  cracke not with the waight, of diuers, and far fetchd daintiel
                  dispute not with gratious bounties. what shall I doe?
                  yf I refuse to touch, & taste these course,
                  & honestie Cated, I fasten my owne fate,
                  & soe with willingnesse embrace a sinne
                  if I shoulde haue thid from. noe the rate,
                  & liue at this poor rate life can continuue
                  I will not thow it of.

Flaminius: I pitie his
                  to bee thus constance
         —————— Metell: bid your properties Enter
The Late artists wee for subteste nayed. / Sempro: I—haue already aquainted him & Eiuru,
& then the songe.   to; Eiuru,
                                            for musicie & then Enter Flaa
                                                            and roscant

John Milton
1608–1674

'The main benefits of conjugal society', said Milton, 'are solace and peace', and these sentiments derived from personal experience. Classically educated, highly cultured, and travelled (he went to see Galileo in prison in Florence), Milton married the sixteen-year old Mary Powell in 1642. They were together for six weeks before she left him. She abandoned their home in St Bride's Churchyard, off Fleet Street, according to John Aubrey, because 'she found it very solitary; no company came'. It may, therefore, not be surprising to find in part of the *Commonplace Book* illustrated here a preoccupation with matrimony and divorce. Passionate in his defence of the individual in society, Milton produced a flurry of pamphlets on the subject of divorce between 1643 and 1645, *The Doctrine and Discipline of Divorce* having, in its second edition of 1644, an address to Parliament itself. Of course, the time was ripe: the abolition in the 1640s of the episcopacy and the ecclesiastical courts with their fierce control was the biggest disturbance to the marriage laws England had witnessed since the twelfth century. This was to be short-lived, however, for 1660 saw the return to the old order. It was not until 1969, incredibly, that Milton's plea – that full divorce may be allowed in England on the grounds of incompatibility and mutual hatred – became at last enshrined in law. Leo Abse revived Milton's spirit to get the Divorce Reform Bill through Parliament in that year.

In the event, Milton's wife returned to him in 1645. She died in 1652 and he married twice more, wives and children satisfying his scribal needs through the great poems of his later years, including the epic *Paradise Lost*, whose publication in August 1667 had been delayed by both the Great Plague and the Great Fire of 1666. One of the great independent spirits of English literature, fiercely protestant, anti-episcopalian and anti-Royalist (in 1649 he was appointed as Latin secretary to the Council of State), Milton was buried nevertheless next to his father among the Anglican fold in St Giles without Cripplegate in London's Barbican, the spot now marked by an easily-missed inscription at the foot of the pulpit steps. This manuscript was bought by the British Museum Library in 1900.

An engraved portrait of Milton.

Opposite: Milton's *Commonplace Book*, written in Latin and containing references to books on ethical, economic and political matters, was compiled *c*. 1630–1650. The folio relating to divorce, shown here, is from the period 1643–1646. It is in Milton's own strong, purposeful hand, though we have elsewhere the hands of amanuenses upon whom he became increasingly dependent as his sight failed.

in judicia translata esse divortii causa videtr ex quo Canonici lucru inde reportare authoritatemque berniman posse didicerunt Hist. Concil. Trident. 67. p.

Questiones innumeras de divortiis incerta solutione tractant Concil. Trident. l. 8. p. 729 et 737

ritus publici celebrandi matrimonii multis post apostolos seculis introducti sunt Concil. Trid. l. 8. 772.

vide de bonis Ecclesiasticis. Causæ matrimoniales ad civile magistratu spinebant priusquam ecclesiastici p socordiam principu eas earum judicia invasere. Concil. Trident. l. 8. 772.

Carolus magnus uxorem Theodorani repudiat non reddita ejus rei cuiquam ratione Girard. Hist. Franc. l. 3. p. 146. et Hildegardam duxit.

Post quinquennalem mariti absentiam, si incertum fuerit ubi sit, uxori concedit cum alio nuphas facere. Manuelis patriarchæ constantinop: sententia. Jus Græco Roman. p. 239. vixit autem hic patriarcha circa an. 1216.

Religionis causa divortium fieri posse statuit Matthæus Monachus, sive orthodoxus ita vult, non tantum si ab altero deseratr, in illo enim negotio non simplex εὐδοκία infidelis ad cohabitationem requirit, sed utriusq συνευδοκια secundu Pauli sententiam; ait etiam ab Theodoto patriarcha ita statutu vide lib. matrimonial. apud Jus graco Roman. p. 507.

Guntarius archiepiscopus Colomiensis, et Tergaudus Trevirensis Lothanium Lotharingiæ ducem repudiata Tiberga p astradam inducentem approbaverunt. Thuan. l. 78. 655

Pro divortio vide Bodin. repub. l. 1. c. 3.

* Belgii et protestan-
tium defensor ——

x non regi solum, sed civibus
Baro ab Herber de Mesd:

Renatus Lotharingiæ dux repudiata ob deformitatem, et sterilitatem uxore Margareta et vivente ea Philippam superinduxit, nec tamen ejus ex Philippa filius hæreditate dejectus. Thuan. hist. l. 24. p. 734.
Wilhelmus Arausionensis abdicata a se ob mores uxore Anna Mauritii Saxonis 7 viri filia Carlotam Borboniam Monpenseri filiam duxit. Thuan. hist. l. 60. p. 72.
Joannes Basilii filius Moschorum dux, uxore repudiata, quod, quoties vult, illi moribus patrii licet, novam ducit. Thuan. hist. l. 72. p. 471.

Propter impedimentum naturale Vincentius Mantuæ princeps Alexandri Farnesii filiam repudiat alia superinducta. Thuan. l. 80. p. 783.
Henricus 4us Galliæ rex Margaritam uxorem ob mores quamvis cognationis obtentu repudiabit multisq exemplis id sibi quoq licere demonstrat, quod alii ante se reges varias ob causas fecissent. Thuan. hist. l. 123. p. 885.

Sir Thomas Browne
1605–1682

'Were the happiness of the next world as closely apprehended as the felicities of this, it were a martyrdom to live.' Thomas Browne's words, from his short treatise *Urne-Buriall*, epitomise his fascination with what lies beyond the observable world. Born in London, Browne travelled widely in Europe before settling permanently in Norwich in 1637 to practise medicine, in which discipline he was widely celebrated: when he received his M.D. from Oxford University in 1637, he had already practised for a period in Oxfordshire, had spent time in the great medical centres of Montpellier and Padua, and had received a doctor's degree from Leyden University.

Browne married Dorothy Mileham in 1641 and the couple had twelve children. His life, from this point, seems (in the absence of a great deal of biographical information), to have been dedicated to the calm execution of his professional and domestic duties, and to his remarkable prose reflections. His first great work, in which he reveals his life to have reached 'a miracle of thirty years', was *Religio Medici* (published in an unauthorised edition in 1642), a wide-ranging exploration of personal faith. *Urne-Buriall*, published in 1658,

is a short work and perhaps Browne's best regarded. Written in a style celebrated for its subtle beauty and power, it takes as its starting point 'the Sepulchrall Urnes lately found in Norfolk' before considering, in an impressively grand historical and geographical sweep, the profound and insistent question of what becomes of us after death. Browne published nothing after this, but corresponded widely with learned men, among them the diarist John Evelyn. A confirmed Royalist throughout the civil war, he was knighted in 1671 by Charles II and died on his birthday on 19 October 1682. He lies buried in the church of St Peter Mancroft in Norwich.

Opposite: This manuscript volume contains a number of drafts of writings by Browne, among them passages incorporated with various alterations in the published version of *Urne-Buriall*. It was one of a number of manuscripts of Browne and of his son and grandson, Dr Edward and Dr Thomas Browne, bought by the collector Sir Hans Sloane after the grandson's death. The first sentence of the passage, written in Browne's difficult hand, reads: 'Could we truly apprehend heaven or were the happinesse of the next world as sensible as that of this it were a martyrdome to live, & to those who conceive not life after death it is an Hell to dye'.

An engraved portrait of Sir Thomas Browne.

Could wee truly apprehend honour ...... of the next worke ... sensible as that of this ... a martyrdome to live; ... to those ... concern not life after death ... an ... to dye twere ...
... wonder but ... spirit of many ... heathens ... durst despise death ... blood not in feare of ... finall dissolution ... they ... durst ...
death when they ... nor life ... would ... scorned to live ... by knowing in ...
... we ourselves ... when ...
better they durst ... and not to ...
... into ...

... not ... valour ... and ...
... not ... nor ... men cowards ...
... of ... contempt of ...
... world ... above ...
... principles ... ...
... of ... ...
... ...
...

John Dryden
1631–1700

Dryden was born into a landed Northamptonshire family whose sympathies during the Civil War were firmly against the King. Indeed, his uncle, Sir Gilbert Pickering, became chamberlain to Cromwell himself during the Protectorate and the elegy illustrated here, 'Heroique Stanza's, Consecrated to the glorious memorie of his most Serene and Renowned Highness Oliver Late Lord Protector of this Common-Wealth etc. Written after the Celebration of his Funeralls', bears witness to Dryden's loyalties at that time.

Cromwell died on 3 September 1658, succeeded to the Protectorate by his son, Richard. His body was embalmed and the funeral in Westminster Abbey was fixed for 9 November but because of the elaborate nature of the preparations, costing an amazing £60,000, it was put off until 23 November. Dryden's opening stanza speaks of the premature effusions of fellow writers who had not anticipated such a delay. He himself was not beyond criticism, however, earning a reputation as something of a politically self-serving creature (and one castigated, while a scholar at Trinity College Cambridge for 'disobediency' and 'contumacy'.) Just one year after his tribute to Cromwell, he was enthusiastically versifying upon 'the Happy Restoration and Return of His Sacred Majesty'. Under the new régime of Charles II, Dryden flourished as a playwright, became Poet Laureate in 1670 and produced a new panegyric in the form of his opera *Albion and Albianus* in 1685, again eulogising the monarch.

Having become a Roman Catholic in about 1686, he lost the laureateship to Thomas Shadwell on the accession of William and Mary, but in these later years he had become a grand old man of letters and was accorded a final resting place, surprisingly, given his faith, in Poet's Corner, Westminster Abbey. Cromwell had been removed from the Abbey in 1661 and we can perhaps look to this manuscript for a lasting contemporary memorial to the Protector.

Opposite: 'Heroic Stanzas', published in 1659, was Dryden's first major work and this manuscript is by far the most important in his hand to have survived; very little else is extant and even this manuscript, thirty-seven stanzas in all, covering four sides, lay unidentified until quite recently. It was among some miscellaneous papers gathered by William Petty, 1st Marquess of Lansdowne, who died in 1805. Petty's collection was acquired for the national collection in 1807 and the Library catalogue published in 1819 failed to identify the manuscript as autograph. It was an Italian academic, Anna-Maria Crinò, who made this important discovery in 1966.

An engraved portrait of the author from *The Dramatick Words of John Dryden*, 1717.

Heroique Stanza's,
Consecrated to the glorious ~~military~~ memorie
Of his most Serene & Renowned Highnesse
OLIVER
Late Lord Protector of this Common=wealth. &c.
Written after the Celebration of his Funeralls.

And now tis time; for theire officious hast
Who would before haue borne him to the sky
Like Eager Romans, ere all ritds were past
Did let too soone the sacred Eagle fly.

2

Though our best notes are treason to his fame
Joyn'd with the loud applause of publique voice,
Since Heavn what praise wee offer to his name
Hath render'd too authentiq by its choise;

3

Though in his praise no Arts can liberall bee,
And they whose Muses haue the highest flowne
Add not to his immortall memorie;
But do an Act of friendship to theire own:

4

Yet tis our duty and our intrest too
Such Monuments as wee can build to raise;
Lest all the World prevent what wee should do
And claime a title in him by theire praise.

5

How shall I then begin or where conclude
To draw a fame so truly Circular?
For in a round what order can bee shewd,
Where all the parts so equall perfect are?

6

His grandeur hee derived from Heavn alone;
For hee was great ere Fortune made him so:
And Warrs, like mists that rise against the Sunne,
Made him but greater seeme, not greater grow.

Katherine Philips
1631–1664

Katherine Philips has only recently emerged as one of the most intriguing literary figures of the mid seventeenth century. She was born Katherine Fowler to a prosperous London cloth merchant and sent to board at a fashionable Presbyterian school in the nearby town of Hackney. It was here that she began to develop the talent for cultivating friendships – especially with women – which would later see her presiding as the 'matchless Orinda' over a select society of erudite and fancifully named friends.

At the age of seventeen, Katherine married the Welshman James Philips, the eldest son of her stepfather. The match seemed an improbable one. While James ('Antenor' in her verse), who was three times her age, successfully pursued high office under Oliver Cromwell, she staunchly defended her independence, aligning herself in print from 1651 onwards with poets espousing Royalist sympathies. However, although political opponents sought to exploit such differences the union proved strong, witnessing the birth of a daughter and a son (who survived only forty days).

With their political fortunes reversed during the Restoration, Katherine put her court and social connections to good use protecting her husband. It was while travelling to Ireland in 1662, to press a claim to lands on his behalf, that she completed a translation of the play *Pompée* by her French contemporary Pierre Corneille. Performed in February 1663, it was the first play brought to the British or Irish stage by a woman. Its great success, swiftly giving rise to editions in Dublin and London, set the seal on her reputation. It also, however, encouraged the appearance in 1664 of a supposedly unauthorized collection of her poems which she insisted was withdrawn, evidently fearing that it might compromise her usual discretion. The first legitimate collection of Philips's verse appeared posthumously in 1667, prepared by Sir Charles Cotterel ('Poliarchus'), a close friend to whom she addressed a series of letters published in 1705. During her lifetime, the majority of her verse was circulated and read in manuscript by an exclusive and carefully chosen audience.

Philips succumbed to smallpox in 1664, which she had only just described, in a poetic elegy to the Earl of Warwick's only son, as 'That fierce Disease, which knows not how to spare/The Young, the Great, the Knowing, or the Fair'. She died in Fleet Street on 22 June and was buried in the church of St Benet Sherehog, barely two years before it was destroyed in the great Fire of London.

A bust of the 'matchless Orinda' as Katherine Philips was known, from the 1667 edition of her poems.

Opposite: This autograph undated fair copy of Philips's Ode 'Upon Mr Abraham Cowley's Retirement' was recently discovered among the papers of the diarist John Evelyn, who may have had it from his father-in-law, Sir Richard Browne.

No, No, unfaithfull world thou hast
Too long my easy heart betray'd
And me too long thy captive made
But I am wiser grown at last
And will improve by all that I have past.
I know 'twas Just I should be practis'd on
                For I was told before
        And told in sober & instructive love,
How little all yt trusted thee have won,
And yet I would make hast to be undone
But by my suffrings I am better taught
And will no more comit yt stupid fault
                Go get some other foole
                Whom thou mayst next cajole
On me thy frowns thou wilt in vain bestow
                        For I know how
To be as coy & as reserv'd as thou.

                    2.

        In my remote & humble seat
            Now I'm again possess'd
            Of that late fugitive my Brest
From all thy tumults, & from all thy heat
I'le find a quiet, & a coole retreat
        And on the fetters I have worne
Look with experienc'd & revengefull scorne
        In this my soveraign=privacy
        Tis true, I cannot govern thee

Thomas Traherne
1637–1674

'An unknown seventeenth-century poet' was revealed to the world for the first time in *The Athenaeum* in 1900. Two manuscript volumes had been discovered quite by chance a few years earlier on London bookstalls, one containing poems, the other a prose work, the 'Centuries of Meditation'. At first thought to be from the hand of Henry Vaughan, they were subsequently discovered to be by Thomas Traherne, son of a Hereford shoe-maker and Rector of Credenhill.

So began the quite romantic emergence of this writer, and the manuscript illustrated here, 'Commentaries of Heaven', continues the tale. It is known to have passed unidentified through London sale-rooms in 1844 and in 1854 (when it sold for two shillings), but in 1967 it was found, amazingly, on a Lancashire rubbish-tip. When the finder emigrated to Canada, it went with him and there, in the University of Toronto, its author was recognised. It was purchased by the British Library in 1984.

Traherne's manuscript, compiled c.1673–74, is an encyclopaedia of religious and moral subjects, all seeds for meditation, evidently curtailed abruptly by his death. Its ninety-four entries proceed alphabetically from 'Abhorrence' ending with 'Bastard'. Indeed, the 'Commentaries' could have opened like the 'Centuries' with the preamble 'An empty book is like an infant's soul...I have a mind to fill it with profitable wonders', for the manuscript is invested with a sacred quality as if it is an end in itself.

Traherne did well for himself. In 1669 he became domestic chaplain to Sir Orlando Bridgeman, Lord Keeper of the Great Seal and Lord Chief Baron at the trial of the regicides in 1660. He and Traherne died within months of each other and both are buried in the little church of St Mary's in Teddington, to which they had retired together, by the river Thames. No portrait of Traherne is known to exist and a tiny contemporary verbal picture of him as 'a man of cheerful and sprightly temper' has to fill the gap.

The little church of St Mary's, a stone's throw from the Thames in Teddington, Middlesex. Both Traherne and his patron, Sir Orlando Bridgeman, are buried within.

Opposite: The folio shown here from Traherne's 'Commentaries of Heaven', c. 1673–74, dealing with the 'Atom' (a 'great Miracle in a little room'), is a typical product of the growing scientific rationalism of the Restoration as, indeed, is the manuscript's projected journey through boundless knowledge. The manuscript is written in a beautifully clear and elegant hand, its author's corrections nevertheless revealing it to be, to some extent, a working document.

Atom.

The Designe.

An Atom is a marvellous Effect of Almighty power, or a great Miracle in a litle Room: perhaps I may say, it is an infinit Miracle in no Room; for it is so small, y^t it taketh up no place at all, but fill oth an indivisible Point of Space: yet is there an unsearchable Abyss of Wonders contained in it; innumerable Difficulties, uses, Excellencies & Pleasures concentering in its Womb, for our Information & Happiness; ye clear Knowledg of wch will make us expert in ye Chiefest Mysteries of GOD & Nature. We may treat of it either Physicaly, or Metaphysicaly: ye Metaphysical notion of it, helpeth much in ye Mysteries of Felicitie, ye Physical in ye Secrets of Nature. In ye Metaphysical Treatice we designe ye Confusion of Atheists, but chiefly ye Accomplishm^t of ye Soul, in Comunion with GOD: in ye Physical Consideration of it, an Hypothesis; (so much desired by learned men) wherby to Explicate ye Phænomena of Nature, as they are observable in ye Univers, for ye Compleating of ye Body of Natural Philosophie, so far as we are able to contribute therunto. for ye least things being ye Basis of ye Great, & ye Seed of all, these Atoms are of important Consideration, bee. ye clear Sight of wch is like ye Knowledge of first Principles, aiding us in ye Discovery of all Causes & Effects whatsoever. In ye Delineation of wch wth out taking notice of other mens Errors, we shall draw a clear & even Rule, wch will measure it self, & others Deviations.

Its Etymologie.

Atom is a greek Word derived from a. priv: & τεμνω, Scindo, signifying a Part of Matter y^t cannot be cut or divided asunder.

Its Nature.

An Atom, according to ye true & full Importance of ye Word, is a Material particle absolutely incapable of being Divided And in this Sence ye Word is taken by Philosophers. Its Nature is made up of its Essence & Affections.

Its Essence.

Concerning ye Essence of an Atom litle can be said, but y^t it is a Material Existence, invisible & Indivisible, having neither Bulk nor figure, but apt to assist as a Part towards both. Of its Affections more may be Spoken.

Its Obscuritie.

An Atom is like ye Heavens, a certain kind of retired Quintessence, far removed from all Elementary Qualities. The Affections wch are generaly observed in other things appear not in y^t; for Want of wch it is inter non Entia, to a vulgar Soul. Common People cannot so much as Shape ye Maner of its Existence. It is difficult wth C^m to believ ye Realitie of such a Creature: much more to apprehend its Inclinations & Properties, Matter, Forme, Qualitie & appearances. Tho by Nature ye Soul was made Capable of Managing any Argum^t, from a Theme infinitly great, to an Object infinity Small; nothing by Vastness exceeding its Capacitie, or by litleness evading its Acuteness. An Atom poseth ye Wits of ye most curious among men, & feedeth ye Intelligence of ye Sublimest Angel.

Its Claritie

To men, restored to ye Claritie of their Knowledg, an Atom is an Object as apparent as ye Sun; every Qualitie in it being as obvious, as ye figure & Color of a most Solid Bodie. The vail, or Miste being removed in ye Purity of infinit & Eternal Light, ye Soul apprehendeth it as effectualy as ye Ey, or Hand, doth things fitly proportioned to C^m for notwithstanding its Nakedness, in being divested of all those Accidents wth wch we commonly converse, it hath a fulness of Attributes by wch it may be Known. Its Original Order, Existence, Use & End, Operations & Circumstances (perhaps innumerable) may be

Samuel Butler
1612–1680

'And having thus lived to a good old age, admired by all, though personally known to few, he departed this life in the year 1680, and was buried at the charge of his good friend Mr. Longueville, of the Temple, in the yard belonging to the church of St. Paul's Covent-garden, at the west-end of the said yard, on the north side, under the wall of the said church, and under that wall which parts the yard from the common highway.' Thus concludes the biographical introduction to an 1805 edition of Samuel Butler's 'Hudibras', a satrical poem originally published in two parts between 1662 and 1663 and responsible for such well-known phrases as 'Look a gift horse in the mouth', 'Make the fur fly' and 'Spare the rod and spoil the child'.

Butler gives full vent to his Royalist sympathies in what is a bitterly satirical masterpiece of the Civil War period. The poem's eponymous anti-hero is comically cast in the shape of a self-serving and foolish Cromwellian colonel. The character's literary debt is to Cervantes's *Don Quixote*, but Butler draws more specific inspiration from the unfortunate puritan Sir Samuel Luke, one of a number of influential figures with whom he found employment as a clerk or attendant.

Butler's somewhat pathetic fate is perhaps ironic given that his most famous work found favour not only among the public, but with those powerful members of the Restoration establishment it set out to please. Although King Charles II himself – who, in the poet's own words 'never ate, nor drank, nor slept,/But Hudibras still near him kept;/Nor would he go to church or so,/But 'Hudibras' must with him go' – rewarded him with various grants of money, these were evidently not enough to compensate for a disastrous financial situation. His wife's fortune was lost through poor investments and he failed to profit properly from his literary success owing to numerous piracies.

Butler lived the latter part of his life in obscurity and relative poverty, but could rely, at least, upon one good friend: in addition to making proper arrangements for his funeral, so the lawyer William Longueville supported the author in these last years, which found him dwelling in Covent Garden's Rose Street – a place deemed fit, by one near contemporary, 'for mechanics only and persons of meane quality'. In return for his kindness, Butler appointed Longueville his heir and inheritor of all his worldly possessions. These amounted to no more than his literary remains, described by Roger North as 'loose Papers and indigested'.

A portrait of Samuel Butler from a 1715 edition of *Posthumous Works in Prose and Verse* – many of which are spurious.

Opposite: The volume which includes the page shown here is thought to represent about half of the manuscripts Butler left to his friend Longueville; the whereabouts of the rest of the 'loose Papers', if they survive, remains a mystery. This manuscript is almost entirely in Butler's own hand, the rarity of which is demonstrated by the fact that only one other autograph document (four lines in Britain's Public Record Office), has been hitherto identified. Among the many lines of verse and prose passages which make up this volume can be found these 'Additions to Hudibras'.

Additions to Hudibras

The Knight upon a Turne of State
...his tail not to come to late
But in betraying his own side
...timely treason saves his tide
...cause, & covnant in the lurch
...sets up for ye King, & church,
...true & faythfull, to deal against
...nsciences, & is highly advanc'd.

Then why should wee believe our sense
...trust its false Intelligence
...that tells us this or yt part akes
...only Imagination makes?
...Peevish ignorant & Brainsick
... th'utter barrister of Swanswick
...as one yt did observe much more
...these who saw more so before.

...count the foreleg of a Cripple
... moments of mann'd People
...Sun goes not so well as does
...witnesses Pendulum Clocks.
...some in turning of a love
...but torment & vex it more
...all yt world there is no need
...Prone t'excess then Avarice
...neither cares for fine nor Cloathing
...Nature's content wth little & wth nothing
...had they had their Right they ought
...Popish & malignants thought
...comets Marching in ye Sky
...Baggage & Artillery
...worst affliction may be born
...easier then Contempt & Scorn.
...A Tradesman to win a Custom Able
...as the face to th' better Table
...For though Pythagoras disallows
...That Plumes should be put out in Flames
...Yet nothing cooks a lovers roste
...Like Bashrad... & Defeat.

...scholar do it every day
...light to ye need... ...
...The Pettifogger damns his Souls
...Papist & knave to cheat a soul
...Merchants venturing through ye main
...rocks & Pirates for game.

This Months husband's... ...
... this Tinker err cast his own
... hast from Rest but even turne while
...Reverend Age as well ye might

For it his Gentleman a Glazier
... Rob Rob & the old Level born
...And in this Cider of his Child
...Returne some Directions yet at home

C Madam I am yr ... ... servent
And humble very & servant

Men break their eyebles wth ye Crofse
That witches may be at a loss
Yt yd should finde them out & nigg it
To crofs ye soar in like a Pigat
Frayle as the Tablet on wch Nature
Do's draw her Pictures standing water
Made Boys as skilful in all Knowledge
As men are now at Grefsham Colledge
Did not Momppus in ye moone
See all yt upon earth was done?
Did not the moon eclypsd foretell
The Macedon kings overthrow?
And was not only the Portent
But reall cause of the event?
Jesoldemans merely by their Cunning
In our Profession overrunne him
And if wee can eth'eclypse foretell
Why should wee no th'event as well?
Some deaf men can (they say) see words
Yt those that speake 'em have no... to eare
Others can heare a violin
Holding between teeth a Pin
...him that dares th' Inrosselle Mountain
Wth all Philosophy do's contayne?
Or like ye Painter yt design'd
A Noyse, or he yt drew ye winde
When over one anothers head
They charge & Rumble at once like Swine
Since here tofore did so aster
Then women should prolong to war
They would not suffer ye Bawdeth time
To sweare by Hercules ye Name
...th' kt at this worke Puts will Ire
Like Metles twist then Red as fire
To have ye old Cause for better or worse
Like an old whore wth money in her Purse
Did not th' Philalgers perswade
The netherow None to evade
The dire event a Star did seeme
To foretell purposely at home
To frustrate all ye designes of State
And turn storm all upon ye State
...for some by foretelling to ...
...th' Art of telling my foote of Hell

The Eighteenth Century

Although later observers have liked to view the early eighteenth century as the Age of Reason, the major writers of the period would have been hard-pressed to agree with this notion, for it was the manifestations of unreason that often occupied them in their stinging commentaries on contemporary life. There is only a small step from the great satirical writing of Alexander Pope or Jonathan Swift to the lacerating treatment in paint by William Hogarth of vice, neglect, cruelty and other extremes of appalling inhumanity.

The evidence is that writers of this period needed to retreat sometimes from the world to maintain their equilibrium. This is reflected in a number of manuscripts selected here from the British Library's eighteenth-century holdings, and Pope's translation of *The Iliad* (1719–26) is a case in point. His savage pen laid aside, he immersed himself for many years in the perfecting of Augustan measures, a literary undertaking complemented by his painstaking efforts to fashion a neo-classical retreat from the grounds of his riverside house in Twickenham.

Lady Mary Wortley Montagu's poem is on the very subject of retreat and marks her abandonment of 'mankind's detested ways' for such calm rural pleasures as her 'rose and jessamin trees'. Robert Burns's celebrated poem 'The Cotter's Saturday Night' goes even further, being a paean to the virtues of domestic comfort and family piety. Perhaps in a similar vein, the gentle William Cowper's expression of friendship towards William Hayley sprang from a sense of gratitude for the homely and the familiar in what he saw as an otherwise bleak world.

Indeed, the quiet pleasure of friendship runs like a thread through the writing of the period. The ideals of order and control made the passions highly suspect and their expression ill-bred; we find none of that in the manuscripts here illustrated. Swift's somewhat cool treatment of Esther Vanhomrigh, Samuel Richardson's gentle words to Anna Meades, Johnson's affectionately shared experiences with Hester and Henry Thrale, Thomas Gray's decorous words to James Dodsley – all the voices in these pieces are far different from the public oratory of

John Dryden's 'Heroique Stanza's' on one side and the earnest tone of Percy Shelley's 'Mask of Anarchy' on the other. It is as if we have reached a plateau of rest in our literature. Even Daniel Defoe, a somewhat shadowy personality, speaks as a family man here, while Laurence Sterne's irony is muted, self-deprecating and amused. These manuscripts have the hushed quality of the parlour about them.

Sentiment, often associated only with the latter end of the century, actually informs, in varying degrees, much of the whole period's offerings here but, of course, we move into new and startling realms with William Blake. We may like to consider the domestic scene of Blake and his wife Kate working together on his prints – or, to the amazement of their neighbours, walking together naked in their back garden – but the areas of the imagination opened up by this writer's noble and yet humble vision seem to have emerged from no earthly parlour.

Whatever fearful alarms came from France in 1789, it may have been a comfort to many an Englishman to know that King George III and Queen Charlotte took joy in simple family evenings round the spinet in their little house at Kew and that this country presented no more alarming a tricoteuse than William Cowper's beloved companion Mrs Unwin.

Jonathan Swift
1667–1745

Swift's letter to 'Vanessa', dated 12 August 1714 and illustrated here, was written at a time of great political ferment in the country. Queen Anne had died eleven days before and George I had been proclaimed King. The Whigs had been assured of continued supremacy in Parliament and Swift, a committed Tory journalist and apologist since 1710, had vowed to quit England for Ireland. He was to return to English soil only twice after that.

Born in Dublin into a Protestant Herefordshire family who had only just settled in Ireland, he had embraced the new order when William and Mary ascended the throne in 1688 and had moved to England where he entered the service of Sir William Temple, a retired diplomat. In Temple's enlightened and rather precious household he learned at first hand the machinations of government and the trappings of society, a good grounding for the trenchant lampoons and biting satires he was later to produce.

His writings, of which a number survive in autograph manuscripts, are the product of an acutely solipsistic mind and one wonders how romantic involvements could be accommodated into his world. Indeed, his masterpiece of 1726, *Gulliver's Travels*, is notable not only for its strong misanthropic vein in general, but for the revulsion with which it treats sexuality and sexual relations in particular. The nearest we come to a manuscript of this work is a printed edition of the text bearing Swift's own annotations (in Armagh Public Library). Considerable vagueness surrounds his attachment to Esther Johnson, known to him as 'Stella', another member of Temple's household. She was dear to him, dear enough for his remains to be laid eventually next to hers in St Patrick's Cathedral, Dublin. But did they ever marry?

Similarly, what was the nature of his relationship with 'Vanessa'? She was actually called Esther Vanhomrigh and he met her in about 1707. Childlike, passionate and self-willed, she can be seen in Swift's clandestine replies to her letters as an embarrassment, even a danger. He ultimately pushed her out of his life. She died in 1723.

The letter shown here is one of forty-four (covering the period 1711 to 1722), gathered into a volume which for many years disappeared. Sir Walter Scott published them in 1814, but only from inaccurate copies, and they did not appear in print in their original form until 1923, having been bought by the Library in 1919. Their earlier history has never been fully established.

This engraving of a melancholy Swift, after a painting by Benjamin Wilson, is found in a commentary on Swift's life and writings published in 1752.

Opposite: Swift's letter to 'Vanessa' was sent from Wantage four days before he left for Ireland, in 1714, and addressed to her 'at Mr Handcock's in Little Rider Street, near St James's Street, London'. Written in Swift's small neat script, the letter urges discretion and is left deliberately unsigned.

I had yr Letter last Post, and before you can send me another, I
shall set out for Ireld: I must go and take the Oaths, and the sooner
the better. I think since I have known you I have drawn an old house
upon my Head. You should not have come by Wantage for a thousand
Pound. you used to brag you were very discreet; where is it gone? It is
probable I may not stay in Ireland long, but be back by the beginning
of Winter. When I am there I will write to you as soon as I can
conveniently. but it shall be always under a Cover; and if you write to
me, let some other direct it. and I beg you will write nothing that is
particular, but which may be seen, for I apprehend Letters will be opened,
and Inconveniencies will happen. If you are in Ireld while I am there,
I shall see you very seldom. It is not a Place for any Freedom, but
where every thing is known in a Week, and magnified a hundred Degrees.
These are rigorous Laws that must be passed through: but it is
probable we we meet in London in Winter. or if not, leave all to
Fate, that seldom cares to humor our Inclinations. I say all this out
the perfect Esteem and Friendship I have for you. These Publick
Misfortunes have altered all my Measures, and broke my Spirits. God
Almighty bless you;   I shall, I hope be on horseback in a Day after
this comes to yr Hand.   I would not answer your Questions for a
million; nor can I think of them with any Ease of Mind. adieu.

Alexander Pope
1688–1744

With the establishment of the Protestant succession under William and Mary in the very year of Pope's birth, Catholic families such as his were certainly faced with severe disadvantages. They were denied admission to university, forbidden to hold public office and to own land and even to live within ten miles of London. Add to these privations Pope's own physical disablement and we can understand the compensatory mechanisms at work in his proud and sensitive nature: his immense ambition, his alliance with established literary and political coteries, his lacerating treatment of adversaries in his writing.

But he also sought peace. The classical studies of his youth bred in him an appreciation of Arcadian pleasures, most apparent in his early *Pastorals* of 1709 and in the celebration of the Thames in his *Windsor Forest* of 1713, but equally evident in his choice of rural Twickenham, fifteen miles to the West of London, for a home in late 1718. He was to remain here for the rest of his days and his final resting place can be found in the Parish church marked by a small slab bearing the letter 'P'.

By 1718 Pope was famous and to consolidate his position he had started a kind of scholastic sabbatical – lasting ten years – in which he translated Homer's 'Iliad' and 'Odyssey', published in parts between 1715 and 1726. Surprisingly for such an august and awesome literary endeavour, the manuscript drafts of the works are really rather homely, for Pope seized scraps of paper of any size and put even the blank sides of old letters to good use.

Illustrated opposite is an extract from Book 16 of the 'Iliad' written on the reverse of a letter addressed to him from the Duchess of Hamilton, complete with wax seal. The circle in a square among the lines of Homer points to a third use to which these sheets were put: as scribbling pads, repositories for his designs, made between 1718 and 1720, for his villa and for his five-acre garden facing the Thames. Plans for serpentine paths, parterres and architectural elevations all add an endearing humanity to this most heroic of literary creations.

Pope's keenly intelligent features are well represented in this engraved portrait from his *Works* of 1720.

Opposite: A page from Pope's translation of the 'Iliad', Book 16, lines 426–463. Pope's numerous manuscript drafts for his translations of the 'Iliad' and the 'Odyssey' (making up three large bound volumes), which he bequeathed to a friend, were eventually presented to the British Museum Library, then in its infancy, in 1766.

great at Hector godlike Ajax
[But Still godlike Ajax at great Hector aim'd,
Still pointed toward his breast his Javlin flam'd:
The Trojan Chief experienc'd in the field,
Oer his broad shoulders spread the massy shield,
Observ'd the storm of Darts the Grecians pour,
& on his buckler caught the ringing Showr.
He sees for Greece the Scale of Conquest rise,
yet stops & hums, & saves his lov'd Allies.
As when the hand of Jove a Tempest forms,
Dark oer ye field th'ascending Vapour & blackens heavn w Storms
& shades ye Sun, and blots ye golden skies, Rolls the cloud,
So from the Ships along the Dusky Plain,
Dire Flight & Terror drove the Trojan Train.
Evn the Steeds of Hector fled, thro Heaps of disarray-
The fiery Coursers forc'd their Lord away.
While far behind, his Trojans fell confus'd,
Wedg'd in the Trench, in one vast Carnage bruis'd.
Chariots on Chariots rowl'd, clashing Spoke,
Fly diverse, while ye madding Steeds desert ye Yokes.
In vain they labour up the steepy Mound, their
& Kings oerturn'd lie foaming on ye Ground.
Fierce on ye Rear with Shouts, Patroclus flies,
The Plains tumultuous clamor fills ye fields & skies,
Thick Drifts of Dust involve their rapid flight,
the Plains are lost, and Heavn is snatch'd from sight
Clouds roll on clouds, their dying Lords cast down,
th'affrighted Horse, and thunder toward ye Town.
increase the Rout, was hear the Victor's cry,
Lord the where ye war bleeds, & where the thickest die.
Where Horse & Arms, & chariots lye oerthrown
& bleeding Heroes under ax les Peleus Groan.
No stop, no check, the Immortal Coursers flew,
From Bank to Bank
High-bounding oer ye Fosse, the whirling Car
Smoaks thro ye Plain overtakes ye war
& thunders after Hector, Hector flies:
Patroclus shakes his Lance, but Fate denies.

Allan Ramsay
1686–1758

Allan Ramsay set himself a mission to liberate the spirit of Scots poetry in an age dominated by the strictures of the Kirk. His effort is epitomized in this lively attack upon the corruption of the clergy (opposite). His early ambitions, however, were not entirely of the bookish sort. Born in Leadhills, Dumfriesshire, he moved to Edinburgh where he was apprenticed to a wigmaker, a trade in which he subsequently established himself in the city's Grassmarket. The great intellectual bustle of the capital at the time – one wonders whether he dressed the head of the philosopher Hume, later painted by his famous son, Allan Ramsay the younger – began to seduce him into pursuing his love of the literary.

In 1713 Ramsay helped to found the Easy Club, a Jacobite literary society, and by 1718 he was a bookseller, with successive premises throughout the city; his influential periodical, *The Tea Table Miscellany*, begun in 1724 and continuing until 1737, published traditional ballads and songs which might otherwise have been lost and proved an inspiration to Robert Burns among others. In 1728 he established Scotland's first circulating library and he opened a playhouse in 1736, losing a substantial amount of money when licensing regulations banning the performing of plays outside Westminster forced it to close the following year.

The Library has two full manuscript volumes of Ramsay's work, one comprising the original manuscript of his great gathering of early Scottish texts, *The Ever Green, being a collection of Scots Poems, wrote by the Ingenious before 1600*. This collection, published in 1724, reveals Ramsay's own interest in original literary remains: he worked upon the famous Bannatyne Manuscript to bring to light the works of medieval poets such as Robert Henryson and William Dunbar. In addition to selling, lending and editing books (sometimes rather too freely according to many critics), Ramsay also published his own work, much of which is collected together in the Library's second manuscript volume. *Poems* (1728) is regarded as his best collection of verse and he also turned his hand to drama in *The Gentle Shepherd of 1725*, a pastoral work which brought him much acclaim. In later years he wrote little, observing that 'the coolness of fancy that attends advanced years should make me risk the reputation I had acquired'.

Ramsay was fiercely devoted to Scotland and adored Edinburgh which, as he made clear in one typically provocative and lively poem, he considered a far better city than Rome, Paris or London. He died aged seventy-two at his home near the Castle and was buried in the churchyard of Greyfriars where there is a monument to his memory.

A somewhat whimsical portrait of Ramsey from a 1758 edition of his pastoral comedy *The Gentle Shepherd*, published in Glasgow.

Opposite: The Library owns two substantial volumes of manuscript verse by Allan Ramsay. One comprises his great gathering of early Scottish poems 'wrote by the Ingenious before 1600' which he published in 1724. The other volume contains drafts and fair copies of Ramsay's own work. Ramsay enjoyed writing provocative poetry and illustrated here is a neatly satirical attack upon the corruption of the clergy.

On the Clergy's minding themselfs mair
than their flock

Wae to the Herds of Israell
that feed nae right the flock
but dauntylie Batten themsell
syne do the people mock

The silly sheep are a' forlorn
and fawn to woraff a prey
Thea Herds hae teendit a' the Corn
the sheep can get nae Strae

They Gatherd up their Woo & Milk
of nae mair took they Cure
but Cled themselfs with costly silk
and siclike cled their whoor

Therfore says God I will require
my sheep out of their Hands
and give them Herds at my dsire
to teach them my Commands

And they shall nowther feed themsell
nor yet hunger my sheep
I shall them frae my Kirk expell
and give them swine to keep

Daniel Defoe
1660–1731

Much of Defoe's life was passed in the shadows. He was at various times a tradesman whose Tilbury brickyard helped build the walls of St Paul's Cathedral, a spy whose work played a part in forging the 1707 Union of Scotland and England under Queen Anne, a soldier, a bankrupt, a political satirist pilloried and imprisoned (twice) for his views, and a journeyman writer – a kind of early hack. Shining radiantly among his achievements, nevertheless, are his great works, *Robinson Crusoe, Moll Flanders* and the *Tour through Great Britain*, all published between 1719 and 1726 and all revealing his close knowledge of contemporary mores and of humanity in general.

Defoe was a committed dissenter born at the Restoration into a family loyal to the memory of Cromwell and was thus an outsider, often on the run and little known to his contemporaries. He avoided portraiture and the accompanying image is rare indeed; one wonders whether it is even his true likeness. His real name was actually Daniel Foe and he often disguised his handwriting.

The manuscript illustrated here, however, replete with elisions and shorthand code, is in his own natural hand and shows the facility of his method of composition. It is an unfinished tract, written in 1729, and is the last of a series of four manuals giving advice on family life and morals. One was a pioneering tract on a happy sex life.

Defoe sent the work off to the printers and shown here is a corresponding pageproof, preserved with the manuscript and bearing his autograph emendations. The original manuscript bears the title 'The Compleat English Gentleman' yet he nowhere corrects its title *The Compleat Gentleman* at proof stage to include the word 'English' and the abbreviated title may have been his preferred choice. He died before the work could be published and the manuscript remained in the family until 1831. It was purchased by the British Museum Library in 1885 and first published in 1890.

Defoe, born and educated in Stoke Newington, which was then on the northern outskirts of London, lies near John Bunyan, William Blake and Isaac Watts, in the Dissenters' cemetery at Bunhill Fields in London. The memorial placed there in 1870 was almost immediately stolen only to emerge in 1940 among the rubble of a Southampton air raid.

This rare engraved portrait of Defoe appears in a collection of his *Works* which he saw through the press in 1705.

Opposite: Defoe's treatise *The Compleat Gentleman* (in manuscript entitled 'The Compleat English Gentleman'), one of five autograph prose works by the author in the Library's collections, defies easy reading. The handwriting is crabbed and idiosyncratic and is laced with abbreviations and shorthand symbols – as befits a man with a highly secretive nature.

that there seems to be an Implacable Animosity between them — they will tear Satyr
: into One another or at least W:ar for a time

Now this comes Exactly within: Censures & I am passing w: so much justice upon
the tenor. If the antient Nobility had either any Superious Personal Merit upon of their
Own upon: foot of & they could justly Rate themselves above: other: or if
Modern Nobility lay und: any Scandal upon: foot of & they could be reproach'd
as Unqualifyd for a Nobility, they had no Merit but their Money or were really
Personally Unworthy being Ennobled: this W: in Either Case justifye: Censurers
will: & they treat them

But I Suppose now: a Noble Venetian of: antient Creation Suppose a Contarini the Bragadini: Boccalini: Cornari or: Morosigi Suppose
him a Bully a Rake a B...... or a W...... or an E...... a man Usless to:
Common wealth Degenerate Vitious Unworthy of: Honour: Titles & he bear
— & he inherits but knows not how to Deserve Suppose him Dishonouring his Glori
: ous Ancestors by: his Deficiency of: Vertues Courage Learning — fidelity to his
Country & justly Raisd: his ancestors to: Dignity of Counsellor — rankt them
among: Nobility

Suppose on: Contrary a Nobleman of: Modern Creation, — allow him to be
a Person of Merit Wise Prudence Learning able for Council for Embassy for Conf
: Dency; a Man of Conduct in: field Brave Enterprising Experience: faithfull
— Worthily Honoured — Noble on all those accot: besides: advancing so much
Money for: Public Service in a time of Exigence

Now, here is the: The first of those — all those Contrary Extremes of: shall Censure: Case for: Moor
Antiquity of their Creation; How absurd is: pride of: this — how Contrary to: Nature of the
thing? : First has nothing to Value himself upon but: remote Vertues of his forgotten
Ancestors, & weigh no more in: Scale of his: ffonal Merit than: Eculehood of his
Arms painted upon Silk W: weigh against: other mans 100 thousand Duckats

In a Word: Case has: Merit: First: Antiquity, pray & has: best Claim to: Honour
: our: First has Family w: out Vertues; Case has: Virtue to Build a Family: First
Ought to be: Case of his Family as: Case is: First Noble man of his

yet thus it is at Venice &: antient Nobility look upon: Modern Nobility w: utt
: most Contempt, So as they will hardly keep: Court: or give them: Civilitye of their rank
if they meet g: in: streets Let us bring: Case nearer home

In Poland this vanity of Birth is still worse, his there Carry it to such a monstrous Ex
: travagance: Name of G: Title of a Starost Palatine or a Castellan gives: man a
Superiority Over all: vassals & Common people infinitely greater than: of: or ten
: poor power w: more Absolute power — make them more inserable
than: Either of Grand Seignior or: Cham of Tartary: into much: they frequently
: Murther them: transfer on them as Dogs — frequently and when they do are Accountable
to no body nor are calld to: acco: for it So much as: give a Reason for it. Now

Lady Mary Wortley Montagu
1689–1762

The early family papers of the Dukes of Marlborough were allotted to the Library in 1978. Among the papers of Sarah, wife of the 1st Duke, was discovered this autograph poem by Lady Mary Wortley Montagu. The 'Lady' of its title may have been Sarah herself, for Mary refers in her letters to 'a long intimacy' between them.

She was born Mary Pierrepont, a daughter of the Duke of Kingston, as he became later, and thanks to a liberal upbringing, she emerged a gifted woman, independent, eccentric, vigorous and volatile. She found friendship in kindred spirits like the Duchess and Mary Astell, the defender of women's rights in her day. Mary's husband Edward Wortley Montagu was a Member of Parliament and, on George I's accession in 1714, a Commissioner in the Treasury. She herself was often at court and a particular friend of the Princess of Wales. The poem illustrated here refers to Mary's court life and was certainly written before she left England (and even her husband) in 1739 for twenty-three years of self-imposed exile. Her literary circle in this country had been glittering: she was a friend of Alexander Pope, was admired by Richard Steele, editor of *The Tatler* magazine, and she was a second cousin of the novelist Henry Fielding. An enigmatic quarrel with

Pope, however, ended their relationship and she certainly brought the odium of others upon herself by the sheer force of her personality. The poem glances at this factor in her life.

Mary's courage in the face of adversity and danger had been reflected in her wonderful letters from Turkey in 1717 and 1718. It was there that she encountered inoculation against smallpox and had her own son take advantage of the discovery, encouraging the practice in a sceptical England. Was it rumour and 'mankind's' detested ways' that drove her out of England in 1739? Her later years were spent in decaying Italian *palazzi*, where she found some simple satisfactions and solaces: 'I have mix'd in my espaliers as many Rose and jessamin Trees as I can cram in'. Only the thought of her daughter, Lady Bute, and of the newly opened British Museum, she said, would lure her back. She did return in 1762 but by then was terminally ill. She died in London and was buried in the Grosvenor Chapel in Mayfair.

This wonderful portrait of Lady Mary Wortley Montagu, taken from an edition of her letters published in 1764.

Opposite: This manuscript of the autograph poem 'To a Lady advising me to Retirement' has all the appearance of a fair presentation copy, an observation which suggests that it may well have been composed and written down specially for Sarah, Duchess of Marlborough, in whose papers it was discovered.

To a Lady advising me to Retirement

You little know ye Heart that you advise
I view this various scene wth equal Eyes
In crowded Court I find my selfe alone
& pay my Homage to a nobler Throne

Long since ye value of this World I know
pity ye Madness, & despise the Show
well as I can my tedious part I bear
& wait Dismission without painfull fear

Seldom I mark Mankinds detested ways
not hearing censure or affecting Praise
And unconcern'd my Future Fate I trust
To that sole Being, Mercifull & Just.

Samuel Richardson
1689–1761

The autograph letter illustrated here is addressed to Anna Meades, a writer and one of Richardson's 'Songbirds', young lady admirers, often Bluestockings, whose company he cultivated. It was written very near the end of his life when, it has been suggested, he suffered from a form of Parkinson's Disease, but his beautifully controlled hand betrays none of that. The fastidious attention to details of punctuation, paragraphing and calligraphy reflects not only Richardson's literary practice but also his business practice.

As a model of superlative careerism, Richardson's life is distinguished. The son of a London joiner, he was largely self-taught. He was apprenticed to a printer when he was seventeen and became a freeman of the Stationers' Company nine years later. Within six years he established a business of his own, both printing and publishing and, by dint of sheer industry, eventually obtained the lucrative commission of printing the House of Commons journals. By 1754 he was Master of the Stationers' Company.

That a man with such a background should suddenly produce a work like *Pamela*, written in the space of two months in 1739–40 and printed, as with all his works, by himself has been the object of amazement. In this novel his perceptive delineation of the moral growth of his heroine is remarkable and the book was wildly and widely acclaimed, achieving six editions within a year. *Clarissa* (published in 1747–48) is a study of even greater intensity, and established Richardson, we can now see, as one of the chief founders of the modern English novel.

Although a good number of his letters survive, nothing has been traced of the manuscripts of Richardson's three novels, excepting an autograph transcript of a series of passages from *Clarissa* (at the Victoria and Albert Museum, London) and fragments from his long, last novel *Sir Charles Grandison* of 1753 (at the Victoria and Albert Museum and the Pierpont Morgan Library, New York).

Richardson died of apoplexy on 4 July 1761. One may find his memorial slab attached to the outside wall of St Bride's Church, off Fleet Street, but the precise location of his remains is unclear.

An engraved portrait of Samuel Richardson, inserted in a 1751 edition of *Clarissa*.

Opposite: All of Richardson's novels are epistolary. He had much practice in the form, for he wrote love-letters for girls in the neighbourhood when he was a boy, and in this late manuscript of an autograph letter to Anna Meades, of 1757, purchased by the British Museum Library in 1869, we can still see his deft handling, manipulation even, of an admiring correspondent.

Dear Madam,   Sept. 5. 1757.

I mentioned to your Rev'd Friend an important Reason, why, at this Time, my Daughters could not embrace, as they wished to do, your kind Offer of corresponding with one of them. The Affair is not yet quite settled; but soon will; and perhaps an Opportunity will be given, on your Return to Town of beginning the desired Correspondence by a Personal Acquaintance on both Sides. Mean time, my dear Anna must not think so highly, as she seems to do, by her unmerited Compliments, of her admiring Friend.

Admiring Friend I justly call myself, on having attentively perused the Manuscript you put into my Hands. How so young a Lady arrived at a Knowlege of Men and Manners so extensive, is matter of agreeable Surprize to me; and I congratulate you on the Felicity of your Pen.

I made some few Observations, as I read; which cannot be so well understood, as by a personal Explanation; and I hope for the Pleasure of another Interview on your coming to Town, for that purpose.

It is a Custom with my Wife and Daughters in long Evenings to sit round a Table employ'd in Needleworkes; while some one of them, in turn, reads to the rest. The Summer, and the concerning Affair I mentioned to your worthy Friend, have not, since I had the Favour of your Papers, allowed of this agreeable Amusement; and therefore they have not yet read the MS. Soon will this Custom be resumed; a Personal Acquaintance will perhaps facilitate the kindly desired Correspondence, between you; and in the Interim, I shall be chiefly obliged to you, if you will at your Leisure, give me your pretty Hist. brief, and your Progress in Knowlege, Step by Step, by which you arrived so early at so much easy and natural Excellence.

Do not, dear Madam, charge with impertinent Curiosity, in this Request.
         Your sincere Friend, and
            Humble Serv.t
London,   S. Richardson.
Sept. 5. 1757.

Laurence Sterne
1713–1768

Sterne, born the son of an army subaltern serving in Ireland and educated at Cambridge University, became a country parson in Stillington, Yorkshire. He owed his position, at least in part, to the connections of his wife Elizabeth, whom he drove to distraction with his philandering. In 1760 he published, at his own expense, the first two volumes of the whimsical yet stylistically innovative *Life and Opinions of Tristram Shandy, Gentleman*, and was immediately lionised by London society.

His *Sentimental Journey*, which followed in 1768, owes something to his travels in France in 1765–1766, but it is far from being mere reportage. On one level it is a response to Smollett's *Travels through France and Italy* published in 1766, but even more it is a highly imaginative and ironic presentation of a man of high moral values (himself, no less, in the form of Parson Yorick). It lays bare, through the most commonplace of events, his susceptibility to self-delusion and in its comic vision anticipates Jane Austen. Depending on the reader's viewpoint, one may be moved by the book either to tears or to hilarity.

The work was originally intended as four volumes, but only two were completed before Sterne died, insolvent, in London's Old Bond Street. The manuscript, which was purchased by the British Museum Library in 1853, covers the first volume (that for the second survives at the Pierpont Morgan Library, New York, in what is believed to be a transcript made from the lost original). It is an autograph draft with quite a number of emendations, as prepared for the press, and is highly legible and fluid in form. An earlier owner has interleaved the folios with illustrations cut from early editions and one such quirky example is shown here.

There was something oddly Shandean about Sterne's end which came shortly after *A Sentimental Journey* was seen through the press. His newly buried corpse was seized by body-snatchers and sold to Cambridge University, before being recognised during actual anatomy-classes and returned to London. In 1969 the remains were again disinterred, Yorick-like, and laid finally to rest in the parish at Coxwold in Yorkshire, to which he had been appointed perpetual curate in 1760.

A quizzical looking Sterne, taken from a Dutch edition of the writer's works of 1779.

Opposite: The manuscript of volume one of *A Sentimental Journey* is possibly the earliest surviving example of a novel written in the author's hand. It served as a printer's copy, as is suggested by its polished state. Here a young woman inspires in the hero Yorick a state of emotion intense enough to lead him to exclaim (over the page), 'Good God! how a man might lead such a creature as this round the world with him!'

The Remise Door
Calais.

When I told the Reader that
I did not care to get out of the Desobligeant
because I saw the monk in close conference
with a Lady just arrived at the inn —— I
told him the truth; but I did not tell
him the whole truth; for I was full as much
restrain'd by the appearance and figure
of the Lady he was talking to. Suspicion
cross'd my brain, and said, he was telling her
what had pass'd: something jar'd upon it
with in me —— I wish'd him at his convent.

When the heart flies out before the un —
-derstanding, it saves the judgment a world

Thomas Gray
1716–1771

Apart from a two-year sojourn in London to be near the British Museum, newly opened in 1759, 'with all its manuscripts and rarities by the cart-load', as he put it, Gray spent most of his adult life in Cambridge. He entered Peterhouse College in 1734, later transferring to Pembroke and in 1768 becoming Professor of Modern History.

His singularly uneventful and retiring life was in fact consumed by an indefatigable quest for knowledge, so that he became, in one friend's estimation, perhaps 'the most learned man in Europe'. Thoroughly versed in this country's literature, he was at the same time an antiquary and a botanist, a musician and a classical scholar, an entomologist and an expert on painting and architecture. This background of vast, eclectic learning is only partially reflected in the manuscript presented here.

The manuscript, which comprises seven folios, is a list of instructions to James Dodsley, his publisher, for a new edition of his poems appearing in July 1768. Gray's fastidiousness is most evident in his handwriting, meticulous punctuation, literary citations and in his careful distribution of copies. The edition was to contain republications of past work including the 'Elegy written in a country churchyard' and three new poems including 'The triumphs of Owen' whose last stanza appears at the head of the folio shown. The volume was also in the press of Robert Foulis, a Scottish publisher, coming out two months later. Gray accepted no money from either Dodsley or Foulis.

Thomas Gray, an engraving taken from an original portrait painted by J. G. Eckhardt for Horace Walpole in 1747.

Opposite: Gray's manuscript instructions to his publisher for the new edition of his poems appearing in 1768 bespeaks the quietness of his study or the gentle domesticity of his mother's home at Stoke Poges, Buckinghamshire, in whose churchyard they are both buried. It was bought for one guinea by James Bindley, a book-collector, in 1807 and was later acquired by Samuel Rogers, the poet, for eighteen guineas. Rogers's great-niece, Laetitia Sharpe, presented it to the British Museum Library in 1912.

Talymalfra's rocky shore
Echoing to the battle's roar.
Where his glowing eye-balls turn,
Thousand banners round him burn.
Where he points his purple spear,
Hasty, hasty Rout is there,
Marking with indignant eye
Fear to stop, & shame to fly:
There Confusion, Terror's child,
Conflict fierce, & Ruin wild,
Agony, that pants for breath,
Despair, & honourable Death.

    *   *   *

Note. The Dragon-Son ⟩ The red Dragon is the device of Cad=
:walader, w.ch all his Descendents bore on their banner

      10.

l.1. —————————— the knell of parting day.
       ———— squilla di lontano,
   che paia 'l giorno pianger, che si muore. Dante.
                      (Purgat: L.8.)

l.92. Even in our ashes live &c:
   Ch'i veggio nel pensier, dolce mio fuoco,
   Fredda una lingua & due begli occhi chiusi
   Rimaner doppo noi pien di faville. Petrarch: Son: 169.

l: penult: There they alike &c:
       ———— paventosa speme. Petrarch: Son: 114.

I hope, you have not begun to reprint: but if you have,
you must throw the notes, &c: to the end, or where you please,
omitting the ~~~~~~ mottoes, w.ch do not much signify.

When you have done, I shall desire you to present in
my name a copy to M.r Walpole in Arlington-street, another
to M.r Daines Barrington (he is one of the Welch Judges) in the
Inner-Temple; & a third to M.r J: Butler at Andover: whe=
:ther this latter Gentleman be living or not, or in that neigh=
:bourhood, I am ignorant: but you will oblige me in making
the enquiry. if you have no better means of knowing, a
line directed to the Post-mistress at Andover will bring
you information. after this you may (if you please) bes=
:tow another copy or two on me. I am

P.S: It is M.r Foulis of Glasgow,   Your obed.t humble Servant
that prints them in Scotland: he has
been told, that you are doing —   Gray.
the same. I have desired, he would=
not print a great number, & could
wish the same of you.

Samuel Johnson
1709–1784

Dr Johnson was the son of a Lichfield bookseller. Poverty, melancholia and illness beset his early years, but on going to London in 1737 he established a living by contributing abundantly to *The Gentleman's Magazine* and later editing his own periodical, *The Rambler*, written almost entirely by himself. His great achievement, however, accomplished between 1746 and 1755, was the *Dictionary of the English Language*, a work unrivalled until the appearance of the *Oxford English Dictionary* in 1884. Almost the whole of Johnson's magnificent enterprise was carried off in his house – which may still be visited – in Gough Square, off Fleet Street.

Domestic life and travel vied in his affections. His Hebridean and Scottish tours are well known from his own descriptions and from those of his biographer, James Boswell. But he was famously happy being in London with his companions, his wife, his cats or, between 1766 and 1783, with Henry and Hester Thrale, his friends in Streatham where he had his own room.

The manuscript illustrated here is from Johnson's diary of a tour in north Wales made with the Thrales in 1774. The right-hand column is particularly interesting: at Holywell the party visit a copper-foundry where Johnson's characteristic demand for truth and exactitude is manifest. It is a kind of bridging moment in our literature, for here, in effect, he tries to 'peep', as he puts it, into the early workings of the Industrial Revolution. Boswell, who did not know of the manuscript's existence, barely comments on the tour.

Sadly, Johnson's connection with Streatham collapsed after Henry Thrale's death in 1781 and Hester Thrale's subsequent marriage to Gabriele Piozzi in July 1784 (which wounded Johnson deeply). Five months later, having destroyed a mass of private papers, Johnson himself was dead. He was granted burial in Westminster Abbey. The manuscript was inherited by his servant, Frank Barber and, after passing through a variety of hands, was acquired by the British Museum Library in 1839.

An engraved portrait of Samuel Johnson taken from his *Dictionary of the English Language in Miniature*.

Opposite: The entry for 3 August 1774 in Dr Johnson's diary of a tour in north Wales. For some reason (perhaps practical, perhaps cosmetic), Johnson has folded his sheets of writing paper vertically down the middle creating two columns of script. Despite the fact that the manuscript accompanied its author *en route*, it is remarkably well preserved. Neither does Johnson's neat regular hand appear to have suffered from whatever makeshift studies (tavern tables?) he used to set down his observations.

August 3. We went in the coach to
Holywell. Talk with Mistress about Flat_
bury — Holywell is a Market town
neither very small nor mean. The
Spring called Winifred's Well is very
clear, and so copious that it yields
one hundred tons of water in a minute. It is all at once a very great
stream which rushes perhaps thir—
by yards of the roompien... a mile
and before in a course of two miles
eighteen miles more. In descent it very
quick. It then falls into the Sea. The
Well is covered by a lofty circular
arch supported by pillars, and over
this arch is an old Chapel, now a
School. The Chapel is separated by
a wall. The Bath is completely and
indecently open. A Woman bathed
while we all looked on. In the Church
which makes a good appearance, and
is surrounded by galleries to receive a

numerous congregation, we were present
while a child was christened in Welsh.

We went down the stream to see a
prospect in which I had no part. We
then saw a brass work where the lapis
calaminaris is gathered, broken, washed
from the earth and the lead, the lead
... the lead was separated I did
not see, then calcined, afterwards ground
fine, and then mixed by fire with the
copper. We saw several furnaces with
melting pots, but the construction of
the fireplaces I did not learn.

At a copper work, which receives its pigs
of copper, I think, from Warrington, we
saw a plate of copper put hot between
steel rollers, and spread thin. I know
not whether copper rollers were fit to a certain distance, as I suppose, or acted only by its
weight.

In the same work I saw round bars formed
and by a notched hammer and anvil. Then
I saw a bar of about half an inch, or more

Robert Burns
1759–1796

In 1815 a marble group was commissioned for Burns's mausoleum, newly built above the poet's grave in St Michael's Churchyard, Dumfries, Scotland. It was to portray the Muse of Poetry discovering Burns at the plough. The image of the 'Ploughman Poet', though well established by this time, was to be thus encouraged and nurtured throughout the nineteenth century.

It is not, of course, an entirely accurate image. His childhood was indeed spent among the rural retreats of Alloway where his father was head gardener to a local estate, but his father also had his own small plot and built the cottage, which survives to this day, with his own hands. One dominie who taught the boys said, 'In this mean cottage I really believe there dwelt a larger portion of content than in any place in Europe'.

It is this picture of content which infuses Burns's poem 'The Cotter's Saturday Night' and illustrated here we have the first of three folios of an autograph fair copy of the poem. The poem was the centre-piece of his first volume, *Poems, chiefly in the Scottish Dialect*, published in Kilmarnock in 1786. It is addressed to Robert Aitken, a successful lawyer of Ayr whose sound criticism Burns valued and whose industry in gathering the names of about a quarter of the subscribers ensured the volume's publication.

The poem bespeaks the study as much as the field. The verse style owes much to earlier models and the content recalls Fergusson's 'The Farmer's Ingle'. The Scots dialect is modified with a canny eye on an English market and in truth we have here the product of a sophisticated literary awareness. This is not to decry it. The poem has worn well through its annual recitations at Burns Night suppers.

Despite his erudition and the great favour he found among the cultured citizens of Edinburgh, Burns was never really able to make financial capital from his verse and, employing the skills learned helping his father, continued to work the land, at a leased farm in Dumfriesshire, until 1792. For the remaining three years of his life, married and with four children, he worked in the excise office in Dumfries.

A portrait of Burns taken from the *Collected Works* of 1834.

Opposite: This manuscript, the first page of an autograph fair copy of Burns's poem, 'The Cotter's Saturday Night', was bought by the Library from Peter Cunningham in 1855. His father, Allan, had edited Burns's works in 1834 and had actually walked in the poet's funeral procession. In the nineteenth century Burns's distinctive bold slanting hand invited the attention of the forger Alexander Howland 'Antique' Smith, whose natural tendency (unlike Burns) to dot his 'i's too far to the right contributed to his undoing.

The Cotter's Saturday-night. ___ A Scotch Poem,
inscribed to Robt. Aitken Esq. in Ayr. ___

My lov'd, my honour'd, much respected friend,
 No mercenary Bard his homage pays;
With honest pride I scorn each selfish end,
 My dearest meed, a friend's esteem and praise:
To you I sing, in simple Scottish lays,
 The lowly train in life's sequester'd scene;
The native feelings strong, the guileless ways,
 What Aitken in a Cottage would have been,
Ah! tho his worth unknown, far happier there I ween! ___

November chill blaws loud wi' angry sugh,
 The short'ning winter-day is near a close,
The miry beasts retreating frae the pleugh,
 The blackning flocks o' craws to their repose;
The toil-worn Cotter frae his labor goes,
 This night his weekly moil is at an end,
Collects his spades, his mattocks, an' his hoes,
 Hoping the MORN in ease an' rest to spend,
And weary o'er the moor his course does hameward bend.

At length his lonely Cot appears in view,
 Beneath the shelter of an aged tree;
Th' expectant wee-things, toddlin, stacher through
 To meet their Dad, with flichterin noise an' glee.
His wee-bit ingle blinking bonilie,
 His clean hearth-stane, his thrifty wifie's smile,
The lisping infant prattling on his knee,
 Does a' his weary kiaugh an' care beguile,
And make him quite forget his labor an' his toil.

William Cowper
1731–1800

Cowper's first volume of poems was not published until he was fifty-one. By then he had passed through three periods of intense melancholia and had twice tried to commit suicide. He had also embraced evangelical Christianity – and had shaken it off. A childhood marred by the very early death of his mother and by vicious bullying at school left their mark in the form of acute anxiety and fear of personal commitment. By 1782 he had arrived at a plateau of security in his troubled life, finding solace and comfort in the friendship of the widowed Mary Unwin with whom he lived first at Olney and then at nearby Weston in Buckinghamshire. We find Mrs Unwin in a letter he wrote in 1783 sitting 'knitting my stockings at my elbow with an industry worthy of Penelope herself'.

The poem illustrated here was written in 1792 at Weston soon after he met William Hayley, a cheerful and congenial man and a poet successful enough to be offered the laureateship (which he declined), but conservative enough to be reviled by Byron. Hayley, like Mrs Unwin, was a source of security and in fact obtained a government pension for Cowper shortly after the poem was written. Cowper addresses him as 'my dear Brother' in letters sent at this time. For all its genuine warmth,

the poem, as seen here in this draft, is consciously crafted. The sonnet form needs scrupulous care and we can see the labour involved in the creation of the last six lines. It is a decorous warmth. The finely tuned artifice of Pope is nowhere to be found but we are some way off naturalness of tone.

Immediately after Cowper's death – he was buried near Mrs Unwin in East Dereham Church in Norfolk – Hayley wrote a biography of his friend, published in 1803. The manuscript of Cowper's poem went into the possession of George III's physician, Dr Edward Ash, and came to the Library from a descendant. The Ash family, according to a note appended to the manuscript, once possessed Mrs Unwin's knitting needles.

A portrait of William Cowper by Lemuel Francis Abbott.

Opposite: Cowper's sonnet of friendship addressed to the poet William Hayley survives in two autograph versions. One, the finished 'presentation' copy , is to be found in a letter from Cowper to Hayley probably written on 3 June 1792, and is in the Library of Princeton University. The other, at the British Library and shown here, reveals Cowper working towards this final fair copy, and is dated 2 June 1792. It forms part of a manuscript volume containing some sixty-two autograph poems (and translations of poems) by the author.

Sonnet

Address'd to William Hayley Esqr. June 2. 1792.

—

Hayley – thy tenderness fraternal shown

    In our first interview, delightful guest!

    To Mary and me for her dear sake distress'd,

Such as it is has made my heart thy own;

still   Though ~~heedless now~~ of new engagements grown;

    For threescore winters make a wintry breast,

    And I had purpos'd neer to go in quest

Of Friendship more, except with God alone.

    But Thou hast won me; nor is God my Foe,

Who eer this last afflictive scene began

    ~~That he might sent Thee to~~   *dreadful*

    ~~Sent Thee before~~ to mitigate the blow

    ~~Whom kind~~ My Brother, by whose sympathy I know

    ~~By true participation of my woe~~,

~~Has~~ Thy true deserts ~~firstly thy deserts~~ infallibly,

~~And taught me all thy worth at once~~ to scan,

Not more t'admire the Bard than love the Man.

—

William Blake
1757–1827

William Blake, now recognised as one of the most visionary of literary and artistic figures, found no fame in his lifetime. It seems extraordinary to think that the man who gave us the words for 'Jerusalem' and 'The Tyger' and whose radiantly beautiful paintings and engravings are so instantly recognisable, should have experienced such a sad lack of interest when he presented his work before the public in his one-man exhibition of 1809. Yet the neglect of Blake by his contemporaries is perhaps not really so surprising. At odds with a world in which he saw the forces of science and materialism triumphing over the spirit, he stood, intellectually and politically, out of his own time.

Sent to a drawing school on the Strand at ten and apprenticed to an engraver at fourteen, Blake lived almost his entire life in London, whose exterior and interior landscapes haunt his work. The sinuous neo-gothicism which flexes and bounds through his art took its cue from the monuments in Westminster Abbey which he spent hours studying in his youth, and he once claimed to have seen angels on Peckham Rye. Blake married Catherine Boucher in 1782, having wooed her with some of the poems which were to appear in his first volume, *Poetical Sketches*, of 1783. He taught 'Kate' to read and she assisted him in their print-shop in Soho – as did William's brother, Robert, for one short year before succumbing to tuberculosis in 1787.

Commissioned as an engraver and illustrator by others more commercially successful than himself, Blake gradually developed his own innovative printing techniques which he used to publish, in tiny numbers, his own beautiful 'illuminated' editions. Most famous among these are his *Songs of Innocence* (1789) and *Songs of Experience* (1793). His work progressed in conditions of poverty, with the couple moving first to Poland Street, in Soho, and subsequently to Lambeth, just south of the Thames. Blake's one long sojourn outside London, in Felpham on the South Coast, included an incident which epitomised his relationship with the hated forces of authority. Blake came to blows with a soldier who had ventured into his garden. The intruder, manhandled back to his lodgings by an adversary renowned for his strength, subsequently accused Blake of sedition – a capital offence eventually rejected in court. In the closing years of his life, Blake's brilliance was recognised and protected by a dedicated coterie, including Samuel Palmer and George Richmond. The patronage of the artist John Linnell ensured Blake's ability to continue working. When he died, aged seventy, it was apparently while singing 'Hallelujahs and songs of joy and triumph'.

A portrait of William Blake taken from the frontispiece to the 1893 edition of his Collected Poems, edited by W.B. Yeats.

Opposite: This notebook of poems, prose and sketches was kept by William Blake from about 1787–1818. It was at one time owned by the painter and poet, Dante Gabriel Rossetti and is sometimes referred to as the 'Rossetti notebook'. The notebook contains over fifty poems from which Blake selected just eighteen for his *Songs of Experience* (1793). Included on one of the manuscript's most fascinatingly complex pages are versions of 'London' and 'The Tyger', the latter certainly among the most famous of English lyrics.

London

I wander thro' each dirty street
Near where the dirty Thames does flow
And mark in every face I meet
Marks of weakness marks of woe

In every cry of every man
In every voice of every child
In every voice in every ban
The mind forg'd manacles I hear

How the chimney sweepers cry
Blackens o'er the churches walls
Every blackning church appalls
And the hapless soldiers sigh
Runs in blood down palace walls

But most the midnight harlots curse
From every dismal street I hear
Weaves around the marriage hearse
And blasts the new born infants tear

I slept in the dark
In the silent night
I murmerd my fears
And I felt delight

In the morning I went
As rosy as morn
To seek for new joy
But I met with scorn

So Nobodaddy
Father of Jealousy
Why dost thou hide thyself in clouds
From every searching eye

Why darkness & obscurity
In all thy words & laws
That none dare eat the fruit but from
The wily serpents jaws
Or in his own eyes

The modest rose puts forth a thorn
The humble sheep a threatning horn
While the lily white shall in love delight
Nor a thorn nor a threat stain her beauty bright

When the voices of children are heard on the green
And whisprings are in the dale
The days of youth rise fresh in my mind
My face turns green & pale

Then come home my children the sun is gone down
And the dews of night arise
Your spring & your day are wasted in play
And your winter & night in disguise

Are not the joys of morning sweeter
Than the joys of night
And are the vigorous joys of youth
Ashamed of the light

Let age & sickness silent rob
The vineyards in the night
But those who burn with vigrous youth
Pluck fruits before the light

The Tyger

Tyger Tyger burning bright
In the forests of the night
What immortal hand or eye
Could frame thy fearful symmetry

Burnt in distant deeps or skies
The cruel fire of thine eyes
On what wings dare he aspire
What the hand dare seize the fire

And what shoulder & what art
Could twist the sinews of thy heart
And when thy heart began to beat
What dread hand & what dread feet

What the hammer what the chain
In what furnace was thy brain
What the anvil what dread grasp
Dare its deadly terrors clasp

Tyger Tyger burning bright
In the forests of the night
What immortal hand & eye
Dare frame thy fearful symmetry

The Nineteenth Century

The nineteenth century, whose authors are all too often gathered up by commentators as 'Romantic' or 'Realist' repays the setting aside of literary critical generalisations in favour of the close scrutiny of its manuscript remains. William Wordsworth, we gather from his intensely subjective vision, 'wandered lonely as a cloud' in his quest for inspiration. Yet the manuscript of his *Poems, in Two Volumes* (1807) bears witness to a far from isolated effort in getting his ethereal words into print. Here we see the everyday evidence of postage, transit parcel and stray pieces of stitching; the industry not only of the poet himself, but his family. Even the famous record of his lonely wanderings comes down to us (as it came to his printer) in the hand of his wife Mary, complete with bodged first line.

Did Keats's poetry come, as he thought all poetry should, 'as naturally as the leaves to a tree'? The manuscript of 'Hyperion', abandoned after several pages of deletions, reworkings and additions would suggest that, in this case, it certainly did not. Bearing this in mind, it seems ironic that one of the most perfect 'finished' of all literary manuscripts, Lewis Carroll's 'Alice's Adventures under Ground', was never intended for publication as *Alice's Adventures in Wonderland* (1865), one of the world's best-loved children's books.

Well into the seventeenth century the circulation of poems by means of manuscript copies rivalled their dissemination in print. By the early nineteenth century there had been a complete reversal of this position, with the published rather than the manuscript record now the means by which works were read. Perhaps it was for this reason that the period saw an unparalleled interest in the collecting and preserving of authors' manuscripts as prized (rather than merely useful) cultural artefacts. It is due to the perspicacity of the foreman of Dickens's publishers, Bradbury and Evans, that a manuscript fragment of *Nicholas Nickleby* (*c*.1839–40) has survived. The descendants of Jane Austen long treasured the gifts she made of her manuscripts. We know that the staff of the asylum to which John Clare was committed took care to preserve his remarkable verses, and posterity has Robert Ross to thank for the survival of a number of important manuscripts by his gifted friend, Oscar Wilde.

Nothing better exemplifies the nineteenth-century cult of collecting than the sad story surrounding the death of the poet Percy Bysshe Shelley. After his drowned corpse was recovered from the sea off the Italian coast (a copy of Keats's poems in his pocket), his body was cremated. In a macabre ceremony, which many would regard as the very apotheosis of Romanticism, those gathered around participated in their own grotesque form of souvenir hunt. Byron's request that the poet's skull be kept for him was denied when it crumbled away. The same fate did not befall the heart, however, which 'although bedded in fire – would not burn'. The words are those of another member of the circle, Edward Trelawny, who recovered the mysterious prize. It was next begged from him by Leigh Hunt who at first refused Byron's demand that it be passed to the poet's widow. He eventually relented and, on Mary's death, it was discovered, shrivelled with age, enclosed in a copy of Percy's *Adonais*. There, however, the story does not end. Secure within the extensive, climate-controlled storage facilities of the British Library, further entombed in what might be better described as a mausoleum than a binding, and sharing space with a long letter from Mary recalling her husband's last days, rests a morbid trophy somehow won many years later by the great forger, book thief, bibliophile and inspired collector of nineteenth- and early- twentieth-century literary manuscripts, T. J. Wise. The trophy? Fragments of the ashes of Percy Bysshe Shelley.

Samuel Taylor Coleridge
1772–1834

A clergyman's son, Samuel Taylor Coleridge was educated at Christ's Hospital School, London and Jesus College, Cambridge, which he left without a degree, having enlisted in the 15th Light Dragoons after an unhappy love affair. Rescued from the army by his brother, he married Sara Fricker and planned, unsuccessfully, with Robert Southey to establish a utopian farming community in New England: just one example of the radicalism which characterised his entire life. Coleridge moved, instead, to the West Country, where he walked, preached and wrote some of his most powerful and moving lyrics. Here he met William Wordsworth, with whom he forged a deep and creative friendship, the first fruits of which appeared as *Lyrical Ballads*, which they published together in 1798. After a period in Germany, Coleridge moved with Wordsworth and his sister Dorothy to the Lake District, helping forever to associate its dramatic and beautiful landscape with the Romantic movement.

Although he continued to immerse himself in literary ventures, publishing widely in the sphere of journalism, criticism, poetry and philosophy and editing an influential periodical, *The Friend*, Coleridge was disastrously addicted to opium from about 1803. At Keswick, in 1802, he wrote 'Ode to Dejection' which has been described as possibly his last great poem and which laments the waning of his imaginative powers. Estranged from Wordsworth and destined never to recapture the intense creative vision of earlier days, he suffered his darkest suicidal years in London between 1811 and 1814. Nevertheless, the support of the Morgan family of Wiltshire and, from April 1816, the surgeon James Gillman of Highgate (who offered him lodgings for the remainder of his life), helped to effect a remarkable process of recovery, in which Coleridge grappled with his demons to emerge a sage-like figure whose influence upon English thought and letters remains strong to this day.

'Kubla Khan' is a monument to English Romanticism. For a century after Coleridge's death, the only clear authority for both the verse 'fragment', shown here, and the story of its remarkable inspiration was the author's preface in *Christabel and Other Poems*, where it was first published in 1816:

A fine engraving of Coleridge taken from an edition of *The Complete Poetical Works* dating from 1870.

Opposite: Coleridge's unique manuscript of 'Kubla Khan' does not look, on the evidence of the first page shown here, like the hastily written recollection which he claimed the poem to be. It is probably a fair copy, perhaps written up from the original 'inspired' draft. The presence of minor corrections to the text does rather invite the question as to why one should wish to meddle with a vision!

In Xannadù did Cubla Khan
A stately Pleasure-Dome decree;
Where Alph, the sacred River, ran
Thro' Caverns measureless to Man
Down to a sunless Sea.
So twice six miles of fertile ground
With Walls and Towers were compass'd round:
And here were Gardens bright with sinuous Rills
Where blossom'd many an incense-bearing Tree,
And here were Forests ancient as the Hills
Enfolding sunny spots of Greenery.
But o! that deep romantic Chasm, that slanted
Down a green Hill athwart a cedarn Cover,
A savage Place, as holy and inchanted
As e'er beneath a waning Moon was haunted
By Woman wailing for her Dæmon Lover:
From forth
And from this Chasm with hideous Turmoil seething,
As if this Earth in fast thick Pants were breathing,
A mighty Fountain momently was forc'd,
Amid whose swift half-intermitted Burst
Huge Fragments vaulted like rebounding Hail,
Or chaffy Grain beneath the Thresher's Flail:
And mid these dancing Rocks at once & ever
It flung up momently the sacred River.
Five miles meandering with a mazy Motion
Thro' Wood and Dale the sacred River ran,
Then reach'd the Caverns measureless to Man—
And sank in Tumult to a lifeless Ocean;
And mid this Tumult Cubla heard from far
Ancestral Voices prophesying War.

    The Shadow of the Dome of Pleasure
      Floated midway on the Wave
    Where was heard the mingled Measure
      From the Fountain and the Cave
    It was a miracle of rare device
    A sunny Pleasure-Dome with Caves of Ice!

    A Damsel with a Dulcimer

In the summer of the year 1797, the Author, then in ill health, had retired to a lonely farmhouse between Porlock and Linton, on the Exmoor confines of Somerset and Devonshire. In consequence of a slight indisposition, an anodyne had been prescribed, from the effects of which he fell asleep in his chair at the moment he was reading the following sentence, or words of the same substance, in 'Purchas's Pilgrimage': 'Here the Khan Kubla commanded a palace to be built, and a stately garden thereunto. And thus ten miles of fertile ground were inclosed with a wall.'

The author continued for about three hours in a profound sleep, at least of the external senses, during which time he has the most vivid confidence, that he could not have composed less than from two to three hundred lines; if that can indeed be called composition in which all the images rose up before him as things, with a parallel production of the correspondent expressions, without any sensation or consciousness of effort.

On awaking he appeared to himself to have a distinct recollection of the whole, and taking his pen, ink, and paper, instantly and eagerly wrote down the lines that are here preserved. At this moment he was unfortunately called out by a person on business from Porlock, and detained by him above an hour, and on his return to his room, found to his no small surprise and mortification, that though he still retained some vague and dim recollection of the general purpose of the vision, yet, with the exception of some eight or ten scattered lines and images, all the rest had passed away.

In 1934 the unique autograph manuscript of the poem came to light. At the end of what is, in fact, a rather undistinguished document, Coleridge writes and signs the following note:

> This fragment with a good deal more, not recoverable, composed, in a sort of Reverie brought on by two grains of Opium, taken to check a dysentery, at a Farm House between Porlock & Linton, a quarter of a mile from Culbone Church, in the fall of the year, 1797.

The rather prosaic account of poetic creation differs in several respects from the famous published version. In the latter, the date is given as summer 1797; the author's poor health is described; it is noted that he has retired to the farmhouse (which is more exactly located); it describes the opium as an 'anodyne', and his dysentry as a 'slight indisposition'; he has been reading 'Purchas's Pilgrimage' and, rather than a 'Reverie', falls into a profound sleep; the length of the poem as originally conceived in the vision is given as no less than 'two to three hundred lines'. Perhaps most interestingly of all, the celebrated 'man from Porlock' is nowhere mentioned in the manuscript account.

The discrepancy may perhaps be attributed to mere abbreviation on the part of Coleridge. But there is an irresistible suspicion of embellishment on his part, which, whether by design or not, has certainly enhanced the Romantic conception of the poet's unique apprehension of imaginative forces far beyond the understanding of mere mortals – such as, for instance, the 'nuisancesome' man from Porlock.

Right: In 1951 The Pilgrim Trust presented the British Museum Library with a substantial collection of manuscripts by, or relating to, Coleridge and his family, including some fifty-five notebooks kept by the poet. Shown here is a map (which occasionally confuses left and right) from notebook 'No 2', entitled 'Lakes'. Kept between July and September 1802, the notebook records Coleridge's energetic, solitary and often daring exploration of the mountainous landscape of the Lake District which seemed to him infused with the sublime. His description of Scafell, which he climbed, is somewhat reminiscent of 'Kubla Khan': 'O Scafell, they enormous Precipices – Just by the hollow stones are two enormous Columns. I am no measurer – they were vaster than any that I have ever seen, & were each a stone Mountain they could not be less than 250 yards high.'

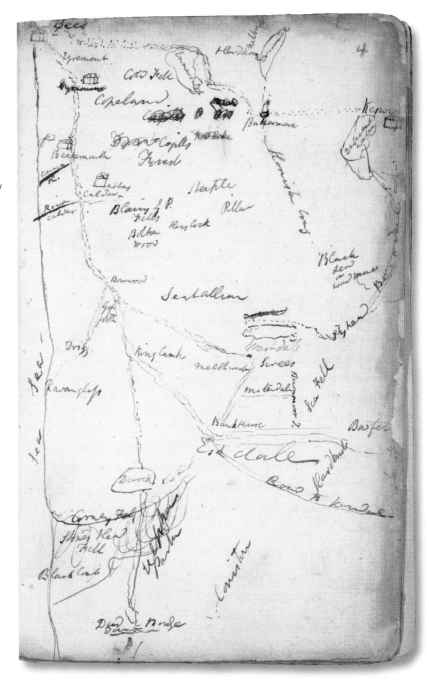

William Wordsworth
1770–1850

Three major episodes in Wordsworth's life had a profound effect upon his development as a poet. First there was the loss of both his parents before he reached the age of fourteen which threw him upon his own resources and made him turn for solace and strength to the beauty and grandeur of the Cumbrian landscape in which he grew up. The second was his series of visits to France beginning in 1790 which nurtured in him republican principles and a respect for the outsider in society, the humble, the unregarded, the rejected. The third was his momentous meeting with Coleridge which led him to examine the growth of his own imagination.

The sum of his thinking was to be put into his vast poem 'The Recluse', begun in 1798 and worked on for years. He saw this poem in the form of a Gothic church: a part of it, *The Prelude*, published posthumously in 1850, was the 'ante-chapel' while another, *The Excursion*, published in 1814, was the 'body'. He considered the smaller poems as 'little cells, or oratories…ordinarily included in those edifices'. One such little cell is his poem 'November 1806', which refers to the overthrow of Prussia by Napoleon's forces at the Battle of Jena on 14 October 1806. It is the last of the twenty-six sonnets 'dedicated to Liberty' published in his *Poems, in Two Volumes* in April 1807.

The poem is to be found on one leaf from the extraordinary manuscript of this collection of poems, acquired by the British Museum Library in 1952. The volume is a gathering together of poems transcribed in 1806 and early 1807 by Wordsworth himself, by his wife, his sister and his sister-in-law while they were all staying, the guests of Sir George Beaumont, at Coleorton in Leicestershire. Coleridge visited at the time and his own scribal contributions are evident. He appears to have brought his own paper, otherwise anything to hand would do, including the blank sides of old letters.

Family responsibilities increasingly diminished Wordsworth's radical views until he became an establishment figure, succeeding Robert Southey as Poet Laureate in 1843. Rydal Mount, his home near Grasmere, became almost a shrine for visiting admirers and today the large number of tourists seeking out his grave in the churchyard there is testimony to his abiding stature in English Literature.

A portrait of William Wordsworth from the frontispiece of *The Poetical Album, and Register of Modern Fugitive Poetry* of 1828–29.

Opposite: Wordsworth's poem 'I wandered lonely as a cloud' was written in 1804. This particular poem was transcribed by his wife Mary, who makes an intriguing false start. No manuscript of the text survives in the poet's own hand. Interestingly, the 1802 journal of Wordsworth's sister, Dorothy, contains expressions which prefigure William's descriptions of daffodils, suggesting that their minds worked in a mutually inspirational way.

'To the Printer
(after the Poem (in the set under the title
of "Moods of my own mind") beginning ~~the~~
"The Cock is crowing" please to insert
the two following ~~properly~~ numbered, & number
the succeeding ones accordingly)

~~I wandered like a lonely~~

    I wandered lonely as a Cloud
That floats on high oer Vales and Hills,
When all at once I saw a crowd
A ~~host~~ of dancing Daffodils;
~~Along~~ the Lake beneath the trees
Ten thousand dancing in the breeze.

The Waves beside them danced, but they
Outdid the sparkling Waves in glee:—
A Poet could not but be gay
In such a laughing company:
I gaz'd — and gaz'd — but little thought
What wealth the shew to me had brought.

For oft when on my couch I lie
In vacant, or in pensive mood,
They flash upon that inward eye
Which is the bliss of solitude,
And then my heart with pleasure fills,
And dances with the Daffodils.

Who fancied what a pretty sight
This Rock would be if edged around
With living Snowdrops? circlet bright!

Jane Austen
1775–1817

Jane Austen was born into a large and affectionate Hampshire family. As a child she was an avid reader and her earliest surviving writings date from her teenage years. A delightful example, pictured here, is her parody of contemporary history textbooks, 'The History of England', written in 1790 by 'a Partial, Prejudiced and ignorant historian', as she describes herself. The illustrations were done by her sister, Cassandra.

Though leading the circumscribed life of a country clergyman's daughter, Austen developed a sharply perceptive view of the follies of mankind. She limited herself to what she knew of her age and society but what she created is a microcosm of the whole world's frailties. Self-delusion, self-aggrandisement and hypocrisy are but a few of the more distasteful traits of humanity to fall under her scrutiny; her ironic detachment and humour, nevertheless, make them joyfully palatable. *Pride and Prejudice* (1813), *Emma* (1815) and *Persuasion* (1818) are among the very greatest of English literary achievements.

It is ultimately Austen's craftsmanship that carries the day. She worked assiduously at shaping her novels, something quite apparent in the manuscript of part of *Persuasion*, also illustrated here. It constitutes what were then – in July 1816 – the two final chapters, numbers ten and eleven. The posthumously published work retains the final chapter, re-numbered as twelve, but discards the other in favour of a new chapter ten and has part of the old chapter ten embedded into a reworked chapter eleven. We can see her structuring processes clearly.

The minute size of the sheets (165 x 92 mm), deliberately cut down from foolscap size, reflects Austen's working practice: she would hide them away when her household or social duties made demands upon her. A slip attached to one of the folios reads 'The contents of this Drawer for Anna' (her niece, Anna Lefroy), a sad reminder of her last days. She died of Addison's disease in Winchester and was worthily granted a resting-place in the cathedral there.

A steel engraving of Jane Austen after a watercolour sketch by her sister Cassandra of 1810.

Opposite: This manuscript, comprising two cancelled chapters of *Persuasion*, was acquired by the British Museum Library in 1925 (having passed to Austen's sister Cassandra after her death). It shows the complexity of Austen's editorial method and represents all that survives of the original manuscript.

Chapter II.

~~Let us conclude our story, then. Who—~~ Who can be in doubt of what followed?— When any two young People take it into their heads to marry, they are pretty sure ~~by perseverance to carry their point, be they ever so~~ by perseverance ~~to~~ ~~opposition~~ — be they ever so poor, or ever so imprudent, or ever so little likely to be necessary to each other's ultimate comfort. This may be bad Morality to conclude with, but I believe it to be Truth— and if such parties succeed, how should a Capt W— & an Emma, fail, with the advantage of Maturity of Mind, consciousness of Right, & ~~an~~ Independant Fortune between them, ~~of~~ ^bd^ of bearing down every opposition?— They might in fact, have borne down a great deal more than they met with, for there was little to distress them beyond the want of Graciousness & Warmth— Mr W. made no objection, & Eliz: ~~too~~ did nothing worse than look cold & unconcerned.— Capt. W— with £ 25,000— & as high in his

John Keats
1795–1821

Keats first appeared in print with a sonnet published on 5 May 1816 in Leigh Hunt's periodical *The Examiner*. His death in Rome on 23 February 1821 and his burial in the Protestant cemetery there curtailed a public poetic working life which spanned barely five years, but the legacy of that intense period is an astonishingly rich one. Although derided by many contemporaries (Byron threatened to skin him), subsequent poets have acknowledged him as one of the finest talents of the nineteenth century and his influence has been far-reaching.

The son of a livery stable-manager – not a humble profession, as has been commonly supposed – he was born in London. He lived in and around the city throughout his life and has come to be closely associated with Hampstead, where his house can still be visited. He originally chose medicine as a profession and began his working life as a dresser at Guy's Hospital. His deeper calling, however, was to poetry, and encouraged and influenced by the poet and liberal journalist Leigh Hunt, he read widely in Elizabethan literature and absorbed the colour of Italian romances.

'Hyperion' was written in late 1818 and abandoned, unfinished, in early 1819. It was a time of considerable personal distress for Keats. Symptoms of consumption began in August 1818 (recognizable to his expert eye) and through the latter months of this year he was nursing his brother Tom, whose early death from the same disease cruelly anticipated his own. Savage reviews of his work had appeared in August and September and in December Keats met Fanny Brawne for whom he developed a tormented passion.

The autograph manuscript of 'Hyperion', shown here, comprises twenty-seven very large folios and is watermarked '1810'. It was evidently intended as a fair copy of the poem but Keats had further assaults on it, often creating improvements which have a Miltonic ring. However, Keats's evident struggle with the text leading to its final abandonment perhaps bears out his famous remark, made only shortly before he began the work, that 'if poetry comes not as naturally as the leaves to a tree, it had better not come at all'.

As for the manuscript's history, it lay unrecognised through much of the nineteenth century. It was probably in Hunt's possession on Keats's death, for his son, Thornton Hunt, gave it to Miss Alice Bird, the sister of Hunt's physician, in about 1862. Only at the turn of the century did she discover that it was in Keats's own hand. It was acquired by the British Museum Library in 1904.

A wistful-looking Keats in a miniature by his friend Joseph Severn.

Opposite: Keats's dramatic manuscript of his unfinished epic poem 'Hyperion' is written, as befits its grand theme, on oversized sheets of high-quality paper. The opening page is shown here. Keats has taken considerable care to write in his best – at times almost calligraphic – hand.

Hyperion Book 1st

Deep in the shady sadness of a Vale,
Far sunken from the healthy breath of Morn,
Far from the fiery noon, and ~~evening~~ Eve's one Star,
Sat grey hair'd Saturn quiet as a Stone,
Still as the silence round about his Lair.
Forest on forest hung above his head
~~Like Clouds that whose bosoms thunderous bosoms~~
Like Cloud on Cloud. No stir of air was there;
~~Not so much life as what an eagle~~
~~No life spread upon a field of green ear'd corn:~~
But where the dead leaf fell, there did it rest
A stream went voiceless by, still deadened more
By reason of his fallen divinity
~~Spreading a shade if~~
Spreading a shade: the Naiad mid her reeds
Pressd her cold finger closer to her lips.

Along the margin sand large foot marks went
No further than to where his feet had stay'd so often
And slept ~~without~~ there since ~~a motion:~~ upon the ground
His old right hand lay nerveless, ~~on the ground~~ listless, dead
Unsceptered; and his ~~white brows~~ eyes were closd;
While his ~~bowed~~ head seem'd listening to the Earth
His Ancient Mother for some comfort yet.

Thus the old Eagle drowsy with ~~his of~~ great grief
Sat moulting his weak Plumage never more
To be restored or soar against the Sun,
While his three Sons upon Olympus stood—

It seem'd no force could wake him from his place
But there came one who, with a kindred hand
Touch'd his wide Shoulders, after bending low
With reverence, though to one who knew it not.
She was a Goddess of the infant world;
~~Scarce by her side the tallest Amazon~~
Had stood a little ~~cloud:~~ she would have ta'en
Achilles by the hair and bent his neck,
Or with a ~~finger can~~ Ixion's toil

*Not so much life as on a summers day
Robs not at all the dandelions fleece

Percy Bysshe Shelley
1792–1822

The decade 1810 to 1820 was, in Coleridge's words, 'an age of anxiety from the crown to the hovel, from the cradle to the coffin'. The English victory at Waterloo did nothing to resolve deep-seated problems at home and the agents of reform clashed hopelessly with an entrenched and intransigent Tory government. Shelley's little tract 'Proposal for Putting Reform to the Vote', an argument favouring an extension of the franchise, was but one of the many dismissed out of hand, but when on 16 August 1819 a crowd of some 60,000 people gathered – peacefully, it should be said – at St Peter's Fields, Manchester, to press for the franchise, the authorities took fright. The local magistrates called in the cavalry, who hacked down over 400 people with their sabres, killing eleven. The magistracy was congratulated by the government.

This, the 'Peterloo Massacre', is what prompted Percy Bysshe Shelley's poem, 'The Mask of Anarchy', a powerful piece of invective written in a popular ballad form. The autograph draft of the poem, whose untitled opening is illustrated here, dates from the autumn of 1819. The manuscript's twelve folios appear to have been torn out of a notebook and its text varies in many places from that printed in the first edition of 1832. The voice is unmistakably Shelley's. Strikingly independent of spirit, he had been a problem to his parents, to his university (from which he was sent down) and

indeed to society whose conventions he ignored. His abandonment of his first wife, Harriet, his flight to the continent in 1814 with Mary Godwin, and their liaisons with Byron and his circle all conspired to shock conventional notions of respectability.

Shelley's death shocked too. He was drowned in the Gulf of Spezia, near Leghorn, in his thirtieth year. His remains were cremated on the beach. Although most of Shelley's ashes were buried in the Protestant Cemetery in Rome (also the final resting place of Keats, a copy of whose poems was discovered on Shelley's corpse), a small phial came to the British Museum Library in 1938, preserved in the binding of a manuscript containing a moving letter from his widow describing his last days.

Shelley, an engraving from the original painting by Amelia Curran, a friend of the Shelleys.

Opposite: The manuscript of Shelley's highly charged political poem, 'The Mask of Anarchy', is written on both sides of ten sheets of paper apparently ripped from a notebook. It contains, as well as his boldly written text, the occasional rather whimsical doodle. The opening of the poem is displayed here.

As I lay asleep in Italy
There came a voice from over the Sea
And with great power it forth led me
To walk in the Visions of Poesy

I met Murder on the way —
He had a mask like Castlereagh,
Very smooth he looked, yet grim;
Seven bloodhounds followed him.

All ghirre fat, & well they might
be in admirable plight
For one by one & two by two
He tossed them human hearts to chew
Which from his wide cloak he drew

Next came Fraud She had on
Like — Eldon, an ermined gown
his big tears for he wept well

John Clare
1793–1864

In 1841 John Clare was committed to Northampton Asylum, where he remained until his death some twenty-three years later. Here he wrote some of his most poignant and celebrated poems. Born at Helpstone, Northamptonshire to a poor farm labourer and his illiterate wife, from the age of seven Clare worked in the fields. He read widely, taking advantage of his father's enjoyment of popular poetry and chapbook (folk) literature; his discovery of Thomson's *The Seasons* at the age of thirteen inspired him to begin composing verse. Initially a private exercise affording a 'downright pleasure in giving vent to my feelings', his honest articulation of country life caught the imagination of a sophisticated reading public glad to discover, in the innocent voice of a 'peasant poet', a worthy successor to Robert Burns. Such fashionable interest, which perhaps failed to take into account the genuine depth of the writing, soon waned, however, and the success of *Poems Descriptive of Rural Life and Scenery*, published in 1820, was never matched by subsequent volumes.

Clare's drift back into literary obscurity together with his luckless attempts to establish himself as a farmer (having worked as a gardener and, for a short while, a soldier) may have played a part in the increasing fragility of his mental health, but his earlier life was not without melancholy. In particular, although he later married Martha Turner in 1820, he never overcame his childhood love for Mary Joyce, whose father forbade their courtship. In 1841, he wandered away from the private asylum in Epping Forest where he had been since 1837, sadly deluded in the belief that he could become reunited with her again. His exhausted return to Northampton was followed by his removal to the county asylum, where he found kindness and support for his writing and was allowed to go about his quiet ways. He died on 20 May 1864 and was buried in the village of his birth.

The poems written by Clare in the asylum survived largely through the good offices of its staff, in particular the House Steward W. F. Knight who began the task, later taken up by other copyists, of transcribing his manuscripts into two volumes. However, the autograph poems shown here date from 1819, a year in which Clare contemplated suicide. In a letter of the same year (which itself bears a poem on its reverse) he sternly instructs the bookseller Edward Drury, who did much to help publish his first poems, as to what he must on no account posthumously print: '...if I knew such things I disapprove of should appear in print after my death it would be the greatest torture possible'.

An engraving of Clare published in 1821, after a painting by W. Hilton.

Opposite: This manuscript belonged, until 1967, in the National Portrait Gallery, where it was displayed with Clare's portrait. 'The Dying Snowdrop' and the sonnet nevertheless went unpublished until the scholar Eric Robinson brought them to light. The two stanzas at the foot of the page are from the poet's 'Song of Praise: Imitation of the 158th Psalm', which appeared in the *Village Minstrel* (1821).

Sonnet   Oct April

Hail to thee Violet sweet Earless spread
Neath each warm bush & cover bidding here
In many a pleasing Walk have I thee td
To seek thy promise of Springs earliest pledge
She modest bays hanging down its head
Unconscious hiding beauties from the eye
So sweetly tossing oer its Graceful form
Shunning each Vulgar gause that cumbers by
Timely stooping from an April shower
As if tue startled by approaching harm   storm
Shrinks from delusion falsely betraying hand
Each bashfull look that shall endearing form
So sweeter I bestow the coy Violet & turn
Tempting the plunderer with a double charm

_____

The Dying Snowdrop   Oct April

Snowdrop I mourn thee oer thy early tomb
Thy withered presence so untimely shed
Killd by the pride that gave thy spotless bloom
Upon the snow bow stoops thy withered head

So artless beauty oftentimes undone
Unconscious obeying oer Seductions heart
Like the poor Lark the Fowlers wile have won
Falls on the spot when proffled of his rest

_____

Praise his name his mercy bless
Ye poor like me in whelvd distress
Thail protection given
When sweet sorrow dies away
Our hopes his promise cant decay
Of recompensing heaven

_____

Thunders that fright the trembling grovn
Ye forked lightnings flashing round
To quench in whelming shower
So shall the this dry present
Though if in rolling rolling winds
While fansomy nature silent bends
To own almighty power

Sir Walter Scott
1771–1832

Shown here is a folio from the manuscript of Scott's novel *Kenilworth*. Vividly evident in this final draft before going to press is the massive impetus of the physical act of writing: Lockhart, his great biographer, said his handwriting reflected his legal training. He can barely stop to close and open a new paragraph and his directive 'NP' (it looks like NL) has to suffice. Interestingly, there are emendations even at this stage – Lady Paulet becomes Lady Paget.

Kenilworth was ready for publication by the end of 1820, a year which had also seen the appearance of Scott's other novels *Ivanhoe*, *The Monastery* and *The Abbot*. This breathtaking output was sustained throughout the author's working life. From childhood Scott was fascinated with his own family history. Born and educated in Edinburgh, his ancestral roots tapped deep into the beautiful Scottish border country whose literary and geographical landscapes he explored with ceaseless energy. His antiquarian enthusiasms expanded to embrace the literature and history of the Scottish people so that he became a mine of knowledge. In 1820 his immense contribution to the nation's literature was recognised by his being given a baronetcy by George IV and he was offered honorary degrees by both Oxford and Cambridge Universities.

The action of the novel is set in 1575. In that year the revels at the Earl of Leicester's Kenilworth Castle actually took place and Scott made use of contemporary accounts but historically the rest of the action is anachronistic, for Ralegh, one of the central characters in the novel, did not appear at court until 1581. Scott's tale is in fact a distillation of the Elizabethan temper but by its great attention to detail – exemplified in this fragment – it achieves the radiance of verisimilitude. Scott's evocations of a picturesque past and portrayals of wild scenery had a huge influence on the romantic sensibilities of the early nineteenth century. Equally his sense of structure and imaginative creation of individual *personae* had a major part to play in the development of the novel form.

He died worn out by his industry, by his extravagant commitment to the beauties of his prodigious home, Abbotsford, near Melrose (which he built for himself between 1817 and 1824) and by his magnificently selfless clearance of the debts he faced on the collapse in 1826 of the Ballantyne printing house in which he had a concern. In that same year his wife died, whom he had married in 1797 and with whom he had five children. He was buried in the ruins of Dryburgh Abbey in the Scottish borders, beside his ancestors, and his manuscript of *Kenilworth*, comprising 170 folios, was purchased by the British Museum Library in 1855.

An engraved portrait of Scott, at work (in the artist's imagination, one suspects) on the manuscript of *Waverley*.

Opposite: A folio from Scott's *Kenilworth*, published in early 1821. The manuscript lacks only a few folios, otherwise presenting us with a remarkable insight into Scott's fervent industry. It was prepared and corrected by Scott for the press and presumably followed a preliminary drafting process.

in that just proportion which was praised alike from malign and slander and insipid praise. He remarked with ready accent the manners of her offered as the clownish and made his own grace. The ... of them united the fashions and even the dress of their ladies were equally his theme and seldom did he conclude without conveying some compliment always couched with delicacy and expressed with ... pusly to the Virgin Queen her court and her government, & he ended by the list of the attendants upon the royal person on such conversation varied by remarks upon ancient elegies and modern authors and mixed wisdom with the lighter talk of a female court. NB. When they returned to the Palace Elizabeth ... It even seemed to him (though that might be crisis from the flattery of his own imagination) that during this their passages she leaned on him somewhat more than the slipperiness of the way necessarily demanded ... by her actions and words, endeavored to express a degree of favour which even in his proudest days he had not ... their attentions ... enjoyed his triumph as one of them court favour had been ... the primary and the ultimate motive of life and forgot in the intoxication of the moment the perplexities and dangers of his own situation. Such strange as it may appear he thought but at that moment of the peril arising from his secret union. Many of the marks of grace which Elizabeth from time to time shewed to young Raleigh...

Fain would I climb but that I fear to fall

The Queen smiled ... twice over with deliberation once to Lady Paulet and once again to herself...

Fain would I climb but that I fear to fall

Might not the answer fit her fault ... than thus
If thy mind fail thee do not climb at all.

119

Mary Shelley
1797–1851

'Singularly bold, somewhat imperious, and active of mind. Her desire of knowledge is great, and her perseverence in everything she undertakes almost invincible.' Thus did William Godwin describe his fifteen-year-old daughter Mary, future wife of the poet Percy Bysshe Shelley and author of *Frankenstein* (1818). Mary's exceptional character sprang from gifted parents. Her mother, Mary Wollstonecraft, who died giving birth to her, wrote the famous *Vindication of the Rights of Woman* (1792), while William established himself as an influential philosopher and radical.

Mary's upbringing fell in part to her stepmother, Mrs Clairmont, with whose daughter, Jane, she travelled to the continent in July 1814. With them was the poet Shelley, to whom Mary had grown increasingly close since their meeting in the Spring of that year. Their friendship developed into profound love and devotion and they married in 1816, shortly after Shelley learned of the suicide of his first, estranged wife. A competition to write a ghost story (with, among others, Lord Byron) in Italy in 1816 resulted in Mary's *Frankenstein*, a powerful gothic fable which was published two years later. It continues to exert a strong (if often misinterpreted) influence on the popular imagination.

The excitement of travel, the deepening of love, the satisfaction of literary achievement and the constant intellectual stimulation derived from the inspirational and eccentric circle of friends among whom she moved, were from this point in Mary's young life offset by a number of cruel blows. She lost two of the children she had had with Shelley: first Clara, who died in Venice in 1818, and then William in 1819, in Rome. A son, Percy, was born to them in the midst of a melancholy which cast its long and ominous shadow as far as San Terenzo, on the Bay of Lerici, to which they moved in April 1822. In this remote spot, Mary suffered a dangerous miscarriage, while Shelley endured strange intimations of his own fate. On 8 July, not long after seeing the ghost of a child in the sea, he drowned while sailing off the coast, leaving Mary to fall upon the support of Byron and his circle in Genoa before her return to England.

Although for the remainder of her years Mary enjoyed a measure of success as a novelist, contributor to periodicals and literary editor, she never surpassed the achievement of her first work. 'Torn by memory', she did her best to keep alive Shelley's literary flame, and to guarantee her son's welfare. If legend is to be believed, she kept with her at all times the remains of her husband's heart, which had failed to burn during his dramatic cremation on the beach. She herself died in London and is buried in the churchyard of St Peter's, Bournemouth, together with her husband's heart and her parents – who were removed there from St Pancras Churchyard shortly after her death.

An engraved portrait of Mary Shelley after the portrait by Rothwell, published in 1889.

Opposite: Mary endured a terrible period of deepening fear between Shelley's embarkation on 8 July for Lerici in the small boat the Don Juan and the discovery ten days later of his body on the shore near Via Reggio. This undated manuscript sets out in fair copy a short poem which explores the themes of loss and hope through the vivid use of night and day imagery.

Ah! he is gone – and I alone;
    How dark and dreary seems the time!
'Tis thus when the glad sun is flown,
    Night rushes o'er the Indian clime.

Is there no star to cheer this night —
    No soothing twilight for the breast?
Yes – memory sheds her fairy light,
    Beaming as sunset's golden west.

And hope of dawn – Oh brighter far
    Than clouds that in the orient burn,
More welcome than the morning star,
    Is the dear thought – he will return!

Mary W. Shelley

George Gordon, Lord Byron
1788–1824

When Byron died of fever in Greece in 1824 the world lost perhaps its most famous modern poet. That he should die in exile as self-appointed head of a 'Byron brigade', formed to lead the Greek battle for independence against the Turks, typifies his boundlessly charismatic and unconventional life. Byron was born in London, the son of a rumbustious, philandering father and a long-suffering Scottish mother descended from the ranks of the minor nobility. Despite a painfully deformed leg, Byron was strikingly handsome, a quality he used throughout his life to seduce a great many admirers. It is probable that one such was his half-sister, Augusta Leigh. The rumours surrounding the nature of their relationship destroyed his ill-advised marriage to Annabella Milbanke and forced him in 1816 to shake the dust of England from his shoes for good. He left behind a daughter, Augusta Ada, whom, like his wife, he never saw again.

By the time of his exile, Byron – boxer, swimmer, traveller, political speaker and from 1798 6th Lord Byron of Newstead Abbey – was already a famous poet, having honed his skills at Harrow and Trinity College, Cambridge to produce, in 1812, the brilliant first cantos of *Childe Harold's Pilgrimage*. He travelled in Switzerland, where he stayed with the Shelleys and Claire Clairmont (who became his mistress and bore him a daughter, Allegra, in 1817) before moving restlessly through Italy and consolidating his literary reputation with the long poem *Don Juan*. Byron played up to his devil-may-care reputation – his mistress Caroline Lamb had declared him 'mad, bad and dangerous to know' – finding it, perhaps, a useful camouflage under which to hide a genuinely melancholy disposition. His last years, if full of resolution to dedicate himself politically, physically and financially to the cause of liberty, were nevertheless tainted with sadness. In 1822 he lost his friend Shelley and received the tragic news of Allegra's sudden death. In February 1824 he suffered a convulsive fit (referred to here in one of his last poems, 'Love and Death') and two months later, weakened by fever and medical bleeding, he died at Missolonghi on the Greek mainland. His body was finally conveyed to the family vault at Hucknall Torkard, near Newstead.

An 1826 engraving of Lord Byron, after a painting by William Edward West.

Opposite: A single manuscript sheet contains drafts of Byron's last poems. 'Love and Death', shown here, was written sometime between 21 February and 9 April 1824. Byron died on 19 April. The poem of unrequited love, which has all the appearance of a first draft, is addressed to Loukas Chalandritsanos, whom Byron cared for in Greece. The poem refers to a series of dramatic events actually experienced by Byron and Loukas.

No 8.

I watched thee when the foe was at our side —
Ready to strike at him — or thee and me —
Were safety hopeless — rather than divide
Aught ~~with~~ dwelt with me ~~our~~ loved — save love out right — Liberty
~~positively not~~ ~~our beloved but~~ thee —

2.

I watched thee in the ~~tempest~~ breakers — when the rocks
Received our ~~bear~~ — out all was ~~terror~~ storm and fear
And bade thee cling to me ~~whatter~~ through every shock —
be thy bark or ~~through~~ every
This arms would bear thee ~~thing~~ ~~part the~~ bier,

3.

I watched thee when the ~~fever~~ ~~had~~ ~~thrown~~
~~gasping~~ my arms — and ~~myself~~ ~~upon~~ the ground —
~~overdone~~
When ~~wth~~ with ~~nothing~~, near to rise
From thence — if them on earth now ~~until~~ fruit,

4. 6

~~has~~ enough and ~~more~~ — and yet thou could'st
are not
~~And~~ never will — Love dwells not in our will —
Nor ~~do~~ I blame thee — though it be my lot.
~~To love thee~~ ~~strongly~~ ~~away~~ ~~vainly~~ — love thee still.

Elizabeth Barrett Browning 1806–1861
Robert Browning 1812–1889

In the summer of 1849, in the small Tuscan town of Bagni de Lucca which Byron had once made his home, Elizabeth Barrett Browning showed her husband Robert a sequence of sonnets secretly written throughout their courtship. Under the last of her now famous *Sonnets from the Portuguese* is written the simple statement 'Married – September 12th/1846'. Why, at this particular point in time, did she decide to reveal her testament of love? Perhaps a period of such great emotional intensity demanded the gesture. A son, Robert Wiedemann (always known as 'Pen') had been born to Elizabeth (now forty-three), after much difficulty, on 9 March, yet barely a week later, their joy was dashed by the sudden death of Robert's mother whom he had not seen for over two years. The younger man – he was thirty-six – must have been greatly comforted by his wife's assurance, which can be read in perhaps the most famous of her sonnets (opposite), that:

> I love thee to the depth & breadth & height
> My soul can reach, when feeling out of sight
> For the ends of Being and Ideal Grace.

Robert and Elizabeth met on 20 May 1845, following a fervid correspondence which had begun early in that year with him famously declaring, that 'I do, as I say, love these Books with all my heart – and I love you too'. The romance blossomed.

Elizabeth's father was opposed to her marrying and so, one week after their clandestine union in St Marylebone Church, they eloped to Italy and settled in Florence, where they made 'Casa Guidi' their home. Elizabeth's literary reputation was by now well established, with her *Poems* of 1844 leading to speculation that she might well become poet laureate. Robert, who like Elizabeth was largely self-educated, was less well known; indeed, his poem *Sordello*, published in 1840, had been poorly received by the critics.

For the next fourteen years the couple remained at 'Casa Guidi', apart from two visits to London (where conciliatory approaches to her father failed) and Paris. Elizabeth's reputation soared with a collected edition of poems (including her sonnets) appearing in 1850 to be followed a year later by *Casa Guidi Windows*, a passionate poetic defence of Italian independence. *Aurora Leigh*, her innovative 'novel in verse' about a woman writer was an immediate success and has come to be seen as an important early feminist text. Her stature was such that she easily shook off censure from the English critics for her pro-Italian, anti-English *Poems before Congress* of 1860.

The American writer Nathaniel Hawthorne described Elizabeth Barrett Browning 'a pale small person scarcely embodied at all', with eyes so bright and dark 'that there is not such another figure in the world'.

Opposite: The manuscript draft of perhaps the most famous of Elizabeth Barrett Browning's *Sonnets from the Portuguese*. The sequence traces her growing love for Robert Browning, who nicknamed her 'my little Portuguese', in reference to her dark complexion.

XLIII

How do I love thee? Let me count the ways! —
I love thee to the depth & breadth & height
My soul can reach, when feeling out of sight
For the ends of Being and Ideal Grace.
I love thee to the level of everyday's
Most quiet need, by sun & candlelight —
I love thee freely, as men strive for Right; —
I love thee purely, as they turn from Praise:—
I love thee with the passion, put to use
In my old griefs; and with my childhood's faith:
I love thee with the love I seemed to lose
With my lost Saints! — I love thee with the breath,
Smiles, tears, of all my life! — and, if God choose,
I shall but love thee better after death.

The following year Elizabeth, always physically frail, succumbed to an affliction of the lungs and on 29 June died in her husband's arms, aged fifty-five. Shattered, Browning left Florence for London, never to return. Relentlessly applying himself to his work, he now began quickly to build upon the success he had achieved with the collection *Men and Women* of 1855, which included perhaps his most famous love poem, 'Love Among the Ruins'. Among the astonishing volume of acclaimed works which ensued (much of it tinged with melancholy and doubt), was his masterpiece *The Ring and the Book*. Browning's epic, philosophically involved poem, woven around a late-seventeenth-century account of murder and published in four monthly instalments from 1868, was inspired by a collection of documents he discovered in a 'square old yellow Book' bought from a market stall in Florence.

Accolades and awards showered down upon Browning in his later years. The founding of a society devoted to him in 1881 was an astonishing, albeit somewhat embarrassing honour. In 1878 he returned to Italy for the first time since the death of his beloved Elizabeth and it was here, in Venice, that he died on 12 December 1889. Browning had said that if he died in Italy he would wish to be buried with his wife. The closure of the Protestant cemetery in Florence prevented this and Pen therefore arranged for his father to lie among the poets in Westminster Abbey.

The English *Dictionary of National Biography* states that 'Browning was below the middle height, but broadly built and of great muscular strength'. His 'full and lustrous' hair is much in evidence in this engraved portrait by J.C. Armytage of 1884.

Opposite: The first page of the manuscript of Robert Browning's epic poem 'The Ring and the Book' inspired by a 'square old yellow book' bought at a market in Florence.

1. The Ring and the Book.

Do you see this Ring?

'T is Rome-work, made to match
(By Castellani's imitative craft)
Etrurian circlets found, some happy morn,
After a dropping April; found alive   5
Spark-like 'mid unearthed slope-side figtree-roots
That roof old tombs at Chiusi: soft, you see,
Yet crisp as jewel-cutting. There's one brick,
(Craftsmen instruct me) one approved device
And but one, fits such slivers of pure gold   10
As this was,—such mere oozings from the mine,
Virgin as oval tawny pendent tear
At beehive-edge when ripened combs o'erflow,—
To bear the file's tooth and the hammer's tap;
Since hammer needs must widen out the round,   15
And file emboss it fine with lily-flowers,
Ere the stuff grow a ring-thing right to wear.
That brick is, the artificer melts up wax
With honey, so to speak; he mingles gold
With gold's alloy, and, duly tempering both,   20
Effects a manageable mass, then works.
But his work ended, once the thing a ring,
Oh, there's repristination! Just a spirt
Of the proper fiery acid o'er its face,
And forth the alloy unfastened flies in fume;   25
While, self-sufficient now, the shape remains,
The rondure brave, the lilied loveliness,

Emily Brontë
1818–1848

Emily has often been acclaimed as the most imaginative of the four Brontë children. After the death of her mother in 1821 she was raised with her brother Branwell and her two sisters Charlotte and Anne by her Irish-born father, the Anglican curate of Haworth. The cloistered life of the children in an isolated village on the edge of the Yorkshire moors brought them very close to each other. They devoured the books in their father's library and began writing stories and poems from an early age.

Eccentric, stubborn and fiercely independent, Emily attended a local school only briefly and was then educated mostly at home: her passionate attachment to the parsonage and its wild surroundings led to acute homesickness whenever she was away from it. She worked for a while as a governess near Halifax and in 1842 spent some time studying languages in Brussels with Charlotte, but seized the chance to return home as soon as she could and spent the rest of her life there, dying of tuberculosis (and refusing to see a doctor until the very end) three months after her brother Branwell, in December 1848.

Emily's only novel, *Wuthering Heights*, although criticised when it was published in 1847 for being excessively violent, morbid and histrionic, is now regarded as one of the masterpieces of nineteenth-century fiction. Virginia Woolf praised it as a work that could 'free life from a dependence on fact'. She is also recognised as one of the most original, lyrical and visionary poets of her time. The poem reproduced here, from her 'Gondal' notebook, is written in the characteristically 'microscopic' hand adopted by all the Brontë children for their imaginative writings. Their father, Patrick, was afraid that this tiny writing would ruin their eyesight and once presented Charlotte with a notebook inscribed: 'All that is written in this book must be in a good, plain and <u>legible</u> hand.' Gondal, an imaginary world created by Emily and Anne, provided the setting for many of Emily's poems; the initials and names attached to them represent characters in the great Gondal epic, of which nothing in prose remains. This world was intensely real to her: in a journal entry at the age of sixteen she interspersed descriptions of music lessons and potato peeling in the kitchen with the excited declaration that 'The Gondals are discovering the interior of Gaaldine'.

This portrait of Emily by her brother Branwell, stored away and forgotten for many years, was not discovered until 1914, eighty years after it was painted as part of a family group, the rest of which has not survived.

Opposite: Shown here is the first page of the manuscript volume containing Emily Brontë's 'Gondal Poems'. Emily notes that the poems were 'Transcribed Feb[r]uary 1844', presumably from her own final drafts, but she continued to make additions down to 13 May 1848. Charlotte has added pencil additions and revisions throughout the manuscript. Not a manuscript trace remains of Emily's most famous work, *Wuthering Heights*.

Emily Jane Brontë.   Transcribed Febuary 1844

Gondal Poems

A. G. A.   March 6th 1837

There shines the moon, at noon of night,
Vision of Glory - Dream of light!
Holy as heaven - undimmed and pure,
Looking down on the lonely moor -
And lonelier still beneath her ray
That drear moor stretches far away

Till it seems strange that aught can lie
Beyond its zone of silver sky =

Bright moon - dear moon! when years have past
My weary feet return at last -
And still upon Lake Elnor's breast
Thy solemn rays serenely rest
And still the Fern-leaves sighing wave
Like mourners over Elbë's grave
And Earth's the same but Oh to see
How wildly Time has altered me!
Am I the being .... years ago.
Sat watching by that water side
The light of life expiring slow
From his fair cheek and brow of pride ?
Not oft these mountains feel the shine
Of such a day - as fading then,
Cast from its fount of .... divine
A last smile on the heathery plain
And kissed the far-off peaks of snow
That gleaming on the horizon shine
As if in summers warmest glow
Stern winter claimed a .... throne -
And there he lay among the bloom
His rich blood dyed a deeper hue
Shuddering to feel the ghastly gloom
That coming Death around him threw -

Charlotte Brontë
1816–1855

Of the Brontës, Charlotte's literary legacy is undoubtedly the richest, yet although her voice is distinctively her own, the source of her inspiration and the pattern of her career make it difficult to isolate her efforts from those of her siblings. Indeed, it was with them that she started to write and recite her juvenile stories, several of which survive in a stupendously small 'print' hand, bound in brown sugar paper.

While Emily and Anne wrote tales of Gondal, Charlotte and Branwell conjured up the kingdom of Angria: each imaginary world a welcome escape, no doubt, from that of the parsonage, with the over-crowded graveyard pushing up against its walls from one side and the moors exposing it to wilderness and the elements on the other. Charlotte left Haworth in 1831 to attend a school in Roe Head, and later returned to teach there before working as a governess. It was in Brussels, where she travelled with her sister Emily to study languages, that she fell in love with her Professor, M. Héger. Her letters to him, rescued from destruction by his wife (who sewed up their torn pieces) are now in the British Library.

Charlotte's unhappy return to Yorkshire was followed by a failed attempt to set up her own school. In 1846 a volume of verse entitled *Poems by Currer, Ellis and Acton Bell* (pseudonyms based on the sisters' initials) appeared, and by this time each of them had written a novel. Charlotte's, entitled *The Professor*, was rejected by her publisher, but her second (and most famous), *Jane Eyre*, appeared in 1847 under the imprint of Smith, Elder & Co., the only publishing house to write her an encouraging letter about her earlier work. *Shirley* followed in 1849, after the early deaths of her brother and sisters, and *Villette* (still under the name Currer Bell) in 1853. In the following year, having turned down three earlier suitors, she married her father's curate, Arthur Nicholls, but died only a few months later, in the early stages of pregnancy.

A portrait of Charlotte Brontë taken from the novel *Jane Eyre*.

Opposite: This emotional passage from the manuscript of *Jane Eyre* describes the moment when Mr Rochester asks Jane, the plain and penniless governess, to marry him. She accepts the proposal with trusting alacrity. The manuscript was written out with amazing speed by Charlotte between 16 and 19 March 1847 and sent to Smith, Elder & Co. on 24 August. It is a beautiful example of what her biographer, Elizabeth Gaskell, described as her 'clear, legible, delicate traced writing'. Although essentially a fair copy transcribed from earlier drafts, Charlotte has been unable to resist the occasional alteration, as is evident here in one of the text's most crucial moments.

His face was very much agitated and very much flushed, and there were strong workings in the features and strange gleams in the eyes.

"Oh Jane, you torture me!" he exclaimed "With that searching and yet faithful and generous look – you torture me!"

"How can I do that? If you are true and your offer real, my only feeling to you must be gratitude and devotion – that cannot torture."

"Gratitude!" he ejaculated, and added wildly "Jane accept me quickly – say, Edward, give me my name, Edward, I will marry you."

"Are you in earnest? Do you truly love me? Do you sincerely wish me to ~~marry you~~ be your wife?"

"I do – and if an oath is necessary to satisfy you – I swear it."

"Then sir – I will marry you."

"Edward – my little wife!"

"Dear Edward!"

"Come to me – come to me entirely now." said he, and added in his deepest tone, speaking in my ear as his cheek was laid on mine, "Make my happiness – I will make yours."

"God, pardon me!" he subjoined erelong "and man, meddle not with me; I have her and will hold her."

"There is no one to meddle sir; I have no kindred to interfere."

"No – that is the best of it." he said and "if I had loved him less

Anne Brontë
1820–1849

Anne Brontë, the youngest of the surviving Brontë children, was greatly influenced by her aunt, Elizabeth Branwell, a fervent Wesleyan who came to live at the Haworth parsonage after their mother's death. Anne was meeker and quieter than her siblings, among whom she felt perhaps the greatest affinity for Emily; together they invented the fantastic Gondal in which to set their stories and poems. Unlike Emily, however, Anne forced herself to go out into the world, first (with her sister Charlotte) to school at Roe Head, and then, in 1839, to work for two periods as a governess, the second time for the distinctly unsympathetic Robinson family at Thorp Green Hall, near York. In 1843 her volatile brother Branwell joined her there as a tutor, and became romantically – and disastrously – involved with Mrs Robinson. The episode must have been acutely painful for his sister and resulted in his returning in disgrace to Haworth, where he took to drink and opium, a combination which led to his rapid decline and death five years later.

Anne's unhappy and difficult experiences as a governess were revisited in her first novel, *Agnes Grey*, published in 1847. This appeared under the pseudonym 'Acton Bell', as did a selection of her poems, including those of her sisters, in 1846. Her second novel, *The Tenant of Wildfell Hall*, drew upon her brother's unfortunate experiences in the portrayal of its main character – a source of inspiration which much upset her sister Charlotte. Later commentators, however, have come to recognise this willingness to grapple with difficult social issues as one of Anne's great strengths as a writer. In *Agnes Grey* she broke new ground in bringing to wide attention the poverty and anxiety suffered by 'droves of spirit-broken governesses'. In this, of course, she wrote from the heart.

Charlotte was at Anne's side when she died of tuberculosis on 28 May 1849. Charlotte, who had taken her to Scarborough, on the Yorkshire coast, wrote to a friend that 'she died without severe struggle, trusting in God – thankful for release from a suffering life – deeply assured that a better existence lay before her.' She was buried in Scarborough, unlike the rest of her family who lie in their vault in Haworth.

The Brontë sisters as painted by their brother, Branwell. Anne is on the left, while the shadow in the centre is where Branwell painted himself out.

Opposite: Reproduced here is the close of Anne's sombre, soul-searching poem 'Self- Communion', which she began in 1847, and the opening of the shorter verse 'The Narrow Way', which she wrote on 24 April 1848. The writing, although clear enough, has a rather stiff quality much in contrast to that of her sister Charlotte.

And still hast borne, and didst
              not faint;—
Oh, this would be reward indeed!"

"Press forward, then, without complaint,
Labour and love — and such shall
              be thy meed."

April 17ᵗʰ 1848
              A. B.

333 lines.

————————

Believe not those who say
            upward
The ~~heavenward~~ path is smooth,
Lest thou shouldst stumble in the way,
And faint before the truth.

It is the only road
        Unto the   perfect
~~That leads to~~ realms of joy;
        he
But ~~they~~ who seeks that blest abode
Must all his powers employ.

Bright hopes and pure delights
~~Above~~ Upon his course may beam,

Charles Dickens
1812–1870

The accession of Queen Victoria on 20 June 1837 saw also the shining star that was Dickens's career very much in the ascendant. *Oliver Twist* had begun its monthly serialization in January that year and, flushed with his success, Dickens moved with his wife and baby into the comfort of a new house in Doughty Street, London (now a delightful museum devoted to the author). In November, two days before the Queen opened her first Parliament, he signed the agreement for the writing of *Nicholas Nickleby* and the first instalment appeared the following March.

For Dickens, of course, it had been no mean feat to reach this point. The son of a kindly but improvident naval clerk whose indifference to thrift brought him to a debtors' prison, the young Charles was to experience a misery that struck deep. One feels that by portraying the fearful abuse of children in his first two novels he was purging something vile from his past. The heightened social conscience he acquired from his apprenticeship as a journalist and Parliamentary reporter lies behind his reproachful reference to 'the monstrous neglect of Education in England' in his preface to the 1848 edition of the novel.

The manuscript of *Nicholas Nickleby* has survived only in fragments. Two are in the United States, one in Doughty Street and the fourth, which for a time had had an owner in Switzerland, was acquired by the British Library in 1971. It owes its early survival to the perspicacity of Charles Hicks, the foreman in the firm of Bradbury and Evans, Dickens's publishers. The manuscript comprises twenty-two leaves of the author's draft of chapter fifteen, with a number of deletions and revisions. Evident from the folio shown here is his reluctance to lose a felicitous phrase, for the crossed-out 'unexpected abstraction' is relocated to an earlier part of the sentence.

Dickens in 1839, taken from the engraving which prefaced the first bound edition of *Nicholas Nickleby*. The original portrait was by Daniel Maclise.

This page from a portion of the manuscript of *Nicholas Nickleby* is full of interest. Dickens's bold and bounding hand applies itself to the page in a manner which shows, even at this early stage in his career, a huge confidence and professionalism. The reference to 'No. V' reminds us that the work first appeared in instalments.

Chapter XV.

Acquaints the reader with the cause and origin
of the interruption described in the last
chapter, and with some other matters ne=
cessary to be known.

Newman Noggs scrambled in violent
haste up stairs with the steaming beverage
which he had so unceremoniously snatched
from the table of Mr. Kenwigs, and
indeed from the very grasp of the water=
rate collector who was eyeing the contents
of the tumbler at the moment of its unexpected abstraction, with lively marks of
pleasure
satisfaction visible in his countenance
and looked not all white edismayed
at the complete abstraction and bore
his prize straight to his own back
garret, where, footsore and nearly
shoeless shoeless, wet, and dirty, jaded,
and disfigured with every mark of
fatiguing travel, sat Nicholas and
Smike, the at once the cause and
partner of his toil, both perfectly

Dickens speaks, at the beginning of the accompanying manuscript draft of his 'Proposals for a National Jest-Book', of Britain's great need over the previous two years for an official joker. They had been grim years indeed: military incompetence and government bungling had led to the disastrous campaign against Russia in the Crimea in 1854 when Balaklava became a cemetery and Scutari a pesthouse. The public mind, chastened by the experience, became possessed of a deep distrust of the military system and of many cherished institutions. But, as André Maurois observed in his lectures on Dickens, the Englishman 'has a longing to believe that all is for the best…in the best of impossible worlds. So whatever is bad ought to be denied. And this is a function admirably fulfilled by humour. It dismisses evil on to a plane of absurdity.'

Dickens, fully acquainted with the world's evils since his poverty-stricken childhood, had by 1856 achieved fame and security. Indeed he was then in the middle of writing *Little Dorrit*, the last of the three great dark novels concerned with social issues. Twelve major novels were behind him and he brought to *Household Words*, published between 1850 and 1859, his customary amazing vigour and intensity.

This manuscript, once in the vast Dickens collection of John Furber Dexter (1847–1927), was purchased by the British Museum Library in 1968. It found an apt home for, as Dickens says on the verso of the folio illustrated here, the collected facetious treasures of a National Jest-Book should be 'preserved, and (in course of time), catalogued by Signor Panizzi in the British Museum'. By the end of his life Dickens himself was a national institution and his impressive burial in Westminster Abbey expressed the national mood.

A photograph of Charles Dickens taken in 1861.

Opposite: Dickens's autograph draft of 'Proposals for a National Jest-Book', in which he asserts that 'it has been ascertained within the last two years, that Britannia is in want of nothing but an official joker', was published in *Household Words*, on 3 May 1856.

Proposals for a National Jest Book.

It has been ~~ascertained~~ ascertained within the last two years, that Britannia is in want of nothing but an ~~able~~ official Joker. Having such exalted office to poke her in the ribs when she considers her condition serious, and to put her off with a wink when she utters a groan, she must certainly be flourishing and it shall be heresy to doubt the fact. By this sign ye shall know it.

My patriotism and my national pride have been so warmed by this discovery that, following out the great ~~noble~~ idea, I have reduced to writing a ~~great~~ scheme for the re-establishment of the obsolete office of court Jester. ~~It would not be~~ ~~Such an office is~~ less expensive ~~these~~ to maintain than a First Lord of the Jokery, and ~~~~ might lead to the discovery ~~~~ of better jokes than issue from that department. ~~~~ My Scheme is an adaptation of a plan I matured some years ago for the revival of the office of Lord Mayor's Fool, a design which, I ~~am authorised~~ ~~~~ mention, would have been adopted by the City of London, but for ~~~~ that ~~immense~~ body, the Common Council, agreeing to hold the office in commission, and ~~to~~ satisfy the public in all their ~~old~~ addresses that perhaps they are never unmindful of its ~~~~ comical duties.

It is not, however, of either of these ingenious proposals (if I may be permitted to call them so) that I now desire to treat. It is of another ~~~~ and far more comprehensive project for the compilation of a ~~great~~ National Jest-Book. ~~~~

Few people, I ~~~~ submit, can fail to have absurdly ~~~~ rich materials for such a collection

Alfred Lord Tennyson
1809–1892

Tennyson grew up in rural Lincolnshire, one of the twelve children of a gifted but emotionally disturbed and sometimes frighteningly erratic clergyman. In later years he said of his wife 'The peace of God came into my life before the altar when I wedded her', something not lightly uttered. With one brother long shut away in an asylum for the insane, another voluntarily seeking help in one, and with a sister-in-law ultimately dying in one after years of suffering, Tennyson had first-hand experience of the disjointed mind.

'Maud' is a complex study of a deranged mind. Of all his poems, this is the one he most frequently chose to read aloud in company – and often in tears. What nerves was it touching on? It is a rich tapestry: its 'hero' is socially displaced, as Tennyson had been in the 1840s; it revolves round a love affair redolent of one he had experienced in the 1830s; it is disturbed by the rancour of mercenary family feuds which he had known in his childhood. Tennyson, nevertheless, disavowed any autobiographical intent at work in the poem and he strongly distanced himself from his hero's idea of finding a resolution in the Crimean campaign.

The poem was published in July 1855 and the manuscript dates from the previous year. Here we have a fair copy of part of one of the lyrics in the poem and a working draft of another. It was written at Farringford on the Isle of Wight, Tennyson's home since November 1853. F. T. Palgrave visited Tennyson several times in December 1854 and it was on one such occasion that the poet gave Palgrave this manuscript. He later tipped it, together with other Tennyson manuscript poems, into his copy of the 1894 edition of Tennyson's *Works* and it eventually came to the British Museum Library in 1941.

This august photographic portrait of Tennyson was taken on 28 February 1877 and included in a short-lived periodical called *The Portrait*, published in the same year.

Opposite: The 'high hall garden', referred to by Tennyson in his fair copy draft of a lyric from 'Maud', looks back to Harrington Hall near his home in Lincolnshire where Rosa Baring stayed. She is thought to be a source for the image of Maud. The heavily worked drafts on the lower part of the sheet belong to a different section of the poem from the fair copy above.

Birds in the high hall-garden
    Were crying & calling to her
Where is Maud, Maud, Maud,
    One is come to woo her

Look! a horse at the door
    And little King Charles is snarling
Go back, my lord, across the moor
    You are not her darling

                    solid ground
Let not the sound earth fail
            fail beneath
And ~~sink~~ under my feet
                    be shrunk
Before my life ~~finds~~ out
What others have found so sweet
Then let come what come may
To a life that has been so sad
I shall have had my day.

                            endure
Let not the sweet Heaven fail
        not
Close & darken above me
Before I am ~~quite~~ quite sure
        sure is one
That ~~much does~~ love me
So Then let come what come may
What matter if I go mad
I shall have lived my day.

Lewis Carroll (Charles Lutwidge Dodgson)
1832–1898

Lewis Carroll was the literary pseudonym adopted by Charles Lutwidge Dodgson, a shy, stuttering and academically gifted mathematics tutor at Christ Church, Oxford University. The son of a curate in Daresbury, Cheshire, he was the third in a lively and happy family of eleven children. The magazines that he edited for their amusement reveal an early fascination with parody, word games and puzzles, all of which gloriously emerge in *Alice's Adventures in Wonderland* (1865).

What might well be regarded as the world's best known children's story began on a boating trip during a 'golden afternoon' in July 1862, with a 'fairy tale' woven from Dodgson's fertile imagination for the three young daughters of the Dean of Christ Church. Alice Liddell, its ten-year-old heroine, begged him to write it out for her (as indeed he did), but it did not appear in published form until 1865, when it was an immediate success. Its sequel, *Through the Looking-Glass, and What Alice Found There*, followed in 1871, with both books memorably illustrated by John Tenniel. Among Dodgson's other works, *The Hunting of the Snark* (1876), a long, fantastical poem, is perhaps the most successful. He was also a prolific letter writer (his register of letters sent and received ran to nearly 98,721 entries) and diarist, and a successful amateur photographer, with a particular gift for photographing his young friends. His charming, often poignant photographs of Alice Liddell are amongst the most famous and sought-after of the Victorian period.

Reproduced opposite is a page from the original manuscript of the first 'Alice' story, entitled 'Alice's Adventures under Ground'. Dodgson took two years to write it out, in a neat hand which would be easy for a child to read, adding his own charming illustrations (here Alice is shown with the 'little magic bottle', the contents of which cause her to start 'growing and growing'). The finished manuscript was bound and finally presented to Alice as an early Christmas present in November 1864. She treasured it for many years until financial difficulties compelled her to sell it at auction in 1928. It was purchased by an American collector but returned to the British people in 1946 by a group of American benefactors in recognition of their strong alliance during the Second World War.

A photograph of Charles Dodgson from 1857.

Opposite: This page from Dodgson's original manuscript of 'Alice's Adventures under Ground', demonstrates the great facility with which he was able to put pen to paper. It is written in what he called his 'manuscript print' hand. Although the charming drawings are Dodgson's own (filled in after he had written the text), he didn't feel they were good enough to publish, and asked John Tenniel to undertake the task on his behalf for this and subsequent books.

than she expected: before she had drunk half the bottle, she found her head pressing against the ceiling, and she stooped to save her neck from being broken, and hastily put down the bottle, saying to herself "that's quite enough— I hope I sha'n't grow any more— I wish I hadn't drunk so much!"

Alas! it was too late: she went on growing and growing, and very soon had to kneel down: in another minute there was not room even for this, and she tried the effect of lying down, with one elbow against the door, and the other arm curled round her head. Still she went on growing, and as a last resource she put one arm out of the window, and one foot up the chimney, and said to herself "now I can do no more — what will become of me?"

Edward Lear
1812–1888

Though Edward Lear was an epileptic, a repressed homosexual and a depressive dogged by feelings of failure and loneliness, he charmed all who met him. To understand why, one need not go much beyond the 'pome' illustrated here with its accompanying self-portrait with Foss, Lear's cat.

One hundred years after his death, a memorial tablet honouring Lear was laid in Westminster Abbey, a long way from his lonely grave in San Remo, about forty kilometres east of Monte Carlo. He would have been surprised that he is commemorated in Poet's Corner, for he saw himself primarily as a painter and the five books of nonsense verse he published between 1846 and 1877 hardly matched, in his thinking, the achievement of his friend Tennyson who lies nearby in the Abbey.

Lear's earliest professional work was as an ornithological draughtsman, concentrating upon the parrot family. Three types of parrot are indeed named after him, so important was his work in this field. But in 1837 Lear abandoned ornithology, concentrating thereafter on landscape-painting and from this point he became a restless wanderer in Europe, North Africa, the Middle East and India. His six travel-books containing his own illustrations were published between 1841 and 1870 and drew even the attention of Queen Victoria, who had Lear give her drawing lessons. Equally important are his illustrations to selected lines from Tennyson's poems.

The letter here was written from the Villa Emily where in 1871 Lear found refuge after so many years of rootlessness. It was built facing the Mediterranean Sea and he eased his solitariness by adding Foss to the household in 1872. However, even as this letter was being written (to the father of the girl who inspired the poem), Lear – who 'weeps by the side of the ocean' – was distressed by the building of a large new hotel, blocking his view completely. In 1880, therefore, he built the Villa Tennyson in an open spot nearby, an exact replica of the Villa Emily, so that Foss might not be unduly disturbed. Foss died, aged fifteen, in 1887. The letter was purchased by the British Library in 1981.

Lear in 1881, from *The Later Letters of Edward Lear*, 1911.

Opposite: Illustrated here is Lear's letter and 'Pome', 'How pleasant to know Mr Lear!', sent to Archdeacon Bevan and dated 14 January 1879. The poem, complete with drawing of himself – 'His beard it resembles a wig' – and Foss – 'His body is perfectly spherical' – varies in several ways from the text as published in 1895.

"How pleasant to know Mr. Lear!"

(From a Photograph.

1
" How pleasant to know Mr. Lear! "
  Who has written such volumes of stuff!
Some think him ill-tempered & queer, —
  But a few think him pleasant enough.

2
  His mind is concrete & fastidious; —
    His nose is remarkably big; —
  His visage is more or less hideous; —
    His beard it resembles a wig.

3
He has ears, & 2 eyes, & 10 fingers, —
  (Leastways if you reckon 2 thumbs;)
Long ago he was one of the singers,
  But now he is one of the dumms.

4
He sits in a beautiful parlour,
  With hundreds of books on the wall;
He drinks a great deal of Marsala,
  But never gets tipsy at all.

5
He has many friends, laymen & clerical;
  Foss is the name of his cat;
His body is perfectly spherical; —
  He weirs a runcible hat.

6
When he walks in a waterproof white
  The children run after him so !
Calling out, — "He's come out in his night=
  =gown, that crazy old Englishman, O! "

7
He weeps by the side of the ocean,
  He weeps on the top of the hill;
He purchases pancakes & lotion
  And shrimps, & it chocolate mill

8
He reads, but he cannot speak, Spanish;
  He cannot abide ginger-beer
Ere the days of his pilgrimage vanish, —
"How pleasant to know Mr. Lear! "

George Eliot (Mary Anne Evans)
1819–1880

George Eliot's *Middlemarch* has been described as one of the greatest works of realism in the English language. Indeed, as an author whose rich and multi-layered narratives are intimately connected with British history and national life, perhaps only Dickens stands as her equal among novelists of the nineteenth century. The very subtitle of *Middlemarch* – 'A study of provincial life' – signals an approach in which profound moral, psychological and political questions are addressed through subtle observations of the local and the everyday. The novel was published in four volumes, 1871–72.

Born Mary Anne Evans (which she later changed to Marian Evans) to a Warwickshire land agent, she was sent to a boarding school whose headmistress inspired in her strong evangelical beliefs. Her thinking later underwent an important transformation, however, in which she held that religious belief is a condition of human rather than abstract concerns. 'One lives by faith in human goodness', she remarked in a letter of 13 March 1870 to her philanthropic friend Jane Senior, 'the only guarantee that there can be any other source of Goodness in the universe'. This very immediate philosophy, together with a deeply held conviction in the importance of duty and service, is perhaps what gives Eliot's writing, above all else, its quality of enduring relevance. Three long stories in the series *Scenes of Clerical Life* (1857–58) were her first pieces of fiction to appear in print and her

standing was immediately established with her first novel, *Adam Bede* (1859), her admiring readers having no idea who she was, or indeed whether she was a man or a woman. The real identity of the mysterious George Eliot, as she had decided to call herself in print, was widely known by the time her second novel, *The Mill on the Floss*, appeared in 1860. Further acclaimed novels followed, culminating with *Daniel Deronda* (1876), although she also turned her hand to poetry. Her last work was the satirical volume of essays *Impressions of Theophrastus Such* (1879), the last chapter of which (like *Daniel Deronda*) makes clear her revulsion for anti-Semitism.

Most of Eliot's literary manuscripts were bound and presented by her to her beloved George Henry Lewes, a man whom she regarded as her 'husband' despite his earlier undissolved marriage to another woman. They were returned to her after his death in 1878. Eliot married John Walter Cross, some twenty years her junior, in 1880, but died only seven months later of a sudden illness. She was buried in London's Highgate cemetery, next to Lewes. Her twenty-four volumes of manuscripts, containing all but three of her novels and poems, were deposited in the British Museum Library, in accordance with her wishes, so that her manuscripts might be available to the British people.

An engraved portrait of George Eliot aged thirty, by G. J. Stodart from a painting by M. D'Albert-Durade.

Opposite: Shown here is the opening chapter of *Middlemarch*, preserved in the original manuscript volumes sent by Eliot to the printer. Even at this late stage she was making changes to the text.

"Since I can do no good because a woman,
Reach constantly at something that is near it."
    The Maid's Tragedy: Beaumont & Fletcher

Miss Brooke had that kind of beauty which seems to be thrown into relief by poor dress. Her hand & wrist were so finely formed that she could wear sleeves not less bare of style than those in which the Blessed Virgin appeared to Italian painters, & her profile as well as her stature & bearing seemed to gain the more dignity from her plain garments, which by the side of provincial fashion gave her the impressiveness of a fine quotation from the Bible, or from one of our elder poets, in a paragraph of today's newspaper. She was usually spoken of as being remarkably clever, but with the addition that her sister Celia had more common sense. Nevertheless Celia wore scarcely any trimmings; & Miss Brooke's plain dressing was due to mixed conditions in most of which her sister shared. The pride of being ladies had something to do with it: the Brooke connexions though not exactly aristocratic, were unquestionably "good": if you inquired backward for a generation or two you would not find any yard-measuring or parcel-tying forefathers; nothing lower than an admiral or a clergyman; & there was even an ancestor discernible as a Puritan gentleman who served under Cromwell, but had afterwards conformed, & had managed to come out of all political trouble as the proprietor of a respectable family estate. Young women of such birth, living in a quiet country town,

& it was only to close observers that her dress differed from her sister's, & had a shade of coquetry in its arrangements

Christina Rossetti
1830–1894

This manuscript is an autograph fair copy of a short poem given by Christina Rossetti to her mother as a Valentine on 14 February 1884. On its accompanying leaf she has addressed her mother as the Queen of Hearts and because there are traces of folds resulting from the triangular envelope-like form of the latter leaf, we can be sure that this was the copy presented on the day.

The Valentine is one of eleven she gave to her mother between 1876 and 1886, all acquired by the Library from the sale of T. J. Wise's Ashley collection in 1938. A pencil note in Christina's hand on a separate sheet declares 'These <u>Valentines</u> had their origins from my dearest Mother's remarking that she had never received one ____ I, her CGR, ever after supplied one on the day; and so far as I recollect it was a <u>surprise</u> every time, she having forgotten all about it in the interim'.

The poem is loving but it is also a sad remembrancer of the domestic events of 1883–1884. Quite typical of its author, it carries no reference beyond the circumscribed world of family experience. The year 1883 saw the centenary of Christina's father's birth and its celebration in his native Italian town but it also saw the deaths of two relatives including her brother William's baby. She also suffered the loss of Charles Bagot Cayley, to whom she had had a tender and serious attachment since 1862. She had in fact made a solitary visit to his grave in Hastings only a month before she presented her Valentine to her mother. As he bequeathed her his writing-desk, one may wonder if the poem was actually written on it.

The marking of significant moments of time was a long-established practice in the Rossetti household; Christina's earliest poem, written when she was eleven, was a birthday tribute to her mother. Mrs Rossetti died, as old as the century, in 1886 and was buried in the family plot in Highgate Cemetery, her steadfastly loyal daughter joining her there eight years later.

An engraved portrait of Christina Rossetti from a drawing of 1877 by her brother, the Pre-Raphaelite artist Dante Gabriel Rossetti, published in *The Family Letters of Christina Georgia Rossetti* in 1908.

Opposite: This is one of eleven Valentine greetings given by Christina Rossetti to her mother. She alludes to the experiences of the family – some joyful, some sad – over the course of the year 1883–1884.

1884.

Another year of joy & grief,
   Another year of hope & fear:
O Mother, is life long or brief?
   We hasten while we linger here.

But since we linger, love me still
   And bless me still, O Mother mine,
While hand in hand we scale life's hill,
   You Guide, & I your Valentine.

Thomas Hardy
1840–1928

Thomas Hardy's parents encouraged early on the signs of creative sensitivity in their son, teaching him the violin and encouraging him to read widely. He went to school in Dorchester and then worked as an architectural assistant, in Dorset and London, until the enthusiastic reception of his second published novel, *Under the Greenwood Tree* (1872), spurred him into becoming a full-time writer. Over the next quarter century Hardy went on to create some of the best-loved novels in English literature, whose grandeur of theme emerges from an intensely human vision; but in 1895 the controversy surrounding the last, *Jude the Obscure*, distressed and disillusioned him so much that he returned to his first love, poetry, winning huge acclaim for his distinctive lyrical style and acute observation of human emotions. His marriage to Emma Gifford, in 1874, at first idyllic, was soon overtaken by great strain and unhappiness; it did, however, produce some of his most moving poems, written after her death in 1912. Two years later Hardy married a younger woman, Florence Dugdale, who was increasingly protective of him as he became a widely revered public figure, showered with medals and honorary degrees.

Reproduced here is a page from the heavily corrected manuscript of Hardy's novel *Tess of the D'Urbervilles*, subtitled 'A Pure Woman'. Its publication in three volumes in 1891 (it first appeared as an illustrated serial in the *Graphic Magazine*) created a sensation, with Hardy pilloried for his 'pessimism' and 'immorality'. Although hurt and offended – 'I have put in it the best of me', he later said – sales surged as a result. The manuscript was presented by Hardy to the British Museum Library, along with that of his novel *The Dynasts*, in 1911. Although its policy was not to accept the manuscripts of living authors, the Library was in this instance pleased to make an exception.

A portrait of Thomas Hardy taken from a 1926 edition of *Tess of the D'Urbervilles*.

Opposite: The impressive complexity of Hardy's working method is much in evidence in this page from the manuscript draft of *Tess of the D'Urbervilles*. Instructions to move text, evidence of repagination, amendments (Tess was originally to be called Rose Mary), additions and determined deletions all point to a tremendous effort on the part of the author. Elsewhere in the manuscript, Hardy has colour-coded (in blue) differences between the texts for publication in serial and book form.

Fred

Tess

~~Poor Tess~~ had never before visited this part of the country, & yet she felt akin to ~~it~~ the landscape ~~scenery~~. Not so very far to the left of her she could discern a dark patch in the ~~landscape~~ scenery, which ~~she did~~ enquiry confirmed her in supposing to be trees, marking the environs of ~~Green~~ King's-Bere ~~hill Regis~~ — in the church of which parish the bones of her ancestors — her useless ancestors — lay entombed.

She had no admiration for them:

Not a single material thing of all that had been theirs did she retain but the ~~an~~ old silver spoon / yet to diverge from the direct route in order to glance a passing courtesy to which they were entitled, and at their resting-place was no serious task for so active a walker. ~~& this it was~~ Tess ~~when to do~~

~~Poor Tess did~~ entered the church about ~~the middle~~ two in of the afternoon, and ~~she stood~~ beheld for the first time in her life ~~upon~~ the spot where her father had spoken or sung ~~painfulness~~ ever since ~~too~~ Parson Tringhams ~~faring~~ announcement.

~~Here~~ Here stood the tombs of the d'Urbervilles — formed of grey Purbeck-marble; canopied, altar-shaped, & plain; their carvings defaced & broken: ½ their brasses torn from their matrices. Of all the reminders that she had ever received that they were ~~practically~~ socially an extinct family there was none so forcible as this spoliation.

She drew near to a dark stone, on which was inscribed:

[Blank line]
[Old English] "Ostium sepulchri antiquæ familiæ D'Urberville."
[Blank line] Tess

~~Poor Tess~~ did not read ~~Latin~~ ~~but she knew~~ that this was the Church. like a Cardinal door of her ancestral sepulchre, & that the ~~all~~ knights of whom her father chanted in his cups lay inside it in their leaden shrouds.

Pooh—what's the good of thinking about them!" she said, with sudden ~~scorn~~ a sigh.
~~She left the church, & resumed her course~~

"I have as much of mother as father in me & she was only a dairy maid". : all my prettiness comes from her.

Oscar Wilde
1854–1900

Oscar Wilde, the epitome of *fin de siècle* aestheticism and the greatest wit and conversationalist of his generation, is still among the most widely read and translated authors in the English language. By turns poet, journalist, writer of short stories, novelist and playwright, he was also a prolific correspondent. Born in Dublin, the son of a distinguished Irish surgeon and a well-known writer and literary hostess who published under the name 'Speranza', he attended a Protestant school. Here he began to excel at Classics and develop a reputation as a gifted conversationalist and story-teller before entering Trinity College, Dublin University. From Trinity, where he came under the spell of a lifelong infatuation with Greek culture and literature, he won a scholarship to Magdalen College, Oxford, where he shunned sport, cultivated a flamboyant aestheticism and proclaimed himself a disciple of Pater and his creed of 'art for art's sake'. He also covered himself in academic glory by winning the Newdigate Poetry Prize and gaining a double first in Classics.

In 1882, a year after the publication of his first volume of poems, Wilde embarked on a hugely successful lecture tour of America, returning determined to conquer the London social and literary worlds. Four years after his marriage to Constance Lloyd, he published in 1888 a volume of fairy stories, *The Happy Prince and other Tales*, originally written for his two young sons. Other stories followed, and in 1890 his disturbing and macabre novel, *The Picture of Dorian Gray*, caused a scandal when it first appeared in the American *Lippincott's Magazine*. In the following year he met Lord Alfred Douglas – the great, but ill-starred romance of his life – and a year later began his rapid theatrical rise with his first successful play, *Lady Windermere's Fan*. Shortly after the triumphant opening of *The Importance of Being Earnest* in February 1895, Wilde took the fatal decision to sue Douglas's father, the violent and erratic Marquess of Queensberry, for criminal libel, and so set in train the sequence of events which led to his own two-year imprisonment for homosexual offences and descent into public disgrace, poverty and exile. His early boast that 'Somehow or other, I'll be famous, and if not famous, notorious' had sadly proved true. A mere twelve years after publishing his first work of fiction, he was dead at the age of 46, buried in a pauper's grave on the outskirts of Paris.

Photograph of Oscar Wilde taken in New York in 1882.

Opposite: The British Library possesses an important collection of Wilde's manuscripts, including poems, letters (among them 'De Profundis,' his long letter to Douglas written in prison), and drafts of his plays. Reproduced here is an early draft, dating from 1894, of his fourth and final West End play, *The Importance of Being Earnest* (subtitled 'A Trivial Comedy for Serious People'). Written very quickly, with many changes and corrections, it is open at the famous 'handbag scene', in which the formidable Lady Bracknell (here called 'Lady Brancaster') interrogates Jack Worthing about his family history.

a Cloak-Room at
a Railway Station might
conceal a social intersection.
It could hardly however
create
a social existence of any
kind, even in the suburbs where
birth is practically unknown.

Do

when you become engaged to be
married you will inform you Father or
of the fact. Its not a thing that
a well brought up girl should know
anything about herself. an engagement
should come on a girl as a pleasant, or
unpleasant surprise, as the case may be. I will
talk to you more
fully about this
subject at home (turns
to Jack.)

Algy (behind the
scenes to Cecily
who is laughing)
Hush!

Lady Bracknell (looks
vaguely about as the
proceeds).

married to Mr Worthy, mamma.

Lady Bracknell.

silly mistaken
You are not really engaged
to Mr Worthy. Such an engagement
is quite impossible. He would be
cruelty. Come over here at once.

Gwendolen

certainly, mamma. (goes
over) But I am engaged to be
married to Mr Worthy.

Lady Bracknell.

Silence, child.
Mr Worthy, apprised of
my daughter's sudden flight by
her French maid whose confidence
I purchased by means of a
small coin, I followed her at
once, by a luggage train. Her
unhappy Father is, I am glad to

The Twentieth Century

In 1923 John Quinn, an American collector of books and manuscripts, sold a number of autograph works he had bought from Joseph Conrad a decade earlier. To the author's considerable irritation, Quinn made a tenfold profit. From the early part of the twentieth century, literary manuscripts began to be collected with a hitherto unknown fervour.

With drafts from James Joyce's *Ulysses* recently being purchased by the Irish government for dramatic sums, and international interest in British writers' manuscripts commensurate with the global reach of English literature, the considerable interest in modern literary manuscripts shows little signs of abating. For this reason, the British Library continues to augment its literary holdings with letters, notebooks, drafts, diaries and an extraordinary assortment of non-print media produced by writers of the twentieth and twenty-first centuries, increasingly augmented by emails, electronic documents, and other evidence of the changing technological nature of literary production. And while the need for an even tighter understanding of institutional collecting parameters is crucial, it is heartening to see how the unexpected and idiosyncratic still sneak into authors' personal archives: a hat worn by G. K. Chesterton, a clay bowl fashioned by Gerald Durrell, the gold Nobel Literature medal awarded to playwright Harold Pinter in 2005, or the label from the bespoke bottles of Spanish sherry selected for the Poet Laureate Ted Hughes.

One of the most moving and impressive group of modern manuscripts to survive anywhere, must surely be those of the soldier poet Wilfred Owen. At the time of his death by machine-gunfire in 1918, just one week before the signing of the Armistice, Owen had seen only five poems into print. Yet among his papers was discovered a remarkable body of work in various states of draft, some written at the front, others worked on with the help of Siegfried Sassoon on paper supplied by Craiglockhart Hospital where both men were sent to recuperate from the shattering effects of modern warfare.

Almost a century later, the manuscripts of writer Harold Pinter, himself a winner of the Wilfred Owen Prize, testify to an undimmed intensity as the writer struggled to compose his Nobel acceptance speech in hospital, unable to travel to Stockholm to receive the prize in person.

The modern literary manuscript often seems to have a remarkably intimate, revealing quality. Philip Larkin, a librarian as well as a poet, recognized this, perhaps, when he set to work censoring the earliest of his poetic notebooks before presenting it to the British Library. Yet even those poems which remain invite us into a privileged personal realm. We see, in 'Wedding Wind', for example, the writer's easy, fluid facility with a conversational idiom twist, flex and tie itself in knots as he struggles to articulate a profound emotional mood towards the poem's conclusion. And to the many who justifiably stand in awe of Sylvia Plath's poetry, with all its raw super-concentrated feeling and barely controlled energy, her manuscript copy of 'Ariel' must come as a revelation, written out, as it is, in a slow, round, childish hand and finished off with a naïve flower motif.

All the manuscripts chosen have the special marks of their respective authors stamped upon them: Virginia Woolf's favoured purple ink, W. H. Auden's syllabic notations, Katherine Mansfield's near illegible scrawl, Dylan Thomas's surprisingly meticulous hand, Ted Hughes's bounding, bible-black, gothic script, Harold Pinter's bold extravagant approach, or the deliberate violence of the layers of text built up by J. G. Ballard . All radiate something of what Larkin called the 'magical quality of manuscripts'.

Sir Arthur Conan Doyle
1859–1930

Sir Arthur Conan Doyle was born in Edinburgh in 1859 to parents of Irish descent. After attending Stonyhurst College, he studied medicine at Edinburgh University. In 1882, after a short-lived venture as a partner in the Plymouth practice of fellow Edinburgh medical graduate George Budd, Conan Doyle arrived in Southsea, where he succeeded in building a medical practice and began to establish himself as a writer. A few years later he married Louisa Hawkins, the sister of one of his patients. Louisa died from tuberculosis in 1906 and he later married Jean Leckie.

Conan Doyle's creation of the cerebral detective Sherlock Holmes and his assistant Dr Watson, who first appeared in his 1887 story, *A Study in Scarlet*, earned him a place in the annals of literary history. The Holmes stories first appeared mainly in the *Strand Magazine* and were later collected in *The Adventures of Sherlock Holmes* (1892), *The Memoirs of Sherlock Holmes* (1894), *The Return of Sherlock Holmes* (1905) *His Last Bow* (1917) and *The Case-Book of Sherlock Holmes* (1927). The ultra-rationalist Holmes was based on Dr Joseph Bell, one of Conan Doyle's tutors at Edinburgh University, who used to astound his students with his ability to make rapid diagnoses from minimal evidence.

Although it is the Holmes stories that have so powerfully captured the public imagination, Conan Doyle wished to be remembered as a writer of historical novels. His historical romances, which he considered far superior to his detective stories, include *Micah Clarke* (1889) and *The White Company* (1891). He also published several influential works of non-fiction, among them histories of the Boer War, in which he served as a volunteer field army surgeon, and of the First World War.

A man of insatiable intellectual curiosity and relentless energy, Conan Doyle played an active role in public life. He twice stood for election to Parliament (although was unsuccessful on both occasions), lent his support to the campaign for the legalization of divorce, and became involved in a number of cases of miscarriages of justice and human rights controversies (including a crusade against the atrocities committed in the Belgian Congo under King Leopold II). In the last decade of his life, he became a worldwide spokesman for the spiritualist movement and published numerous books on the subject, among them *The Case for Spirit Photography* (1922) and *The Edge of the Unknown* (1930).

A photographic portrait of Conan Doyle taken from *Men and Women of the Day*, 1888–1897.

Opposite: Shown here is a page from the manuscript of Conan Doyle's first novel, *The Narrative of John Smith*. Written when he was in his early twenties, the novel (which he described as a work with 'a personal-social-political complexion') was lost in the post on its way to the publishers and never appeared in print during his lifetime. This manuscript, which Conan Doyle reconstructed after the original was lost, was acquired by the British Library at a major Conan Doyle sale held by Christie's in 2004.

"Gout or rheumatism, Doctor?" I asked

"A little of both, Mr Smith" said he

"And pray, sir, what is the exact difference between them?" I continued under a natural impulse to gain a little knowledge in exchange for the red-hot skewer which was transfixing my right foot.

"Why" said my good physician tapping his tortoise-shell snuff box "the one is a punishment and the other is a misfortune — one is in the hands of Providence and the other is in your own. hands. You can't command the weather which governs your rheumatism, but you can command your ~~stomach~~ appetites which governs your gout.

"And so said I "this diabolical pain in my foot is the hybrid form of torture known as Rheumatic Gout which unites ~~all~~ the disadvantages of both diseases ~~with~~ to a dash of malignancy all its own"

"You are certainly suffering from Rheumatic Gout" observed Dr ~~Jackson~~ Turner

"And can only be cured by colchicum?"

"And alkalies" cried the Doctor

"And flannel?"

"And poppy heads!" cried the Doctor

"And abstinence?"

"And a weeks complete rest"

"A week!" I roared, partly from emotion, and partly in response to a twinge which shot through my foot "Do you seriously imagine, Doctor, that I am going to lie upon this sofa for a week?"

"Not a doubt of it" he said composedly. It is astonishing how calm and free from all human weakness, ~~unscrupulous~~ these Doctors can be, until

Joseph Conrad
1857–1924

Joseph Conrad, born to Polish nobility, had endured, by the age of eleven, a harsh exile in the snowy wastes of Russia, the slow and painful death of his mother from tuberculosis and the imprisonment and death of his father. A patchy education under the guardianship of his long-suffering uncle was followed by a move to Marseilles and a reckless period sailing the West Indies in the company – if his later lively recollections are to be believed – of smugglers and gun runners. A half-hearted suicide attempt following heavy gambling losses marked his twenty-first year, as did a decision to reinvent himself as an English sailor. Jozef Korzeniowski became Joseph Conrad, a British citizen who sailed the world for fifteen years. Another astonishing transformation occurred in 1893 when, now a master mariner, he gave up the sea, settled in the southern English countryside with his wife Jessie and two sons, and began to write, in his third language, some of the most celebrated works in the English literary tradition.

Conrad's writing, often drawing upon the strange and disturbing experiences of his own life is, in his own words, profoundly preoccupied with the 'single-minded attempt to render the highest kind of justice to the visible universe, by bringing to light the truth, manifold and one, underlying its every aspect'. For him this truth was often far from palatable. The uncompromising bleakness of much of his writing – perhaps reaching an apotheosis with the short but shattering *Heart of Darkness* – did little to endear Conrad to a mass audience unprepared to grapple with any work of literature whose purpose ventured beyond simple entertainment or instruction. When Conrad finally attained success, chiefly with the populist *Chance* in 1914, he had long since completed his best works, among them *Lord Jim* (1900) and *Nostromo* (1904). In his later years he moved from house to house (mostly in Kent), wrote profitable film scripts and became one of the first authors to benefit from the sale of his manuscripts. He died in Bishopsbourne, Kent, and is buried in Canterbury City Cemetery.

A portrait of Conrad taken on his voyage to America in 1923.

Opposite: Conrad's intensive drafting is shown in this manuscript fragment from *Nostromo*, which appeared in 1904. The process of composition was, for Conrad, typically arduous, and beset with all sorts of difficulties. Nevertheless, he had confidence in the work, writing to his agent in 1903: 'I have never worked so hard before – with so much anxiety. But the result is good. You know I take no credit to myself for what I do – and so I may judge my own performance. There is no mistake about this. You may take up a strong position when you offer it here. It is very genuine Conrad.'

In the Intendencia of Sulaco Charles Gould was assuring Pedrito Montero who had sent urgent for his presence there, that he would never let the mine pass out of his hands for the profit of a government

threat ~~At about that time Charles Gould was bringing forward~~ threat, in the Intendencia of Sulaco when he had ~~been~~ sent for by Pedrito Montero.

"You may feel assured," Charles Gould said, "that I shall not leave ~~nothing~~ ~~with Don Pepe there Charles Gould could tell of the utter~~ the mine behind me for the profit of a government who has robbed me of

~~and complete destruction~~ of the San Tomé mine with the perfect assurance who had ~~broken faith~~ robbed him of it. The Gould Concession could not be resumed. his father had not desired it. The son would never surrender it. He would never surrender it alive. ~~of being taken seriously~~ capable of resuscitating ~~th~~ such an enterprise

had once dead where was the power in all its vigour and wealth out ~~out~~ of the ashes and ruin of destruction? There was none in the country. And where was the skill and capital abroad that would condescend to touch such ~~the very much than the spiritual and temporal governors of the~~ an ill-omened corpse. Charles Gould talked in the impassive tone which had for many years served to conceal his anger and contempt. He suffered. He was disgusted with what he had to say. It was

~~imperium in imperio were looking at each other thoughtfully in Father~~ too much like heroics. In him the strictly practical instinct was in bad accord with the almost mystic view he took of his right. The Gould concession was symbolic of abstract justice. Let the heaven fall. But ~~Mr. So political Charles~~ Gould was talking of it in the audience room of since the San Tomé mine had developed into world wide fame his threat had enough force and effectiveness to reach the rudimentary intelligence of Pedro Montero wrapped up as he was in the futilities of historical anecdotes

~~the Intendencia where he had been sent for by Pedro Montero. A table~~ The Gould concession was a serious asset in the country's finance, and what was more in the private budgets of many officials. It was known. It was said. It was credible. Every minister of ~~interior~~ interior drew a ~~chair a wooden bedstead had been found for His Excellency who after~~ salary from the San Tomé mine, it was natural. And Pedrito intended to be minister of the interior and president of the council. The Duke de Morny had occupied them with profit during the Second French Empire with conspicuous advantage to himself. ~~having had his siesta very necessary after the labours and the pomps of~~ A table, a chair, a wooden bedstead had been procured for His Excellency, who after a short siesta rendered absolutely necessary by the labours and the pomps of his

~~his~~ entry into Sulaco had been getting hold of the administrative machine giving orders

by making appointments ~~and~~ signing proclamations. ~~They were alone in the~~ Alone with Charles Gould in the

audience ~~big~~ room ~~and~~ His Excellency ~~was~~ managed with his well known skill to conceal his ~~greatly struck by the impos~~ annoyance ~~many~~ and consternation. He had begun at first to ~~Sr. Tomé mine~~ He had talked to Charles

~~Gould~~ loftily of confiscation but the want of mobility in the Señor all proper feeling and

Administrador's face ~~affecting~~ adversely his power of masterful expression. ~~the masterful confidence of~~ ended by

had repeated. The Government can certainly bring about the destruction of the San Tomé mine
Charles Gould ~~had said~~ "~~You can certainly destroy it if it likes~~ but without me it can do nothing else". It was an alarming pronouncement and ~~that is all that he can do"~~ it was an amazing pronouncement. well calculated to offend the sensibilities of a ~~vis~~ politician whose mind is bent upon the spoils of victory. And Charles Gould said also that the destruction of the San Tomé mine would cause the ruin of other undertakings, the withdrawal of European capital the withholding most probably of the last instalment of the foreign loan. ~~That field of~~ in an said all these things (which were accessible to his Excellency's intelligence) in a cold-blooded manner which made you shudder.

E. M. Forster
1879–1970

In 1905 the twenty-six-year-old Edward Morgan Forster published his first novel, *Where Angels Fear to Tread*, the first manuscript page of which is illustrated opposite. His story of a belligerent English family gradually educated out of their prejudices while in Italy drew, like his next two novels, *The Longest Journey* (1907) and *A Room with a View* (1908), upon his own experiences: the miserable time he had spent at public school in Tonbridge (which became the small-minded fictional 'Sawston') and his travels through Greece and Italy following four happy years at King's College Cambridge where, he later recalled, 'They taught the perky boy that he was not everything, and the limp boy that he might be something.'

Forster's early years were spent with his mother and a number of aunts at their home 'Rooksnest' in Hertfordshire, just to the north of London. They had moved here after the death of his father and he grew to love it deeply enough for it to become 'Howards End' in his eponymous novel of 1910, a symbol of the continually threatened virtues of continuity and quiet humanity. The novel, which takes as its main theme the resolution of conflicting values, introduced the phrase by which Forster's admired philosophy has come to be defined: 'Only connect!'.

Forster's next novel, *A Passage to India*, which he had started in 1912, did not appear until 1924. Its picture of Empire in decline, which he himself had observed in two visits (the last in 1921 as the private secretary to a Maharaja) was immediately acclaimed a masterpiece. During the novel's long gestation Forster had drafted and then returned time and again to *Maurice*, a story of homosexual love which he circulated privately but which remained unpublished until the year after his death; his own serious relationships began in Alexandria, where he served in the Red Cross during the War, and in the early 1930s he found his long term companion in a young policeman.

A Passage to India was to be Forster's last novel, yet for the remainder of his long years he occupied a position at the very centre of British literary, intellectual and cultural life, issuing numerous essays, biographies, lectures and broadcasts and supporting political and social causes with such an honesty and vigour that the British *Dictionary of National Biography* felt able to describe him as 'the sage of humanism'. He believed perhaps above all else in the importance of personal relations and died, as was his wish, in the Coventry home of his closest companions Bob and May Buckingham. His ashes were scattered in their rose garden.

E.M. Forster photographed in 1910.

Opposite: The opening page of E. M. Forster's first novel, *Where Angels Fear to Tread*. The manuscript was found among the papers of Nathaniel Wedd (1864–1940), one of the Fellows under whose influence he had come while studying at King's College Cambridge. Forster maintained close links with King's throughout his life and the college, which presented this manuscript to the British Library in 1971, holds the most important collection of his papers.

They were all at Charing Cross to see Lilia off — Philip, Harriet, ~~Georgie~~, Irma, Mrs Herriton herself. Even Mrs Theobald, squired by Mr Kingcroft, had braved the journey from Yorkshire to bid her ~~sod~~ only daughter goodbye. Miss Abbott was likewise attended by numerous relatives, and the sight of so many people talking at once and saying such different things caused Lilia to break into ungovern-able peals of laughter.

"Quite an ovation" she cried ~~feeling~~ spreading out of her 1st class carriage. "They'll take us for royalty. Oh Mr Kingcroft, get us footwarmers."

The good natured ~~young~~ man hurried away, and Philip, taking his place, flooded her with a final stream of advice and injunctions, where to stop, how to learn Italian, when to use mosquito-nets, what pictures to look at. "Remember" he concluded "that it is only by going off the track that you get to know the country. See the little towns — Gubbio, Pienza, Cortona, San Gimignano, Volterra, Monteriano. And don't, let me beg you, go with that awful tourist idea that Italy's only a museum of antiquities & art. Italy's living. Love and understand the Italians, for the people are ~~even~~ ~~not~~ more marvellous than the land."

"How I wish you were coming, Philip" she said, flattered at the unwonted notice her brother in law was giving her.

"I wish I were." He could have managed ~~ad~~ it without great difficulty, for his career at the bar was not so intense as to prevent occasional holidays. But his family disliked his continual ~~visits to~~ ~~absences~~ on the continent, and he himself often found ~~took~~ pleasure in the

Kenneth Grahame
1859–1932

Born in Edinburgh, Kenneth Grahame had an unhappy childhood – his mother died when he was a young boy, and his father sent him away to live with his grandmother. The young Kenneth wanted to attend Oxford University, but his family would not support him financially, and he instead became a clerk at the Bank of England, where he was quickly promoted to become the youngest ever Secretary. During this time he wrote two of his early works, *The Golden Age* (1895) and *Dream Days* (1898), both evocative stories about perfect childhoods in the British countryside. The books acted as escapism for Grahame, and played on the contemporary fashion for celebrating a kind of eternal boyhood: an idyllic world full of boating, rambling and nature-worship. Famously, *The Golden Age* was the only book apart from the Bible that Kaiser Wilhelm II kept on his yacht, while Theodore Roosevelt was such a fan that he invited Grahame to the White House. The books, although less well-known now, were to become massively influential for children's writing for years to come.

Grahame's most famous work, *The Wind in the Willows* (1908), was originally conceived as a series of bedtime stories for his son Alistair, but became the perfect expression of Grahame's interest in nature, landscape and pantheism. He wrote that the novel was 'only an expression of the simplest joys of life as lived by the simplest beings'. It is both a celebration of the natural world, and an expression of concern for a modernity that might destroy it, told through the eyes of iconic, immediately engaging, animal characters.

Grahame struggled to find a publisher for the novel, and it was initially disliked by critics, but despite this it immediately became – and stayed – a bestseller, and one of the most important British children's classics. The central characters, Mole, Toad, the Water Rat and Badger, have been loved by generations of children, and been the inspiration for countless adaptations for the theatre and cinema over the years.

A sad epilogue to the story is that Grahame's son Alistair, whose bedtime stories were the inspiration for the novel, died in a railway accident in 1920 at the age of 19, almost certainly a suicide. Grahame wrote no further novels after *The Wind in the Willows*, and died in Berkshire in 1932.

A vintage snapshot print of Kenneth Grahame taken by Lady Ottoline Morrell in 1920–1921.

Opposite: This is an autograph draft of part of the chapter entitled 'The Piper at the Gates of Dawn'. This chapter, significantly placed centrally within *The Wind in the Willows*, features the appearance of Pan, the god of nature in Greek mythology. The passage is somewhat tangential to the story, but was highly important to Grahame's representation and celebration of the natural world. The manuscript was presented to the British Library by the Trustees of the Dorneywood Trust Fund.

Lest the awe should dwell
And turn your pleasure to fret,
You shall look on my full my power at the helping hour
— But then you shall forget

From the helper Lest the limbs shall be ~~adorned~~ & rent
I spring the trap that is set
As I loose the snare you may ~~catch~~ sleeping
~~Yet~~ For surely you shall forget

Helper healer ~~I look above~~ cheer
(~~Helper healing song cheer~~)
Small Each waifs in the woodlands wet
With ~~Stray~~ Strays I find ~~the~~ in it wounds I tend ~~in it~~
Bidding them all forget.

None shall pay for the piper's play
And none shall feel the debt
As I pipe your sadness into gladness

Wilfred Owen
1893–1918

On 4 November 1918, just one week before the signing of the armistice to end the First World War, a young officer and recipient of the Military Cross for 'conspicuous gallantry', was killed by machine gunfire at the Sambre canal in France. The soldier was Wilfred Owen, whose total of five published poems had done little to raise him from literary obscurity at the time of his death, but who has subsequently emerged as the best known of all modern British war poets. He was born at Oswestry in Shropshire and completed his education at London University, following which he travelled to France where he worked as a private tutor. He volunteered for active service in 1915.

In language and style, Owen's work owes more to the poetic idioms of the past (John Keats was a strong influence) than to the hard and fractured forms emerging from his 'modernist' contemporaries such as T. S. Eliot, Ezra Pound and T. E. Hulme. Nonetheless, he developed a high degree of technical sophistication and is credited with inventing 'pararhyme', in which consonants are matched before and after different vowels.

It is, however, the sheer visceral power of the subject matter which truly sets Owen's writing apart; the ability to bring home from the trenches the full brutality and pathos of a war whose 'actualities', as he put it, were at best unknown, at worse ignored, by the 'pulpit professionals' who sent men to their uncertain fates. It has been pointed out that after Owen no one could ever again write poetry which saw in war the possibility of romance and gallantry.

Owen's literary manuscripts, often comprising successive heavily reworked drafts of one poem, were gathered together after his death and brought to wide public attention in editions by the poet Siegfried Sassoon, helped by Edith Sitwell (1920) and Edmund Blunden (1931). Sassoon, also the winner of a Military Cross (which he later threw away in disgust), had already embraced the pacifist cause when, invalided with 'shell-shock', he met the younger soldier at Craiglockhart Hospital, near Edinburgh. It was here, under a diagnosis of 'neurasthenia', that the twenty-four-year-old Owen wrote many of his finest poems. Among them was 'Anthem for Doomed Youth' shown here in a first draft. Sassoon's suggested amendments can be seen in addition to Owen's firm and fluid hand. Despite his encouragement and help in giving the piece its final well-wrought shape, Sassoon was in no doubt as to the essential genius from which it sprang. He recognised 'that my little friend was much more than the promising minor poet I had hitherto adjudged him to be' and that the sonnet in all its 'noble naturalness and depth of meaning...was a revelation'.

A photographic portrait of Wilfred Owen by John Gunsten, 1916.

Opposite: Wilfred Owen's first draft of 'Anthem for Doomed Youth' reveals the young poet working hard to find the final shape of the poem. The draft bears pencil amendments by Siegfried Sassoon, with whom Owen spent time at Craiglockhart Hospital in Scotland. Owen's literary manuscripts were acquired by the British Museum Library in 1934, through the good offices of the Friends of the National Libraries and other generous subscribers.

Anthem for Dead Youth.

What passing bells for these who die so fast?
— Only the solemn monstrous anger of the our guns.
Let the majestic insults of their mouths
blind insolence
Be as the priest words requiem of their burials.
Of choristers and holy music, none;
Nor any voice of mourning, save the wail
The long-drawn wail of high far-sailing shells.

What candles may we hold for these lost souls?
— Not in the hands of boys, but in their eyes
Shall many candles flames shine;
And Women's wide-spread arms shall be their wreaths,
And pallor of girl's cheeks shall be their palls.
Their flowers, the tenderness of mortal minds,
And every slow Dusk, a drawing-down of blinds.

First Draft
(With Sassoon's amendments.)

Katherine Mansfield
1888–1923

Although she often berated herself for laziness and was extremely critical of everything she wrote, Katherine Mansfield's literary output was considerable. Born Kathleen Mansfield Beauchamp in Wellington, New Zealand, she was sent to board at Queen's College, London from 1903 to 1906, then studied music in New Zealand before returning to London in 1908, seeking – as she wrote in her diary – 'Power, wealth and freedom'. She became part of a progressive and liberated literary and artistic set, which included Virginia Woolf and D. H. Lawrence, and began to write poems and short stories for small avant-garde magazines. Her personal life was eventful and difficult, involving an affair and pregnancy (which ended in miscarriage) and an extremely brief face-saving marriage to another man.

In 1911 Mansfield met the writer and editor John Middleton Murry; they finally married in 1918, by which time she was suffering from tuberculosis, which compelled her to spend part of every year in the South of France and Switzerland. Her first collection of short stories, *In a German Pension*, appeared in 1911, *Bliss, and Other Stories* in 1920 and *The Garden Party and Other Stories* in 1922.

Two further collections, as well as various editions of her letters and journal extracts, were published after her death, in Paris, at the age of thirty-five. Murry described his wife as 'the most wonderful writer…of her time' and her influence, particularly on the form of the short story, has been considerable.

Reproduced here is a page from the manuscript draft of a story, dated 15 March 1919. Entitled 'A Suburban Fairy Tale', it appeared in the collection *Something Childish and Other Stories*, published in 1924, a year after her death.

Katherine Mansfield sent this postcard photograph in 1921 to her friend S. S. Koteliansky, the Russian writer and man of letters.

Opposite: Katherine Mansfield's 'A Suburban Fairy Tale' tells the strange, poignant story of a sensitive and timid little boy who is transformed into a hungry sparrow and flies away with his flock, leaving his hitherto complacent parents bereft and horrified. Although she starts relatively neatly, by the end of the story Mansfield's hand is virtually indecipherable.

A Suburban Fairy Tale.

15. iii. 1919.

Mr and Mrs B. sat a breakfast in the cozy red
dining room of their 'snug little crib just under
half an hour's run from the city.'
There was a good fire in the grate — for the dining
room was the living room as well — the two
windows overlooking the cold empty garden patch
were closed, and the air smelled agreeably
of bacon and eggs, toast and coffee. Now that
this rationing business was nearly over Mr B. made a
point of a thoroughly good tuck in before facing
the very real perils of the day — He didn't mind
who knew it — he was a true Englishman
about his breakfast — he had to have it; he'd
carr on without it and if you told him that
these continental chaps could get through half
the mornings work he did on a roll and
a coffee of coffee — you simply didn't know what
you were talking about. Mr B. was a stout

T. S. Eliot
1888–1965

Thomas Stearns Eliot is perhaps the most influential English-speaking poet of the twentieth century and certainly one of its greatest literary and cultural critics. Born in St Louis, Missouri, he was educated at Harvard, Boston, the Sorbonne, Paris, and Merton College, Oxford. Although he generally presented himself to the world with a formal gravity (the philosopher Bertrand Russell commented that his manners were 'of the finest Etonian type') he possessed a strong sense of humour and a love of practical jokes: while working in London as a publisher at Faber and Faber he once set off firecrackers at a board meeting on 4 July.

It was his poetic mentor, Ezra Pound, who encouraged Eliot to settle in England and by 1928 he was famously declaring himself 'classical in literature, royalist in politics and Anglo-Catholic in religion'. In 1915 he married for the first time, and after a brief period of teaching went to work for Lloyds Bank. From 1917, when he published *Prufrock and Other Observations*, he was also assistant editor of *The Egoist* and in 1922 he founded *The Criterion;* his great and controversial poem *The Waste Land* appeared in its first issue, and, after radical editing by Pound, was published in 1922. Eliot completed the poem in a Swiss sanitorium to which he had retreated in the aftermath of an emotional crisis triggered in part by his troubled marriage. In its abstract forms, fragmented meanings and apocalyptic tone, the poem stands as a plangent articulation of Modernism, a complicated, pervasive and avant-garde movement of the early twentieth century in which the scientific, cultural and political assumptions of the previous age were called into question. The manuscript is now in the New York Public Library.

Eliot's continuing versatility is witnessed in his sequence of highly lyrical long poems, *Four Quartets*, which appeared together in 1943, and in his acclaimed poetic dramas of the 1930s and 50s, including the moving and powerful *Murder in the Cathedral*. A classic book of comic verse for children, the delightful *Old Possum's Book of Practical Cats*, appeared in 1939. Eliot became a British subject in 1927, found happiness in a second marriage and, living and working in London for the remainder of his years, was the recipient of both the Nobel Prize for Literature and the Order of Merit. He died in 1965 and was cremated at Golders Green Crematorium.

This portrait of T.S. Eliot was taken by Ida Kar in 1956.

Opposite: Reproduced here is a page from a letter of September 1921, from Eliot to his close friend and fellow writer Sydney Schiff, written at Margate during his recuperation from a severe nervous breakdown. In it Eliot describes his attempts to write what would become *The Waste Land*. He refers to his difficulties in making much progress with the third section, having so far managed only fifty lines; the whole letter has a weary, tense and desolate air which reflects his physical and mental state at that time.

But I have written only some
50 lines, and have read nothing.
literally,— I sketch the people,
after a fashion, and practise
scales on the mandoline.

I rather dread being in town
at all — one becomes dependent,
too, on sea or mountains, which
give some sense of security in
which one relaxes — and hope to
be only a day or two. I hope
to have good news of you both
from Vivienne — she tells me
very little about her own
health, inspite of my complaints. With best love to you
and Violet Yr aff. Tom.

James Joyce
1882–1941

'Stately, plump Buck Mulligan came from the stairhead, bearing a bowl of lather on which a mirror and a razor lay crossed.' So begins James Joyce's most famous novel *Ulysses* (1922), a work that placed Joyce in the vanguard of the literary modernism movement of the early twentieth century, alongside T. S. Eliot and Virginia Woolf. Indeed, *Ulysses* is regarded by many as one of the greatest literary works in English.

James Augustine Aloysius Joyce was born in Dublin in 1882. He was educated at University College, Dublin where he read modern languages and philosophy. In 1902 he left Dublin for Paris, returning briefly a year later at the time of his mother's death. He then left Ireland more or less permanently with Nora Barnacle, the woman he was to live with for the rest of his life, eventually marrying her in 1931. It was during his time in Paris that Joyce became familiar with the work of Edouard Dujardin, whom he credits as influencing the stream of consciousness method he employed in *Ulysses*. Despite living in Paris, Trieste and Zurich for the greater part of his life, it was Dublin that remained the inspiration for his fictional work. *Ulysses* follows the structure of Homer's *Odyssey*, the events of the novel taking place in Dublin on a single day: 16 June 1904. This was the day that Joyce began courting Nora Barnacle, and is now known and celebrated as 'Bloomsday' after Leopold Bloom, one of the principle characters in the novel.

Other notable works by Joyce are *Chamber Music* (1907), *Dubliners* (1914), *A Portrait of the Artist as a Young Man* (1916), the play *Exiles* (1918), and *Finnegans Wake* (1939). After finishing *Finnegans Wake* in Paris, Joyce moved back to Switzerland, where he died in 1941.

A photographic portrait of James Joyce taken in 1928.

Opposite: Joyce's notes from a section of *Ulysses*, with extensive scoring through by Joyce in blue, red and green pencil.

sturgeon type 1st fish
cartilage spine bony plates,
external, tail accretion,
insects, reptiles,
differentiated temperature
oyster beds
coal up to equator
Lepidia 10 footer crabs
Nb carnivorous reptiles
crocodile brain = 100. Brontosaurus
(20 meters)
brain smaller than air needle(s)
flying reptiles.
as simple work
(Belemnite formation)
mount Caledonian.
primeval boreal? tropical continents
middle sea formation
lower silurian none pre conative
all life was extinct
plane of contact, or ecliptic
height — head, chest, belly.
all eyes roll itself
effects of imperfect metamorphosis
6 wings 6 pairs
cervical vertebrae

org. pachyderm, hippo, rhino, tapir.
perissodactyla (3) or hoofed (2)
solipeds (horse) none perissod. pachyd.
ruminants

Rumen ... in upper jaw.
cannot sleep ... teeth sharp
feathers plants teeth sharp
hoops fleet
feel earthquake, eruptions, epidemics

bats, fly low
animals went when storm high
spider cease to weave rain thread
in dry night coming weaves long thread
he if rain if chill snatch = long
oyster paralysis ... naked
spider & snake blue fly
snake ... feeds
Pythian oracle of delphos

Clap your wings and crow.
otter

when bubble
froth leaps out change
bubble ... wee rain
... rep ...

approach
decay
storm to back
breakdown

rock
advance
desire
trail
cavity of bone
primary
archaic
trail till (coal)
subterranean fossil
clears ...
coal.
primitive man

Paleology.
hollow bones
but beaked teeth
no opposum
24 vertebrae in tail

emerged archipelago
His ...
temperature

Persians
temperature = 25° ... 18°
amber = petrified ...
dentition
Labrador at a child

God knows, R & R step R to L well
murder returns ... (to be killed)
murder kills self first
day they ... death breaks

water ... of all things

Virginia Woolf
1882–1941

Virginia Woolf, the daughter of Julia Duckworth and Leslie Stephen, scholar and editor of the *Dictionary of National Biography*, was born at Hyde Park Gate, London. Her literary talents revealed themselves at an early age, when she compiled, with her brother, Thoby, and elder sister Vanessa (destined, as Vanessa Bell, to became an important painter), the witty and inventive home-made periodical, 'Hyde Park Gate News'. By the age of twenty-three she had established herself firmly at the centre of London's literary world, writing for the *Times Literary Supplement* and forming, with her siblings, the influential 'Bloomsbury Group' of writers and artists. She married, in 1912, Leonard Woolf, a writer, journalist and political thinker, with whom she founded the Hogarth Press in 1917. Her first novel, *The Voyage Out*, appeared in 1915.

The ensuing decade saw a stream of increasingly innovative prose, leading to a highly concentrated and exhausting period of creativity in which she composed the major works by which she is best known. The first of these, *Mrs Dalloway* (1925), traces the thoughts, memories and emotions of one character through the course of a single day in London. The novel's inventive narrative technique is brilliantly assured, its evocation of isolation and loneliness moving and beautiful. Indeed, it is hard at times not to associate the heroine's sadness with that of Woolf herself, who suffered mental anguish throughout a life which she eventually took by her own hand in 1941. Woolf's novel, originally entitled 'The Hours', was published in 1925 and helped, in its adventurous treatment of narrative structure and interior monologue, to establish her as an important exponent of the Modernist style. Indeed, by limiting the events of her novel to just one day, Woolf recalls the work of another great Modernist and exact contemporary, James Joyce, whose *Ulysses* was serialized from 1918.

A photographic portrait of Virginia Woolf taken in 1902 by Charles Beresford.

Opposite: The British Library has several important manuscripts by Virginia Woolf. This page is taken from one of three notebooks containing drafts for *Mrs Dalloway* (1925) and for essays published in the periodical, *The Common Reader*. Woolf here sets down, in her favoured purple ink, a wonderful account of what Mrs Dalloway sees on her visit to Mulberry's, the florists, early in the novel.

Monday

by the red faced, button faced Miss Pym, whose hands were
always bright red, as if they had been stood in cold water with the
flowers.

There were flowers; delphiniums, sweet peas; bunches of lilac,
& carnations, masses of carnations. There were roses; there
were iris & lilies. Ah yes — so she breathed in the earthy
garden smell; talking to Miss Pym, who owed her help, & would
therefore always come as the little boy; & come as the boy
always when Mr Dalloway came in; & they let her kind, for
kind she had been, years ago; kind she still was, standing there,
looking older, now this year, turning her head from side to
side among the iris & roses, & nodding tufts of lilac, with
her eyes half closed, snuffing in the delicious scent. And then,
opening her eyes, how fresh, like frilled linen clean from a
laundry laid in wicker trays they looked; & dark &
prim, the red carnations, holding their heads up; &
all the sweet peas spreading in their bowls, tinged
violet, snow white, pale, — as if it were the evening,
girls in muslin frocks came out to pick sweet peas &
roses after the superb summers day, with its
almost blue-black sky, its delphiniums, its carnations,
its arum lilies, was over; ~ now the alarming moment
between six & seven, when every flower — roses,
carnations, irises, lilac, glows whatever its
colour — white, violet, red, deep orange; every
flower seems to burn by itself, softly, purely
with magic fire — in the misty beds, —
here she loved the grey white moths spinning over
the purple cherry pie, the yellow evening primroses!
Don't you get fearfully tired, she said
to Miss Pym. When standing all day
when do you get your holiday?

George Bernard Shaw
1856–1950

Shaw's *Pygmalion* had its first theatrical performance in Vienna (in German) in October 1913, followed shortly afterwards by one in Berlin. Illustrated below is a prompt copy for the first English production, containing Shaw's autograph staging instructions, written while he was directing rehearsals in early 1914. It is interesting to see how he asked Mrs Patrick Campbell, who played Eliza Doolittle, to substitute 'No bloody fear!' for the immortal 'Not bloody likely!' As we know, he returned to his original wording before the first London performance on 11 April 1914.

Twenty years later he was at work on *Pygmalion* again, this time on the screenplay. A folio from the manuscript is shown opposite. It is dated 1 October 1934 (by which time Shaw was seventy-eight) and the film was released in 1938. Though unwilling to attend studio filming, he exerted a strict control, prefacing the manuscript with the injunction that 'the printed play should be carefully kept out of the studio, as it can only confuse and mislead the producer and the performers'. He brings to the scenario a sharp perception of what the camera can achieve. This is the work of an old mind quite at ease in a relatively new medium: in fact he won an Academy Award for 'Best Screenplay of 1938'. Shaw had developed an interest in photography in the 1880s and published his first articles on the subject in 1901. By 1912 he admitted to being a cinema-addict. Interestingly, both he and G. K. Chesterton played the parts of cowboys in a comic skit on the early Western genre directed by J. M. Barrie, in 1914.

Was the theme of *Pygmalion*, in which a working class cockney heroine, Eliza Doolittle, is transformed by a speech coach into a woman able to pass as a duchess, somehow rooted in Shaw's Dublin childhood? From a shabby genteel background he emerged resoundingly with an independent and influential voice – sometimes waspish, often humorous – in journalism in the London of the 1880s. A founder member of the Fabian Society, a campaigner for women's suffrage and a defender of free speech, he was a self-educated man who said he owed all to the Library of the British Museum. His bequests to the institution bespeak his gratitude. The *Pygmalion* manuscripts are among the large collection the Library acquired from his estate in 1960.

A photographic portrait of George Bernard Shaw by Frederick Henry Evans, 1900–01.

Opposite: This page from George Bernard Shaw's screenplay for *Pygmalion* provides an excellent example of his idiosyncratic and easily identifiable hand, the character of which, in its combinations of tight forms and loops, lies somewhere between neat and spidery.

her hat, an old black straw with a
band of violets, indescribable.

② (2)

3. Eliza and her next neighbor, an elderly woman.
The audience now has a better look at Eliza; but her
good looks are not yet discoverable: she is dirty and her
~~uncomb~~ ill combed hair is dirty. Her shawl and skirt are
old and ugly. Her boots are deplorable. The older woman, though
also dirty with London grime, and no better dressed, is slightly
more ~~disciplined by~~ experience). She is busy packing her
basket and covering it. ~~The~~ Eliza is listless, discouraged, ~~and~~
and miserable.

OLD WOMAN. Now then, Eliza; woke up. Its going to rain something
chronic. You going to sit there and get soaked?

LIZA. O Gawd, I ~~aveat~~ avnt sold a bloody thing
since five o'clock, I avnt. Whats the good of doing anything
in this weather?

OLD WOMAN. Come now: talking like that wont elp.
Better get home dry than wet.

The old woman takes up her basket and hurries off.
Thunder, much nearer, after a flash.
Eliza looks up, and hastily stirs herself to pack
her basket — She finishes by putting her hat into the basket
and drawing her shawl over her head. Then she rushes off

Stella Gibbons
1902–1989

Stella Gibbons, poet and novelist, was born in New Malden, London, in 1902. After studying journalism at University College London in the early 1920s, she supported herself by working for publications including the *Evening Standard* and *The Lady*. Her first solely literary work appeared in 1930 when she published a collection of poems entitled *The Mountain Beast*.

In 1928, Gibbons was asked to write summaries of Mary Webb's first novel *The Golden Arrow* (originally published in 1916), which the *Evening Standard* had serialised in response to a sudden resurgence in popularity of the late author. Webb's rich satirical potential appealed to Gibbons, but she disliked the despairing portrayal of relationships in the countryside. Partly as a reaction to this, she wrote what would become her best known work, *Cold Comfort Farm*, a sparkling satire set in a near future in which Lambeth has become the fashionable centre of London, and video phones and private planes are features of everyday life. In the novel, Flora Poste descends on the chaotic mess of her relatives' farm and brings forth order. It has become justifiably famous both for its comedy, and for such famous lines as 'I saw something nasty in the woodshed', the constant complaint of the iconic character Aunt Ada Doom.

In 1934 Gibbons accepted the Prix Fémina at London's Institut Français, and in 1950 she was elected a Fellow of the Royal Society of Literature. *Cold Comfort Farm* continues to be by far her most famous book, although she published almost 30 others, including four volumes of poetry. Her later novels, although less well-known today, included reworkings of fairy tales for an adult market such as *Nightingale Wood* (1938) and *White Sand and Grey Sand* (1958); keenly observed portraits of wartime Britain in *The Bachelor* (1944) and *Westwood* (1946), and a satire of the nineteenth-century British army in her favourite novel, *Ticky* (1943). However, she preferred to be known as a poet, and took her poetry more seriously than she did her novels.

A photograph of Stella Gibbons taken in 1955 by Mark Gerson.

The last page of Gibbons' autograph manuscript of *Cold Comfort Farm*. Only this page and the first page of the manuscript have survived. They were purchased by The British Library from the Arts Council on 30 May 1970.

lips move, and guessed what he was saying×
as the farm chopped away beneath them. He
was occupied with keeping the machine clear of the ~~topmost branches of the~~ elms, and
~~dropped~~ one hand on her's. ~~He~~ could not
    look at her,
~~take his eyes from the~~ steering, but she saw
by his troubled profile that he feared (so
fantastically beautiful was their the night and
~~their~~ (this) ∧discovery of their love) that it might be

some cruel mistake.
    [Flora put her warm lips close to his cap.
" I love you " she said. He could not hear ~~a~~ her
(very well) ~~he~~
~~word,~~ but ∧turned for a second and, (comforted,) smiled
into her eyes.   ×
    [She glanced upwards for a second at the soft
blue
~~summer~~ vault of the Midsummer ~~the~~ (Night) sky. ~~It~~
                    misted   depths.
~~Not~~ Nor a cloud ~~broke~~ its solemn ~~beauty~~. Tomorrow
would be a beautiful day.
                THE END

Dylan Thomas
1914–1953

Dylan Thomas, the son of a Swansea school teacher, spoke no Welsh and often spoke slightingly of Wales, but in his later restless years Wales became for him, as one biographer succinctly puts it, a frame of mind he settled into. The small town of Llaregyb in his *Under Milk Wood* (1954) is an imaginary spot but it takes its life from the real New Quay, and particularly from the real Laugharne.

Thomas first lived in Laugharne from 1938 until 1940. It lies to the north-west of Swansea overlooking the estuary of three rivers that run into Carmarthen Bay. In a letter sent to his friend and fellow poet Vernon Watkins in late August 1944, he said he had written 'a Laugharne poem: the first place poem I've written' and part of it is here reproduced. Although Thomas described 'Poem in October' as a 'new poem', Watkins later recalled its having been first worked on three years earlier – with a first line of 'It was my twenty-seventh year to heaven' – and it may actually have begun life earlier than that in Laugharne itself. Such re-working was characteristic of Thomas; even the title had been once used and later abandoned for another poem first published in *The Listener* in

1934. We can see how meticulously it is written out in this fair copy in a somewhat fastidious naïve hand quite at variance with his notoriously ill-disciplined everyday existence. It was first published simultaneously in *Horizon* and in *Poetry* (Chicago) in February 1945.

Thomas married Caitlin Macnamara in 1936 and worked for the BBC throughout the war years, before returning to Laugharne in May 1949. From then on 'The Boat House', generously lent him by the wife of the historian A. J. P. Taylor, became his main residence, though he never possessed a home of his own. There he wrote *Under Milk Wood* and it was in New York, where that glorious work (originally written for broadcasting) had its first performance, that he died. There were plans to have his remains buried in the garden of The Boat House but he lies not far off in Laugharne Churchyard. His letters to Watkins, written between 1936 and 1952, were acquired by the British Library in 1965.

A photograph of Dylan Thomas c. 1950.

Opposite: This fair copy of Dylan Thomas's 'Poem in October' was sent by him, in 1944, to his friend and fellow poet, Vernon Watkins. Thomas's hand is fastidiously neat and, in its preference of print to cursive, curiously childish. The first five verses of seven are shown.

It was my thirtieth year to heaven
Woke to my hearing from harbour and neighbour wood
And the mussel pooled and the heron
Priested shore
The morning beckon
With water praying and call of sea gull and rook
And the knock of sailing boats on the net webbed wall
Myself to set foot
That second
In the still sleeping town and set forth.

My birthday began with the water
Birds and the birds of the bare trees flying my name
Above the farms and the white horses
And I rose
In rainy autumn
And walked abroad in a shower of all my days.
High tide and the heron dived when I took the road
Over the border
And the gates
Of the town closed as the town awoke.

A springful of larks in a rolling
Cloud and the roadside bushes brimming with whistling
Blackbirds and the sun of October
Summery
On the hill's shoulder,
Here were fond climates and sweet singers suddenly
Come in the morning where I wandered and listened
To the rain wringing
Wind blow cold
In the wood faraway under me.

Pale rain over the dwindling harbour
And over the sea wet church the size of a snail
With its horns through mist and the castle
Brown as owls
But all the gardens
Of spring and summer were blooming in the tall tales
Beyond the border and under the lark full cloud.
There could I marvel
My birthday
Away but the weather turned around.

It turned away from the blithe country
And down the other air and the blue altered sky
Streamed again a wonder of summer
With apples
Pears and red currants
And I saw in the turning so clearly a child's
Forgotten mornings when he walked with his mother
Through the parables
Of sun light
And the legends of the green chapels

Sir John Betjeman
1906–1984

Sir John Betjeman was more than a composer of memorable, popular poems; he was also a writer on British architecture, with a special enthusiasm for great railway stations. It is therefore only fitting that his statue should stand beneath the majestic canopy of the restored St Pancras station complex, the writer having campaigned in the mid-1960s against its demolition.

Betjeman was among the founders of the Victorian Society, which champions the preservation of Victorian and Edwardian buildings, and nostalgia and an attachment to the values of the past infused his work. Its extended form notwithstanding, his verse memoir *Summoned by Bells* is typical of his style. The story of the poet's life from his pre-war childhood in Highgate, North London, with its trips by train to the 'yet unbuilt-on' fields of Middlesex, up to his emergence into 'the opening world' of Oxford is told in simple, accessible language allied to a steady metrical pattern. By 1960, when the book was published, Betjeman was by far the best selling of modern English poets. He held the post of Poet Laureate from 1972 until his death in 1984.

Betjeman consolidated his literary success with a second career as a television broadcaster, mainly on architectural subjects, becoming in the process a well-known media figure. In his later years he made a series of LP recordings for Charisma Records in which his previously published poems were given popular music settings. More recently, Betjeman's poem 'Slough', first published in 1937, was quoted by Ricky Gervais in the hit TV comedy series *The Office* – a small but significant measure of how deeply his work has permeated the British cultural consciousness.

A 1982 photograph of Sir John Betjeman.

Opposite: John Betjeman's typescript, with autograph revisions and re-workings, of the autobiography in verse published in 1960 as *Summoned by Bells*.

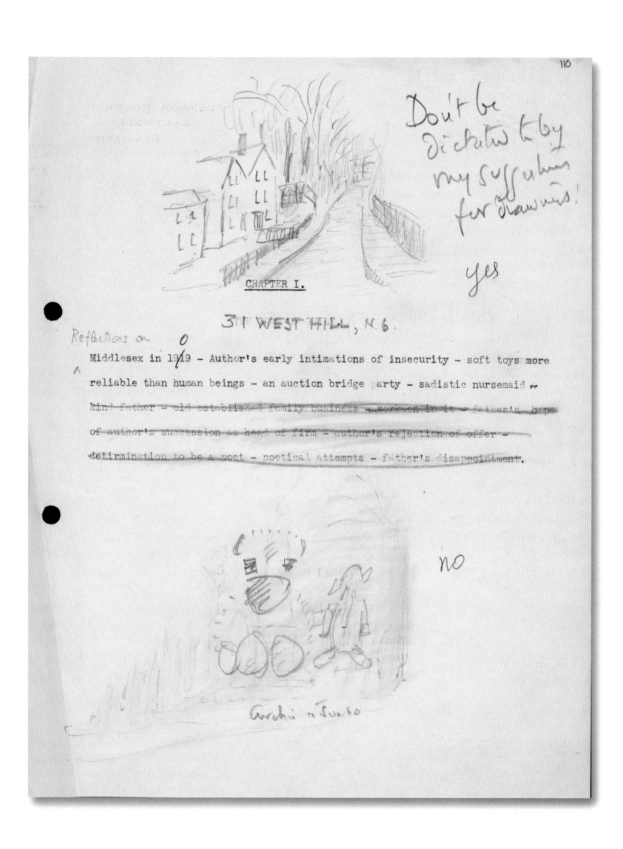

Don't be
dictated to by
my suggestions
for drawings!

yes

CHAPTER I.

31 WEST HILL, N.6.

Reflections on

Middlesex in 19¹9 - Author's early intimations of insecurity - soft toys more
reliable than human beings - an auction bridge party - sadistic nursemaid ~
~~kind father - old established family business - worked in it - father's hope
of author's succession as head of firm - author's rejection of offer -
determination to be a poet - poetical attempts - father's disappointment.~~

no

Archie & Jumbo

Philip Larkin
1922–1985

Although by his death in 1985 Philip Larkin had published just four slim collections of verse (in addition to two early novels), his superb modulation of tone, technical brilliance and ability to speak of both the mundane and the marvellous had endeared him to a broad audience. Larkin's work is at its most visceral when addressing the dismal and the dull, the fear of growing old and death, while his own essential conservatism (he rarely went abroad) is reflected in accounts of contemporary England which strike a bitterly satiric tone. In some of his best poems, however, this darker vision is transcended and redeemed by moments of great lyric intensity.

Larkin was born in 1922 in Coventry where he went to school before attending St John's College, Oxford. After graduating, he began his lifelong career as a librarian, first in Wellington, Leicester, then in Belfast, and finally at the University of Hull, where he ran the Brynmor Jones Library, whose 'high windows' inspired the title of his last collection. He once commented in an interview that 'Librarianship suits me – I love the feel of libraries… And I've always thought that a regular job was no bad thing for a poet.'

Larkin's first collection, *The North Ship*, was issued in 1945, followed by *The Less Deceived* (1955) and *The Whitsun Weddings* (1964) which, with *High Windows* (1974), has proved the most enduringly popular. Less acclaimed were his two novels, *Jill* (1946) and *A Girl in Winter* (1947). Larkin was a shy man who lived an outwardly unassuming life, the routine of which was enlivened by a love of jazz and a series of occasionally outrageous correspondences with friends and fellow writers. Although he never married, he had close relationships with women who inspired some of his most tender poems.

Larkin died on 2 December 1985, his funeral in Westminster Abbey marked with a performance of the jazz he found to be so affirmative. He decreed at the end of his life that his papers should be burnt; many of his diaries indeed met that fate, but other of his manuscripts were, controversially, preserved.

Larkin's commitment to his chosen profession was clearly shown by his involvement, from 1965, in a scheme to secure contemporary literary manuscripts for British libraries. This draft of 'Wedding Wind', written at the age of twenty-four, is from a notebook which he donated to the British Library as part of that project in 1965 – having first cut from it anything he did not wish to meet the public eye. The convincingly intimate voice of the narrator as she wavers between melancholy and joy, the elemental imagery contrasted with domestic detail, the shift from the palpable contexts of the first lines to the metaphysical questionings of the last – all anticipate some of Larkin's late, great verses.

A photograph of Phillip Larkin at work in the Brynmor Jones Library, Hull University.

Opposite: In this draft of his poem 'Wedding Wind', Philip Larkin adopts the persona of a newly wed bride. Her voice, in all its beauty and emotional sincerity, reminds us that Larkin could be sensitive and subtle as well as acerbic and irreverent. The manuscript notebook in which it is written was kept by the poet from 5 October 1944 to 10 March 1950.

The wind blew all my wedding-day

And my wedding-night was the night of the high wind,

And a stable door was banging, again and again,

~~So~~ That he must go and shut it, leaving me

Stupid in candlelight, hearing ~~the~~ rain,

Seeing my face ~~twisted~~ in the ~~brass~~ twisted candlestick,

Yet seeing nothing. When he came back

He said the horses were restless, and I was sad

That any man or beast that night should lack

The happiness I had.

                     Now in the morning

      travelled   with

All's ~~restless~~ under the sun ~~the wind still blowing~~ wind's blowing.

                  floods

He has gone to look at the ~~fences~~, and I

Carry a chipped pail to the chickenrun,

~~Set~~ Set it down, and stare. All is the wind

Hunting through clouds and forests, thrashing

              clothes on the line

My apron and the hanging ~~sheets~~.

Can it be borne, this bodying-forth by wind

    of joy ~~my~~ ~~across time~~ on, ~~like a~~ ~~thread~~

    ~~to the undreamed joy at the root of day and night,~~

    ~~carrying beads?~~ Shall I be let to sleep.

Now this ~~With this~~ perpetual morning ~~shares~~ my bed?

    ~~Will even death conclude...~~

        our

~~Now~~ Kneeling like cattle among new ~~waters of faith~~?

Can

~~Will~~ even death dry up

These new delighted lakes, conclude

           by

Our kneeling as cattle ~~among~~ all generous waters?

                      28 Sept

Terence Rattigan
1911–1977

Between 1936 and 1956, Terence Rattigan was the most successful playwright in Britain. *French without Tears*, his first great success in 1936, and *While The Sun Shines*, in 1943, had more than 1000 performances, a record still unequalled in the West End, and four other plays ran for more than 500 nights, including his finest full-length play, *The Deep Blue Sea*.

But in 1956, when *Separate Tables* had been running for nearly two years, John Osborne's *Look Back In Anger* opened at the Royal Court Theatre to great excitement, and opened up the English theatre to younger, working-class voices. Within two years, the critics had turned against Rattigan, seemingly disliking his ostentatiously wealthy lifestyle as much as his writing. Rattigan's always fragile confidence was undermined and his health began to fail. Although his achievements were honoured with a knighthood six years before his death, it was not until the late 1980s that critics and audiences were prepared to make a more generous reassessment of Rattigan's work.

Rattigan himself once said, 'It is the implicit rather than the explicit that gives life to a scene'. The emotional restraint Rattigan always showed in his writing may have been born of the sexuality he could not express openly in his lifetime, but in his plays this reticence becomes an acute sensitivity to the emotions of others: the schoolmaster Crocker-Harris in *The Browning Version* (1948), or Sybil Railton-Bell in *Separate Tables* (1954) who at last finds the courage to stand up to her bullying mother and remain a friend of the erring Major Pollock. Around Rattigan's centenary year, the triumphant revivals of *After the Dance* at the National Theatre, *Flare Path* at the Theatre Royal Haymarket, and *Cause Célèbre* at the Old Vic showed that the audiences who once prized the writer for his theatrical craftsmanship and his humane response to the emotional dilemmas of ordinary people were not mistaken.

A photograph of Terence Rattigan taken at Claridges Hotel, London in 1973.

Opposite: The page shown here is from Rattigan's personal copy of *Separate Tables* as used in the original production at the St James's Theatre in 1954. It shows the last scene of the play, with Rattigan's handwritten annotations.

oreen   What's the matter with you tonight ? You always say "mea culpa". (She beats her breast in imitation of an obvious Major bon mot)

ajor P.   Do I ? Well — ~~they both mean the same, don't they ?~~ *my fault means the same thing, doesn't it ?*

oreen   I suppose so. (Finishing the serving) *well,* there you are. Now what about breakfast ?

ajor P.   Breakfast ?

oreen   Joe got it wrong about your going, didn't he ?

                    There is a pause. SIBYL is looking
                    steadily at the Major, who now raises his
                    eyes from his plate and meets her glance.

ajor P.   (Quietly)   Yes, he did.

oreen   That's good. (Crosses U.C.) Breakfast usual time, then ?

ajor P.   Yes, Doreen. Breakfast usual time.

                    DOREEN GOES into the kitchen.

                    MAJOR POLLOCK begins to eat his fricassee.
                    SIBYL continues to eat her sweet. A
                    decorous silence, broken only by the
                    renewed murmur of "the casuals" reigns
                    once more, and the dining room of the
                    Beauregard Private Hotel no longer gives
                    any sign of the battle that has just been
                    fought and won between its four, bare
                    walls.

                                LIGHTS FADE AND

            CURTAIN.

            THE END.

Mervyn Peake
1911–1968

As an author, Mervyn Peake is best remembered for his *Gormenghast* trilogy, or *Titus* books as he preferred to call them. Gormenghast – the labyrinthine castle of ancient stones which almost seems to live and breathe – has become seared in the public consciousness as an archetypal symbol of a shadowy bureaucracy. Such is the resonance of the books that they have inspired the coining of a new term – the 'gormenghastly'– which has been applied to fascist regimes and petty officialdom alike.

Peake started his trilogy in 1940, before the publication of J.R.R. Tolkien's *Lord of the Rings* and C.S. Lewis's *Narnia* series. Without magic or supernatural elements, at least in the first two books, Peake's story stands apart from the tales of quests and magic portals that have proliferated in English fantasy writing since the 1950s. In this respect Peake has more in common with Kafka, Dickens and Lewis Carroll, and in his third novel, *Titus Alone*, he veered towards science fiction.

Born in China in 1911, Mervyn Peake was influenced by the contrast between his very English upbringing in a missionary compound, and what he saw as the outlandishness of Chinese society outside its walls. Isolation and islands were to dominate his work, not least in his 1953 novel, *Mr Pye*, which is set on the Channel Island of Sark, where Peake lived for several periods in his life.

Although his characters and settings are often cut off, or set adrift, there is much fun to be found in Peake. His nonsense poetry and his books for children, *Captain Slaughterboard Drops Anchor* (1939) and *Letters From a Lost Uncle* (1948), show the delight he took in adventures, pranks and punning.

Among Peake's 'serious' poetry, his Blitz poems and his responses to a visit to Germany in 1945 stand out as significant works. To consider Peake solely as a writer, though, is to overlook his equally extraordinary work as an artist. Peake trained at the Royal Academy, taught life drawing for most of his career, and illustrated such classics as Lewis Carroll's *Alice* books, *The Rime of the Ancient Mariner*, and *Treasure Island*. When drafting his own work, he would make drawings of his characters as wrote, helping him to visualise them and imagine the kinds of things they might say. It is this symbiotic relationship between the senses – between word, image and sound – that characterises all Peake's work, and marks him out as a true original.

A photograph of Mervyn Peake taken in the garden of his house in Smarden, Kent in 1951.

Opposite: A page from one of the thirty-four extant notebooks for Peake's *Titus* books. This page shows Lord Groan's manservant, Flay, stalking the chef Swelter. The act of drawing stimulated Peake's sensory perception, prompting him to make the revisions seen on the page.

~~The dew settled through the cracks in his~~

The air was sickly with an aftermath
~~and otherwise~~ of the days heat - a clammy, *lifeless,* ~~thunderous~~
~~breathed~~ air, as though it had been
breathed before, *thrice* exhaled & stale ~~and as once exhaled and~~.
Only his feet felt cold, as ~~they~~ they
sank ankle deep in the dew. ~~and as~~
~~as though he trod in his own spit~~
~~tread for though the meadows~~
~~his sweat~~. It was as though he trod through
grass that was ~~heavy~~ with his own sweat
dripped

Lawrence Durrell
1912–1990

Lawrence Durrell was born in India and, apart from his schooling in London and Canterbury, spent most of his life out of England for he felt oppressed and deadened by this country's social *mores*. His first liberation came in 1935 when the family moved to Corfu, the idyllic years there being celebrated in his book *Prospero's Cell* (1945) and in his brother Gerald's *My Family and Other Animals* (1956). By 1935 Durrell had already published some tiny volumes of verse and that year saw the publication of his first novel, *Pied Piper of Lovers*.

The great adventure of this period is encapsulated in the photograph of Durrell on board his boat, the Van Norden, named after a character in Henry Miller's *Tropic of Cancer* (1935). Miller's influence on Durrell was huge. They met in 1937. The Second World War saw the departure of the Durrells from Greece. Durrell himself was in Cairo and Alexandria during the conflict and it was in the rich ambiguity of Alexandrian life, its squalor, its allure, its brutishness, its lyricism, that Durrell was to find inspirational sources for the four novels known as the *Alexandria Quartet*, his most notable achievement, published between 1957 and 1960.

Durrell's drafts for the first two of these novels, *Justine* and *Balthazar*, came to the British Library by bequest in 1995 among the large collection of Durrelliana gathered by his most loyal friend, the antiquarian bookseller, Alan Thomas. Shown opposite is a folio from one of the *Justine* notebooks whose inner front cover declares that the work was begun in Venice on 21 January 1954, based on notes made in 1946–47 with some passages from 1943. In the same notebook we can also see (left) the kind of idle sketch he turned to slightly better account in his painting exhibitions under the pseudonym Oscar Epfs. Below it is the outline of his daughter Sappho's hand and one may wonder if this was the source of the cover design for the first edition in 1957.

France became Durrell's adopted home. He died in Sommières, near Nîmes, where he had lived since 1966 and his remains are in the nearby cemetery of the chapel of St Julien de Salinelles.

This photograph of Lawrence Durrell is taken from a negative discovered among his papers.

Opposite: This manuscript notebook contains one of two drafts of *Justine* acquired by the British Library as part of Lawrence Durrell's large archive in 1995. Here we can plainly see (thanks to the change of pen) Durrell returning to, correcting and continuing his work.

And Melissa? She lacked the insight of Justine into my human case. She only knew that my strength supported her where she was at her weakest — in her dealings with the world. She indeed loved me for every sign of my human weakness — disorderly habits, incapacity over money affairs, and so on. She loved my weaknesses because here she could feel of use to me; Justine brushed all this aside. I interested her only in this one particular which I could not offer her as a gift or she steal from me — my real self. This is what is meant by possession — to be passionately at war for the qualities in one another; to contend for the treasures of each others' personalities. How can such a war be anything but destructive and hopeless? ~~The greater insight of the~~ ~~XXXXXXXXXXXXXXXXXXXXX~~ Justine with the more deeply divining sense of the powers had isolated what was dear to her in me; Melissa accepted everything, even the pain I caused her without criticism, unflinchingly, as part of my weakness.

Yet, so entangled are human motives — it was really she (Melissa) who had driven Nessim from his refuge in the world of fantasy towards an action which he knew we would all bitterly regret. For it was she who would, overmastered by the impulse of her unhappiness one night approached the table where he was sitting alone before his world of circumspect one pensively watching the cabinet, and blushing and trembling under false eyelashes, blurted out the words "Your wife is no longer faithful to you" — a phrase which fell and remained quivering in Nessim's heart like a thrown knife. It is true that for a long time now his dossiers had been swollen with reports of this dreaded fact; but these reports themselves seemed somehow to lack a personal application. They were like the reports one reads in a newspaper of some huge earthquake which has destroyed a country and rendered a million people homeless. The difference was now that he was face to

John Osborne
1929–1994

The events of 8 May 1956 revolutionised the British theatre and the life of John Osborne, and for a long while it seemed that both were to be inextricably tied to the legend of '1956 and all that'. The date marked the opening night of the unknown Osborne's play *Look Back in Anger* at the then unfashionable Royal Court theatre in London. The play was widely seen to herald a new energy and political awareness in British theatre.

A legend soon grew around the young Osborne's overnight success but, unbeknownst to critics, he had been writing for the theatre since the late 1940s, and by the time of *Look Back in Anger* had already had two plays professionally produced; these unknown works were thought to have been lost until copies were discovered in the British Library archives in 2008.

Following the success of *Look Back in Anger* in Britain and overseas, Osborne was appointed by the media as the leader of the so-called 'Angry Young Men' school of young, male, working-class writers. This revolutionary label, however, masked Osborne's attachments to traditional elements of English life and culture, apparent in his follow-up work, *The Entertainer*, which mixed awareness of Brechtian theory with an affectionate recall of earlier music hall traditions.

During the 1960s, Osborne's work was at the forefront of the new wave of British writing, and with *Luther* (1961), *Inadmissible Evidence* (1964), and *A Patriot for Me* (1965), he wrote plays that challenged both dramatic and social conventions; the overt depiction of homosexuality in *A Patriot for Me* was disallowed by the official censor, the Lord Chamberlain, and performance only enabled by turning the Royal Court theatre into a private members' club.

Although Osborne enjoyed considerable success in the cinema (he won an Oscar for the 1963 film *Tom Jones*) and, later, with his uncompromising autobiographies, his writing for the theatre lost some of its vitality and urgency during the 1970s. By the time *Look Back's* central character, Jimmy Porter, was resuscitated in the late play *Déjà vu* (1992), Osborne was a marginalised figure. However, despite a growing critical counter-revisionism that questioned the revolutionary nature of *Look Back in Anger*, a series of acclaimed revivals in recent years, alongside productions of rediscovered early work, has reestablished his reputation as a leading figure of post-war British theatre.

A photograph of John Osborne taken in 1956.

Opposite: Laurence Olivier, the leading light of an earlier generation of British actors, was reluctantly persuaded by American playwright Arthur Miller to go to see *Look Back in Anger*. Impressed by the play's young writer, he reportedly asked Osborne to write him a new role. The resulting play, *The Entertainer*, saw Olivier reconnect with a younger generation through his acclaimed creation of the washed-up music hall entertainer Archie Rice. The draft shown here is an early version sent by Osborne to Olivier, and discovered in the latter's archive at the British Library.

CAST IN ORDER OF APPEARANCE

1 BILLY RICE.

3 ~~MICK~~ ARCHIE RICE

4 PHOEBE RICE

2. JEAN RICE

5 FRANK RICE

6 WILLIAM (BROTHER BILL) RICE.

7 GRAHAM DODD.

THE ENTERTAINER

Stevie Smith
1902–1971

In her essay 'Too Tired for Words', published in *Medical World* in December 1956, Stevie Smith relishes the thought that death summoned at command is 'a great relief to the tired' and, speaking of God in that same essay, she adds 'when I am dead I hope that he will eat Everything I have been and have not been'. These thoughts evidently possessed her considerably in late 1956, for we can see them again in the letter illustrated opposite, addressed to her friend Sally Chilver and sent on 20 November of that year. 'Death as end and remedy', she writes. But after she had sought such a remedy in an unbalanced moment in 1953, she was filled with remorse about the pain she had inflicted on the person she most cared about, her aunt back home in Palmers Green.

This trim suburb of north London had been Stevie Smith's home since she was three and, comfortable in its discomforts ('…the lavatory cistern floods the garden…', she writes in this letter), it remained so until her death from a brain tumour in Ashburton Hospital, near Plymouth. She was much occupied with what to her were deeply satisfying domestic duties and with caring for her aunt, but she nevertheless held down a secretarial job in Covent Garden for thirty years, published three novels between 1936 and 1949, eight volumes of poems, all illustrated with her own drawings, between 1937 and 1969, and various essays and reviews.

Though actually quite a gregarious woman (she had her home telephone number put into her entry in *Who's Who*), she found intimacies beyond friendship quite suffocating and she was aware that she was limited in her ability to portray love between couples – 'that troubled stirring world of Two's' as she puts it earlier in the letter. The two 'new' poems embedded in the letter to Chilver show her own strange – one might even say lonely – experiences of the emotion. The manuscript was given to the British Library by Sally Chilver in 1980.

A photograph of Stevie Smith.

Opposite: In this page from a letter to Sally Chilver, Stevie Smith includes two new poems, one of which, 'My Heart Goes Out' appeared in her radio play *A Turn Outside*, broadcast on 23 May 1959. Smith uses a ballpoint pen. Invented in its modern form in 1935 in Prague, and marketed in New York from 1945, it was still a relatively new instrument.

2.

I do not quite catch it. But I know
it means a lot to some people, so I
suppose it does mean a lot. Now (of
course) I must tell you my new
ones. (¹) ~~My Heart goes out~~ It Filled My
Heart with love

(When I hold in my hand a
soft & crushable animal, & feel
the fur beat for fear, & the
soft feathers, I cannot feel
unhappy.) [N.B. This is a sort of
introduction or sub-title.]

In his fur the animal rode & in
his fur he strove
And oh it filled my heart, my heart,
It filled my heart with love.

(2)   My Heart Goes Out

My heart goes out to my creator in love
Who gave me Death, as end & remedy.
All living creatures come to quiet Death
For him to eat up their activity
And give them nothing, which is what
they want although
When they are living they do not think so.

(what I like about this, is that
it's so apt to be 'my creator-in-law')

Laurie Lee
1914–1997

Writer and poet Laurie Lee grew up in Slad, a small village in the Cotswolds. In his memoir, *Cider with Rosie*, he describes with warmth his childhood there. Lee's picture of a slower, quieter, semi-feudal rural Britain, far away in time from both the bustle of modern life and its many comforts and conveniences, was an instant success, being reprinted three times in the month following its first publication in 1959. Decades later, with over six million copies sold, its appeal shows no sign of fading.

Ten years later, Lee published *As I Walked Out One Midsummer Morning*, an account of how, at the age of 19, he left his countryside home 'to discover the world'. Lee travelled on foot, first to London and then around Spain, supporting himself with odd jobs and the small change brought in through busking with his violin ('Slow melodies were best, encouraging people to dawdle.'). Another immediate bestseller, the book stands as a classic of twentieth-century travel writing. At the tale's close, the Spanish Civil War is breaking out, and the narrator is repatriated courtesy of a Royal Navy warship. *A Moment of War*, the concluding volume in Lee's autobiographical trilogy, tells of the events following his return to Spain in 1937 to join the International Brigades.

Lee died in his home village at the age of 82 and was buried, according to his wishes, in the local churchyard. Five months after his death, a memorial service was held at St James's Church in Piccadilly. The author himself was heard on tape, speaking at first, then playing an old Spanish tune on the violin.

A photograph of Laurie Lee taken in 1956 by Ida Kar.

A draft opening of *As I Walked Out One Midsummer Morning* by Laurie Lee. This manuscript dates from around 1947 and is completely different from the opening page in the version eventually published some twenty years later.

Chapter 1.

Just as we die many times in our lives, so are we several times born and begin an epoch when all familiarities disappear & everything in the world is viewed as by a child — strange, new & double-sized.

Just as we die many times in our lives, so are we several times born. Love, Illness, or a strange country mark the starting places, when all the familiarities of experience disappear & the whole range of everyday it & nightlit living is viewed again, as by a child — magic, terrible, & double-sized.

When I landed in Spain on the dawn of that July day, 1935, I felt the second birth in all my senses. I was alone, ignorant, & mute as a babe — I knew not a word of what the world talked round me. But also enjoyed without knowing it the supreme strength of ignorance: optimism & a belief in luck.

a child enjoys only its or make signs for its unwell imperative food, drink or sleep

But I also enjoyed the supreme strength of that ignorant innocence — optimism and a belief in luck.

It was early & almost dark when out of the blue unconscious rocking of sea & sleep I was simultaneously woken & hooked to the soil of that country by the dramatic thunder of the iron-covered anchor going over the side. I awoke with a curious reluctance, protesting, with a nostalgia for the deep blue sleep, unwilling,

Sylvia Plath
1932–1963

Sylvia Plath was born in Boston, Massachusetts. The death of her father, a German immigrant Professor and entomologist, in 1940, had a profound effect upon her and his image haunts her later poems. An excellent student – talented, clever and attractive – in 1952 she won a *Mademoiselle* magazine fiction award, and spent some time in New York as a guest editor. Despite her many shining qualities, she was troubled. When she graduated from Smith College, Massachusetts, in 1955, she had already survived severe bouts of depression, two suicide attempts, hospitalization and electro-convulsive therapy. A year later, she married the poet Ted Hughes, whom she met in England while a Fulbright scholar at Newnham College, Cambridge. After teaching together in America, they returned to England in 1959, living in London before moving to Devon in 1961. Her first volume of poetry, *The Colossus*, appeared in 1960, and her autobiographical novel, *The Bell Jar*, was published under a pseudonym (Victoria Lucas) in 1963. Less than a month after its publication, early in the morning of 11 February, during the coldest winter experienced in England for many years, she committed suicide. Tired and worn down after a severe bout of influenza, and suffering from a recurrence of her depressive illness, she had been living alone in London with her two young children after separating from Hughes.

In 1965 Plath's best known collection of poems, *Ariel*, established her reputation as one of the most powerful poets of the twentieth century with its vivid, rich, turbulent poems of fury, ecstasy and anguish; as she herself explained: 'The blood jet is poetry/There is no stopping it.' A friend, the poet Anne Sexton, wrote that 'These last poems stun me. They eat time.' The stanzas reproduced here, heavily revised in her distinctive, rather girlish hand are from a poem entitled 'Insomniac'. It was completed in May 1961 and won a prize at the Cheltenham Literary Festival that summer. On receiving the prize, Plath wrote to the judges 'I am happy to hear…that sleeplessness has its own very pleasant reward' – although 'sleeplessness' might be regarded as a rather understated way of referring to the mental anguish depicted in the poem. Always her own sternest critic, Plath was a constant discarder of her own work (which was written on any paper that came to hand – including, on occasion, the backs of her husband's early drafts). These impressive and heavily revised stanzas, signed at the top of the page, did not appear in the poem's final version.

A photographic portrait of Sylvia Plath.

Opposite: This is the first of several pages of a draft of 'Insomniac' by Sylvia Plath, a prize-winning poem submitted to the Cheltenham Literary Festival in 1961. It shows the opening of a poem which, in its alterations, corrections and additions, seems as restless as the subject it treats.

Insomniac

The night sky is only a sort ~~sheet~~ only a sort of carbon paper,
Blueblack, with the much-poked periods of stars
letting in light, peephole after peephole —

A bone white   The light ~~and too~~, like death, behind all things.
    ~~He is~~ under the eyes of the stars, the ~~busy~~ moon's victim
    ~~of a moon that craves her light into the world~~
    ~~of the / aluminium - cold mournfully suffers~~
    ~~cold,~~

He suffers his desert silences; sleeplessness
Stretching ~~like / irritating fine~~ sand in all directions
        ~~is~~ / a fine,

Over & over the old, granular movie
Exposes embarrassments — the mizzling days
Of childhood & adolescence, sticky with dreams,
Parental faces on tall stalks, alternately stern & tearful;
A garden of buggy roses that made him cry.
His forehead is bumpy as a sack of rocks.
~~the~~ Memories ~~jostle~~ each other/like obsolete film stars.

                    but Grau-room

he is immune to
    ~~He~~ pills: a ~~softhess wants~~ red, purple, blue —
    ~~they bloomed like~~
    ~~The eloquent~~ ~~pellets of oblivion~~   protracted
                            void
How they lit the tedium of the ~~various~~ evening!   ~~he   Won but
    ~~How meany~~   whose ~~edge~~   influence   p
those   planets, ~~humming~~
sugary   ~~And a ~~/ sweet~~ baptised in~~
    ~~Silent fiction life~~ no life at all for a while,
to the   ~~Apt~~ a sweet, drugged wakening, ~~like~~ a forgetful baby.
    He ~~this is 18~~   immune to ~~Dawn~~ their poppy-cheerful colour
                    to him no good.

W. H. Auden
1907–1973

Wystan Hugh Auden gave his name to a generation of poets who, during the 1930s, sought to reconcile the chaos they perceived in the 'public' world around them with their own 'private' vision. Stephen Spender, Louis MacNeice, Cecil Day Lewis and Christopher Isherwood all formed part of a closely-knit group characterised by left-leaning principles which formed a counterpoint to the plangent and uncompromising position adopted by their Modernist predecessors.

Of a solid middle-class background, Auden was educated at Gresham's School in Norfolk, and Christ Church College, Oxford University. He published his first volume of verse in 1930. His homosexuality and residence in America during the Second World War caused him some difficulty among the reading public but his return to Oxford in 1956 as Professor of Poetry signified a widening respect for his assured, distinctive voice.

In a letter of 19 August 1963 to Cecil Day Lewis, Auden wrote: 'I have no manuscripts in the ordinary sense of the word. I keep a working notebook in which poems are sketched out. For the most part, these sketches are illegible to anyone but myself:

further, they are almost always incomplete, for the final revisions are made in my head or on the typewriter.' Scholars were able to judge Auden's words at first hand when, in the mid-1960s, an important notebook which he had kept since 1947 came to the British Library under a scheme initiated by Philip Larkin to preserve modern literary manuscripts.

The fascinating complexity of Auden's method is well illustrated here in one of many heavily revised drafts of the poem 'To-Night at Seven-Thirty', probably written in 1963 as part of a profound and touching sequence 'Thanksgiving for a Habitat' in which he questions where, how and, quite simply, why we live.

W. H. Auden on Fire Island near New York, in 1946. The photograph was taken by his good friend, the Irish writer James Stern.

Opposite: Auden's poetic drafts often bear a series of dots and dashes together with alphabetic and numeric schemes, indicating the importance he attached to rhyme and metre in the process of composition.

bite — a tablet.... when to stop,

a temporal re-presentation of to interrupt,

The feast is a human invention. The life of a plant
Is one long meal; no movements interrupt theirs,
To sleep or mate, or while predators must grab a bite
And bolt it when they get the chance let
the carbon eat alone — even the pack-hunters
like dine en famille do not invited guests
A feast the can still feast or share
as .... a ... implies / placement

of placement period — placards has never unto
A great thing is life's first
our temporal celebration awareness.
of the shared silence

I see a table	a	4
Facing a wall	b	10
dinner table, ...	a	4
At which the guests a dinner ...	c	12
Make the eye grateful	b	4
	d	12
So Eating as	d	12
For life, speech as a representing	e	12
of the shared silence	e	7
	c	12
	f	10
	g	8
	f	9
	g	6

Harold Pinter
1930–2008

Presenting the 2005 Nobel Prize in Literature to Harold Pinter, Per Wästberg of the Swedish Academy noted that: 'with his twenty-nine plays and about a hundred that he has directed or acted in, he has made the theatre his own domain'. Not only a writer of some of the most significant and celebrated plays of the twentieth century, Pinter was thoroughly implicated in all aspects of dramatic creation as an actor, director, and designer of his own and others' work.

The son of a tailor, Pinter was born in East London and educated at Hackney Downs Grammar School. He was published as a poet in so-called 'Little magazines' during the late 1940s, and his first play, *The Room*, was performed at the University of Bristol in 1957 while he was still acting in regional repertory theatre. It was followed in 1958 by *The Birthday Party*, now regarded as one of the seminal plays of the twentieth century but which, on the occasion of its London opening, was greeted with horrified incomprehension by the critics, one writing of '*non sequiturs*, half-gibberish and lunatic ravings'. However, after the distinguished reviewer Harold Hobson wrote a highly appreciative piece, in which he praised Pinter's mastery of impalpable terror, the tide quickly turned, and many critical and commercial successes followed. The term 'Pinteresque', with its connotations of nameless menace, erotic fantasy, obsession, jealousy and family rivalries, has now entered the English vocabulary to the extent that it is occasionally used by people who have never seen a Pinter play.

Pinter's later work, from the 1980s onwards, is more spare and politically charged, with plays such as *One for the Road* (1984) and *Mountain Language* (1988). However, Pinter's earlier work was equally political, demonstrating a challenging, provocative scrutiny of power relations and justice from the start. The PEN/Pinter literary prize was established after his death, and every year honours those writers who, in the words of Pinter's Nobel Lecture, demonstrate an 'unflinching, unswerving fierce intellectual determination… to define the real truth of our lives and our societies'.

A photographic portrait of Harold Pinter.

Opposite: Pinter's archive of poems and playscripts was acquired by the British Library in 2007, where it is used by literary researchers from all over the world. Reproduced here is the first page from the earliest draft of one of his most powerful and frequently acted plays, *The Homecoming*, first performed in June 1965. The play still shocks audiences with its stark portrayal of what the critic Michael Billington called 'the naked violence of family life and…the primal, atavistic power of the female'.

(Evening)

Son 3 jotting notes on sports page. Enter Father.

F. - What have you done with the scissors ?
          p.
     I want the scissors.
3. - What for ?
F. - What have you done with them ?
3. - What do you want the scissors for ?
F. - ~~I want to cut something out.~~ I want to cut something
     out the ~~bleeding~~ paper. ~~You bastard.~~
          p
3. -I'm reading the paper.
F. - Not that paper. The sunday paper.
          F. sits.
F   - I think I'll have a fag.

          p.
     There's an advertisement in the paper about flannel
     vests. Cut price. Navy wear. I could do with a few of
     them. Give me a fag.
          p.
     Give me a cigarette !   ~~Pass it~~ I've got enough
                                                            to do.
3. + ~~Why should I give you a cigarette ? I've got enough~~
     ~~to do.~~
F. - Look what I'm landed with. ✓ ~~A pair of bastards. Well,~~   (I'm sorry
     you can drown in your own blood, anyway. ~~You can drown~~   I told
     ~~in your own blood. As far as I go.~~ And the other one.
     ~~All these tough boys.~~ You and your bleeding bastard
     ~~brother. Lousy stinking prostitutes.~~   (crumpled.
                    p. takes fag from pocket what's the matter
     I'm getting old, my word of honour. ✓You think I wasn't
     a tearaway ? I could have taken care of you, twice over.
     I'm still strong. You ask your uncle Sam what I was.
     ~~I was a villian.~~ At the same time I always had a kind
     heart. I used to knock about with a man called Berkowitz. ✓
     I called him Berki. Come on Berki, where you going
     tonight ? Coming up West tonight ? Go round the back
     doubles, do a few snooker halls, run in a couple of
     tarts. I still got the scars. We used to walk back to
     back, Berki and me. The terrible twins they used to call
     us. He was six feet tall. But even his family called
     him Berki. He had a big family, mind you. But even his
     old man called him Berki. Of course the old man was a
     ~~Berkowitz too.~~ They were all Berkotitzs, ~~it goes without~~
     ~~saying.~~ But he was the only one they called Berki. ~~His~~
     ~~other brothers we called Berks. Anyway, he's dead.~~ One
     of his sisters died in prison. The other one died in
     hospital. We went to see her. She was dead ~~whenx~~ by the
     time we got there.

                    p. she   such a bad, your ~~mother~~
     Mind you, your ~~mother was a good~~ woman, ~~even though she~~
     ~~was too honest.~~ Even though she made me sick she wasnt
     a bad bitch. ~~Not that you two care a fart about your~~
     ~~mother. Where did you put those bastard scissors ?~~
3. - ~~Why dont you shut up ?~~   I gave her the best years
     plug it, will you,   of my bleeding life,
     you stupid sod.   anyway.?
     I'm trying to read the paper.

MacGregor

a tearaway
called my boy

He was fond of
your mother.
Berkowitz was.
Always had a
good word for
her.

B. S. Johnson
1933–1973

For writer B S (Bryan Stanley) Johnson, 'telling stories really is telling lies', and throughout his relatively short writing career between 1963 and 1973, Johnson struggled with the consequences of his rigid understanding of the form. At times, his insistence on the artificial nature of storytelling threatened to overwhelm his novels; two thirds of the way through his second novel, *Albert Angelo*, the narrator pulls his story up short, and addresses the reader directly as the author: 'f**k all this lying... what's the point in covering up covering up covering over pretending pretending'.

Johnson was born into a working-class London family in 1933, and having left school at sixteen, graduated from King's College, London as a mature student. A strong (often autobiographical) sense of place is apparent in his work, from the precise observations of the area of North London in which Johnson lived in *Albert Angelo*, to a sometimes affectionate portrait of Hammersmith (where he grew up) in *Christy Malry's Own Double-Entry*.

For Johnson, the great nineteenth century realist novel had had its day, and his work was committed to revealing the artificiality of the traditional novel. This commitment to what he saw as the 'truth' of story-telling resulted in a fierce autobiographical core to his 'fiction', and also extended to a keen interest in the physical form of his works.

Frustration at the constraint of a fixed linear narrative imposed by bound pages led to the publication of *The Unfortunates* as a series of loose leaves in a box; whilst the unusual typographical layout of *House Mother Normal* allowed each character's thoughts to be experienced simultaneously in a series of vertical columns on the page. Such invention caused confusion to the traditional gate-keepers of literature: book-sellers reportedly sent back copies of *Albert Angelo* (which features a hole cut into the pages), while librarians were known to have carefully rebound the loose leaves of *The Unfortunates*.

Johnson also worked in theatre, film, television, and published two volumes of poetry, but commercial success was limited during his lifetime – to his great disappointment. In the years since his early death in 1973, however, he has developed a growing following, and his reputation as 'Britain's one-man literary avant-garde of the 1960s' was confirmed by Jonathan Coe's acclaimed biography, *Like a Fiery Elephant* (2004).

A photograph of B. S. Johnson taken by Mark Gerson.

Opposite: *Albert Angelo* was partly based on B. S. Johnson's experiences as a supply teacher in North London, and includes exact transcripts of exercises that Johnson set his pupils. The illustration is of the famous hole cut into the pages of the book, which allows the reader to anticipate a future event in the novel.

"Kindly get stuffed," said the waitress.

"Only time I did touch them, hurt them," Albert resumed, "was today, for the first time. I was giving a bloody brilliant lesson on architecture — it was brilliant, too — and the bastards still weren't paying attention and still mucked about, and I lost my temper and said they were a lot of peasants. That they resented, being called peasants, that touched them, that hurt them. They copied chunks out of the Bible for the rest of the lesson, and I could feel the resentment in the room. It wasn't the copying out of the Bible, I'm sure, they probably hated that less than me rabbetting on about architecture, but being called peasants. Perhaps it has country bumpkin associations for London kids. Strange that it should be the only thing to touch them. But you know what I've decided to do in the last few days of term? I'm going to give them time and paper to write down exactly what they feel about me, with a guarantee that there will be no complaints or recriminations from me, whatever they say. This I hope will work out their hatred of me without it actually needing to come to violence. How about that for an idea, then?"

3 leaves ?

*   *   *   *   *

N.B. Holes pp. 142-145. To achieve this effect, the matter will be cut or added to as demanded by the printing. Extra matter (or a space) will be provided to show through left-hand pages.

(to a depth of two inches) from which he died instantly.
Christopher Marlowe, Poet, February 1564 to May 1593.

Holes to come at bottom of page as indicated.

Jean Rhys
1890–1979

Ella Gwendolen Rees Williams (who published under the pseudonym Jean Rhys) was born in Dominica in 1890. Her father was a Welsh doctor and her mother a Creole of Scottish extraction. Hoping to develop a career on the stage, she entered the Academy of Dramatic Art in London in 1909, although she was withdrawn after only two terms on account of failing to lose her Caribbean accent. She subsequently found work as a chorus girl and a film extra, experiences on which she later drew in her fiction.

In 1919 Rhys married Willem Johan Marie (Jean) Lenglet, a Dutch journalist and writer, and for the next decade lived a nomadic existence on the Continent. Encouraged by Ford Madox Ford (who became her patron and later her lover), in 1927 she published her first collection of short stories, *The Left Bank: Sketches and Studies of Present-day Bohemian Paris*. Rhys had already begun to develop her own stream of consciousness technique, a fragmented narrative style that continually shifts between past and present and merges the primary voice of the narrator with a multitude of other voices.

The novels Rhys published over the following decade – *Quartet* (1928), *After Leaving Mr Mackenzie* (1930), *Voyage in the Dark* (1934) and *Good Morning, Midnight* (1939) – attracted a mixed critical reception. Although praised for their exquisite artistry, her treatment of the darker side of sexual relationships proved challenging for some readers. All four novels portray displaced women who exist precariously on the margins of respectable society. Questions of race and gender, a preoccupation with the figure of the outsider, and the workings of power recur and are developed throughout her work.

After 1939, Rhys's books went out of print and she disappeared completely from public view. Nearly twenty years later she was re-discovered (living a largely reclusive life in the West Country), and in 1966 she published *Wide Sargasso Sea*, which brought her international acclaim. Set in the West Indies shortly after the abolition of slavery, the novel tells the story of Antoinette Bertha Cosway, a young Creole heiress who becomes the mad Mrs Rochester in Charlotte Brontë's *Jane Eyre*. Her final collection of short stories, *Sleep It Off Lady*, appeared in 1976, and *Smile Please*, her unfinished autobiography, was published posthumously in 1979.

A photographic portrait of Jean Rhys by the celebrated photographer Fay Godwin.

Opposite: A page from the draft of the beginning of Part Two of *Wide Sargasso Sea*. Published in 1966, Rhys had begun work on the novel during the 1930s and only completed it after much revision and agonized rejection of earlier versions. At the end of the draft of the final chapter of this section, she has noted plaintively: 'The rest of the book can be dictated. I will get it done somehow.'

Part II
Continuation of Chapter IV
to be inserted after "I dont say nothing Reslie"
Space

A large table covered with a red fringed cloth made the
small room seem hotter - the only window was shut.
'I put your chair near the door' Daniel said 'a breeze
comes from underneath.' But there was no breeze .
not a breath of air .

'When I hear you coming I take a good shot of rum'
'and then I take a glass of water to cool me down', but it dont
cool me down it run out of my eyes in tears & lamentations

'Why you dont give me an answer when I write to you
the first time' he went on talking without waiting for
an answer, his eyes fixed on a framed text hanging on the
dirty white wall 'Vengeance is Mine' 'You take too long
Dad' he told it.' I hurry you up a bit'. then he wiped
his thin yellow face & blew his nose on a corner of the
tablecloth .

'They call me Daniel' he said, still not looking at me
'But my name is Esau. & All I get is curses & get outs
from that same devil my father. My father old Cosway,
with his white marble tablet in the English church at
Spanish town for all to see. It have a crest cut & a motto
in Latin & words big black letters I never know such lies.
I hope that stone tie round his neck & drag him down to
hell in the end 'Pious' they write up, Beloved by all -
Not a word about the people he buy & sell like cattle .
'Merciful to the weak' they write up. Mercy! The man
have a heart like stone . Sometimes when he get sick
of a woman which is quickly he give her like his first
my mother, even he give her a hut & a bit of land for
herself (a ja'din some call that) but it is no mercy, its

Angela Carter
1940–1992

Angela Carter's work mixes elements of Gothic fantasy, fairytale and science fiction, and her oeuvre ranges across short stories and novels, poetry and non-fiction. She is particularly remembered for *The Bloody Chamber* (1979), her re-worked collection of traditional fairy tales, and for her two late novels *Nights at the Circus* (1984) and *Wise Children* (1991).

Born in Eastbourne, Carter's first novel, *Shadow Dance* (sometimes reprinted as *Honeybuzzard*), was published when she was a student at Bristol University in 1966. She published a further two novels, *The Magic Toyshop* (1967) and *Several Perceptions* (1968), before moving to Japan in 1969. The time that Carter spent in Japan had a definite impact upon her development as a writer, and her portrayal of the foreignness of English and Western culture stems from her early experiences in an environment so different to her own. The influence of Japan can be seen in the semi-autobiographical collection of short stories, *Fireworks* (1974), and in her journalism, which included an attack on sado-masochistic comic books that was later expanded into *The Sadeian Woman*.

A lifelong cinema fan, Carter was influenced by European cinema and French surrealism. Theatre, music halls and circuses figure in her last two novels, *Nights at the Circus* (1984) and *Wise Children* (1991). In *Wise Children*, Carter explored the demise of British imperial power and the decline of theatre through the lives of Dora and Leonora Chance, music hall performers and the illegitimate twin daughters of the great Shakespearean actor, Sir Melchior Hazard. The novel's narrator, Dora Chance, laments the societal changes that she sees around her, regretting the loss of London institutions such as the Lyons Corner houses. The novel has a mock Shakespearean plot, which includes disguises, false trails, a search for parentage and no less than four sets of twins. As Carter herself explains in notes that she made in preparation for the novel, it is a 'comic family saga that … [uses] the theatre, both legitimate and vaudeville, and the plays of Shakespeare, as a metaphor for some aspects of British Society in the last century'.

A photographic portrait of Angela Carter by Fay Godwin.

Opposite: This early draft of chapter one of *Wise Children* shows Carter's careful re-working of the text as she sought to find the correct tone for Dora's narration. Carter's archive held at the British Library includes working notes and multiple drafts for almost all her literary works.

<u>Wise Children</u>: One.

~~Overture & beginners~~

Why is London like Budapest? Because it is two cities divided by a river.

*

You used to be able to make a crude distinction - the rich lived on the North bank, amongst pleasant verdure with abundant public transport, & the poor lived on the South bank in circumstances of arid deprivation, condemned, x to wait for hours at windswept bus stops whilst partially feral cats marauded dustbins & the sounds of marital violence made the night hideous. ~~as they echoed through the~~ Things are more complicated, now; ~~the Thames~~ "posts" the division a little less clearcut - there's been a diaspora of the affluent, they've scattered all ~~over~~ over the city, that's what happens when property values go through the roof, ~~isn't it~~ And what does the robin do then, poor thing.

Bugger the robin. x If our mum hadn't had the sense to buy this house, knock down price, during the Blitz, ~~if she hadn't~~ we'd be ~~put~~ on the streets now, Nora & me, pushing our worldlies up & down on supermarket trollies, reduced to sucking on the bottle for comfort like babes unweaned x & no doubt intermittently bursting into uninvited song xx when finally allowed admittance to the night shelter & so chucked out to freeze on the midnight street again. That's the apolyptic scenario, of course; bt we always knew we had the house to fall back on, see, so we never bothered to put a bit away. Easy come, easy go, that was the motto of the Chance girls. The "Lucky Chances." x when our giros came in
xx out of pure joy & relief *
x if they wanted release from the transpontine limbo

Ted Hughes
1930–1998

The poet, Edward James (Ted) Hughes was one of the most influential literary figures of post-war Britain. His verse challenged the studied indolence and urbanity which had come to define the poetic voice of the post-war generation.

Born in Yorkshire, whose tough, unforgiving landscape remained a lasting influence in his work, Hughes emerged as a major poetic force with his first collection *The Hawk in the Rain*. This appeared in 1957, the year after Hughes married the American-born poet, Sylvia Plath. The couple's relationship, and particularly Plath's death in 1963, inspired controversy in the decades that followed; Hughes's life was further overshadowed by tragedy in 1969 with the deaths of his partner Assia Wevill, the couple's daughter Shura, and Hughes's mother. The publication in 1970 of Hughes's dark allegorical poetic vision, *Crow*, without the redemptive elements that he had originally planned, may be seen in part as a result of this.

Hughes's oeuvre was rich and diverse, ranging as it did from poetry such as *Crow* and *Remains of Elmet*, an exploration of the Calder Valley of his childhood, to his work for children including *The Iron Man*. Theatre collaborations with Peter Brook and others, translations of classical texts and foreign poetry, and his term as Poet Laureate (he succeeded John Betjeman in 1984) brought Hughes's work to a still wider audience. However it was his last major collection, *Birthday Letters*, that was published to the greatest public and critical acclaim in 1998.

In the eighty-eight poems that make up *Birthday Letters*, Hughes explored his relationship with Sylvia Plath, often addressing her directly. In 'Your Visit' he writes 'You are ten years dead. It is only a story./Your story. My story'. Drafts, correspondence, and associated material in the British Library's Hughes archive provide a unique insight into the creation of the collection, from earliest jottings through to discussions with publishers. In particular, they provide an insight into the conception of the poems, which began as a 'written conversation' with Plath as early as the 1970s.

The acquisition of the final portion of the Hughes archive by the British Library in 2008 built upon literary drafts purchased in the 1960s, and collections of correspondence with important figures such as Olwyn Hughes and Leonard Baskin. Such collections have made the Library an important centre for Hughes scholarship.

Fay Godwin's photographic portrait of Ted Hughes.

Opposition: The draft shown here from the *Birthday Letters* material is an early, untitled version of 'Fulbright Scholars', written in a school exercise book.

Stopping, in the Strand, I saw a picture

~~Stopping, in the Strand, I studied~~

I

Where was it, in the Strand?
Somewhere near it. A display
Of news-items in photographs.
For some reason I noticed it.
A picture of that year's intake
Of Fulbright scholars. Or some of them.
Were you there? I studied it,
Not too minutely, thinking
Which of them might I meet?
I remember the thought. Not
Your face. No doubt I scanned particularly
The girls. Maybe I noticed you.
Maybe I weighed you up, feeling unlikely.
Looked at your loop hair, loose waves ——
It would appear blonde —— and your grin.
Your ~~exaggerated~~ American ~~smile~~ grin.
Then I forgot. ~~Yet~~ I remember
The picture, the Fulbright scholars,
With their luggage. I was walking
Sore-footed, in hot sun, hot pavements.
Was it then I bought the peach?   Now is still
In the Strand, near Charing Cross Station,
The first fresh peach I ever tasted.
At twenty five I was ~~dumb~~founded afresh
~~With~~by my ignorance of the simplest things.

J. G. Ballard
1930–2009

James Graham Ballard was born in Shanghai in 1930. He grew up in an affluent expatriate bubble with Chinese servants and an American car, a Packard, in which he was chauffeured daily to the Cathedral School. But the city's teeming lawlessness and destitute poor were never far away, and a curious, young Ballard would secretly explore the city on his bicycle. In 1943, however, life changed abruptly when the occupying Japanese army interned Shanghai's international community, and the Ballard family was confined in Lunghua Camp for more than two years. The author's adolescent experiences provided the raw material for *Empire of the Sun* (1984), Ballard's most acclaimed novel, and the self-acknowledged emotional centre of his work.

Immediately after the war, Ballard continued his education in England as a boarder at the Lees School in Cambridge. Compared to Shanghai, post-war England seemed grey and pinched, and bore no resemblance to the country he had imagined. He was later to remark: 'as a writer I've treated England as if it were a strange fiction'. In 1956, Ballard published his first science fiction stories, developing a distinctive style that owed much to his interests in surrealism and human psychology. His early novels turned the familiar formula of the cosy catastrophe on its head: the protagonists of *The Drowned World* (1962), *The Burning World* (1964) and *The Crystal World* (1966) do not overcome the destructive forces that threaten; they embrace them.

In the mid-1960s, Ballard's writing took an experimental turn, and *The Atrocity Exhibition* (1970) collected a number of shorter works in this vein. He then turned his imagination upon the 'strange fiction' of contemporary England, publishing in quick succession *Crash* (1973), *Concrete Island* (1974) and *High Rise* (1975). In *The Kindness of Women* (1991), an autobiographical sequel to *Empire of the Sun*, Ballard further shaped his public persona, drawing out the patterns of deep metaphorical connectedness that mark his writing. His final sequence of novels subverted yet another popular genre: detective fiction. The central characters in *Cocaine Nights* (1996), *Super-Cannes* (2000), *Millennium People* (2003) and *Kingdom Come* (2006) follow chains of clues that lead only to themselves; to the gradual recognition, that is, of a psychological and complicit affinity between the pursuer and the pursued.

A photographic portrait of J. G. Ballard by Fay Godwin.

Opposite: The British Library was allocated the archive of J. G. Ballard under the Acceptance in Lieu scheme in 2010. The archive contains two drafts of *Crash*, the earliest of which is intensively revised on the front and back of almost every sheet of paper. The novel's dark and erotic conjunction of celebrity (Elizabeth Taylor), consumerism and fatal car crashes evoked Andy Warhol's *Death and Disaster* (1962-64), Reyner Banham's paean to *Los Angeles* (1971), and the silver-finned American cars of Ballard's Shanghai boyhood.

machine sprung from a trap. An hour later
at his body under the police arc-lights.
The grotesque postures of his legs and arms, and the
face, to the soft palate reminded me of the
wounds he had collected in his gallery, the photographs of
crash injuries, that covered the walls of his apartment. I looked
down at his penis. Engorged with blood, his penis had become
inflated to twice its erect size. Ten yards away, the film
actress stood below the revolving light, trembling on the arm
of her chauffeur whinnying before a dead
Vaughan had died at the moment of orgasm.
Before this Vaughan had been involved in many crashes.
When I think of Vaughan now I see him two months earlier at
the foot of the flyover, in a rehearsal of his own death. A young
man and woman were being helped from their car by
drivers who had stopped. My first sight of
Vaughan was through the fractured windshield of the heavy saloon
car. His white face, with its eyes and slack mouth,
was lit by broken rainbows. I pulled the dented door
frame. He sat motionlessly on the broad seat, hands at his
sides covered with blood from his injured kneecaps. Vomit stained
the lapels of his leather jacket,
across the steering column and
instrument panel. His buttocks were clamped together
as if they had seized while the last drop from his vesicles.
Before he would allow me to move him
the zip of his trousers. Scattered on the floor beside him
were the photographs of the death-crashes of Jayne Mansfield and
James Dean which I had reproduced for him that morning at my
office.
For Vaughan the car-crash and his own sexuality had
a final marriage, the logic of that strange eroticism which
carried him to his death over the railing of the flyover.
I remember him with the
the crushed rear compartments of wrecked cars in used-car lots,
and the photographs of these young women in the grotesque
postures of intercourse, their tight faces and uncomfortable
thighs lit up by his polaroid flash like the startled
survivors of some submarine disaster. These strange young women
seemed cousins of those in the gallery of crash injury
photographs which Vaughan collected. Vaughan was fascinated
by the buboes of gas bacillus infections that ballooned in
bubbles on the legs of injured young women, facial

Dame Beryl Bainbridge
1934–2010

Having been shortlisted for the Booker Prize on five occasions without winning, in 2011 Beryl Bainbridge was posthumously awarded a special Booker 'Best of Beryl' Prize for her 1998 novel, *Master Georgie*.

Bainbridge grew up in Formby, Lancashire, and was educated at the Merchant Taylors' School in Liverpool. She began her career as an assistant stage manager at the Liverpool Playhouse, where she subsequently acted, and later performed at a number of repertory theatres around Britain. After the collapse of her short marriage to the painter Austin Davies, Bainbridge moved to Camden, North London in the early 1960s, where she lived for the rest of her life. She was awarded a DBE in 2000.

Bainbridge's literary career began with the publication of *A Weekend with Claude* in 1967, although her first novel, written during the 1950s, was *Harriet Said*, which failed to find a publisher until 1972. While many of her earlier novels were autobiographical in character, from the late 1970s the novels took historical settings. Among these are *Every Man for Himself* (1996), which takes place on board the *Titanic*, and *According to Queeney* (2000), which explores the relationship of Samuel Johnson and Hester Thrale. Bainbridge adopted a thorough – if on occasion idiosyncratic – approach to research: while working on her 1984 novel *Watson's Apology*, which reconstructs a real life murder committed by a Victorian clergyman, she went to the Isle of Wight and lay on the vicar's grave, in the hope of receiving a message from the body below.

As well as numerous works for stage and screen, Bainbridge produced some memorable work for television, notably two series in which she travelled across England: *English Journey* (1984) in which she followed in the footsteps of J.B.Priestley; and *Forever England* (1986), which explored the differences between the north and south of the country.

Bainbridge's writing is characterised by its sparseness and economy of style, as well as its black comedy that sometimes verges on the macabre. Populated by a cast of eccentric characters who lead unstable, distorted and suffocated lives, her novels juxtapose the mundane and the absurd and show up the violence beneath the surface of daily existence. A pervasive idea in her writing is succinctly articulated by the narrator of *Watson's Apology*: 'Tragedy, though hard to contend with, was an affirmation of life'.

Dame Beryl Bainbridge at the Poetry Olympics festival, London, c. 2000.

Opposite: A page from Bainbridge's first published novel, *A Weekend with Claude* (1967). Bainbridge was a ruthless editor of her own writing, composing 20 or so pages and then cutting mercilessly until she was left with only a few paragraphs.

A weekend with Claude

~~as of tea~~ ~~Just a moment my lamb~~

Kneeling as he was Claude felt the photograph in his
pocket stiff against his skin, and beneath that his
heart beating, beating rather rapidly with the effort
of stooping. It didnot seem such a long time since he had been
young, or younger, since he had been two stones lighter
since his wife had gone away: She had walked so deliberately
out of the shop door, and yet he could not believe she would go without even a coat
~~without a coat even~~, and he had followed her
down the street to the bridge, ~~over which she crossed~~, and then stopped
and watched her walk away from him over the
river, her hands by her sides. He had remembered
that when he first ~~met her~~ had seen her it had been by a river, and she
had been sitting in the grass ~~with~~ in a dress with a collar that did not quite fit ~~yellow hair hanging onto~~
~~her shoulders~~, and he had thought I will make you my
wife. It was not so much love at first sight, as the
decision of a man who knew a beautiful thing when he
saw it and wanted to own it. For which he had paid,
not in money but in ~~misery~~ unhappiness, because later he had
~~several years and several children later~~, ~~to~~ found
he had never possessed her at all, that she was a stranger
to him. He had been so ill for the year following her
departure over the bridge, out of his ~~life and his~~ reach,
that at he had not been aware of the gradual accumulation
of flesh. ~~It had been almost.~~

Timmy was left standing by the doorway, without contact.
He had the feeling that if he spoke he would get no reply.

However he said — Anything very interesting old man.
And to ~~suck up~~ ~~fill~~ the silence ———— in which Claude went
on unwrapping plates ———— Shall I make out a
cheque for the desk now Mr White.

~~Yes if you~~
Claude had rolled up the sleeves of his check shirt and his
enormous squat forearms were ~~stood~~ elbow deep in newspapers.
~~Between his~~ ~~lips he had sucked in a tendril of beard.~~
~~His~~ ~~He did not look up. Yes if you like ~~~~

Sir Tom Stoppard
1937–

Tom Stoppard first came to prominence with his play *Rosencrantz and Guildenstern are Dead*, premiered at the Edinburgh Festival in 1966, and a triumph at the National Theatre in 1967. It introduced audiences to his spectacular verbal dexterity, and his ability to take a familiar or even over-familiar scenario and infuse it with entirely new life.

Over the next fifteen years Stoppard's plays enjoyed almost uninterrupted critical and public acclaim: *Jumpers* (1972), *Travesties* (1974); *Night and Day* (1978), and *The Real Thing* (1982) won between them nine major awards in Britain and the United States, including two Tony awards for the best play of the year.

While Stoppard had consciously avoided serious political and social issues in his early work, by the late 1970s he was deeply involved with human rights issues, especially in relation to the old Soviet Union and the Eastern bloc. In 1977, he met the future Czech president Václav Havel, much of whose writing Stoppard later translated into English.

The citation for one of Stoppard's many awards describes him as 'a master playwright whose plays return repeatedly to the past as part of his ceaseless search for meaning in a bewildering universe', although some of his later plays have been found bewildering in themselves. One writer said of *Arcadia* (1993) that it was 'too clever by about two and three-quarters', but the play was a success with audiences and won three major awards. *Arcadia* is one of three plays represented in the British Library's holdings of Tom Stoppard manuscripts, acquired in 2004. The others are *The Invention of Love* (1997), based on the life and work of the poet and classical scholar A. E. Housman, and his hopeless love for his Oxford friend Moses Jackson, and the trilogy of plays *The Coast of Utopia* (2002), which deals with the origins of modern political radicalism in early-nineteenth-century Russia.

A photographic portrait of Sir Tom Stoppard by Fay Godwin.

A page from Stoppard's research notes for *The Coast of Utopia*, first performed in 2002. The trilogy covers the lives of a group of friends – writers, critics, and political philosophers – who live in Russia during the reign of Tsar Nicholas I, and in these particular notes the author lists in careful detail events taking place at Premukhino, the country estate of the anarchist and philosopher Michael Bakunin, and concurrently in Moscow.

PREMUKHINO   MOSCOW, etc.

1833 —   AUG:
         Michael returns from school aged 19,
         └ Accepts Lyubov's engagement, stays till   by letter
         December. Père pays debts (19)

         [Nicholas's first kiss]

1834   Early in year, Michael expelled — briefly to Prem to say
         Dec: Varvara marries Dyakov.   Goodbye, Varia in   [June, Michael expelled, to Lithuania.
                (22)   June to Lithuania   In Spring, Lyubov met Nicholas in
                                               much older   Moscow.

1835   ★ Jan: Michael "descends" to Prem, stays   [Feb: Michael, Lyubov and Tatiana
from Schilling to   till Feb, to Moscow with Lyubov + Tatiana   to Moscow. Natalie B. matchmakes
Kant (aeco 26)   Michael meets Nicholas.   Lyubov and Nicholas.
to Fichte (31)   March: Lyubov + Tatiana return, Michael   Lyubov + Tatiana return to Prem. March
                                                                      Natalie falls in love with Michael,
                     a week later ... Letters from Natalie (in M's pocket)   who leaves for Prem a week with his
                     affront the sisterhood. Michael declares for   sisters.
                     spiritual love only.

                     Oct: Nicholas comes for ten days, studying
                     Kant with Michael.

                     Nov: Varvara's son born. Michael and Nicholas
                     exchange letters on Kant. Dahin, dahin!

1836   Jan: Michael flees from job arranged by Père. He was   [Michael lodges with Stankevich,
                    terrified of suicide. Letter to Varvara "I recover   meets Belinsky. Stankevich connection (p.67)
         March   Michael's letter to Tatiana.   my periods"   Michael "moth teacher"
Alexandra B. to Prem   ★ Varvara one body at Prem without Dyakov.   (Chaadev Letter?)
                     — Michael campaigns against husband.   Fichte is the new philosophy.
                                                                     Michael's first publication in Telescope
         May Michael returns to Prem. Varvara still there.   St Nicholas to Caucasus for health.
                                                                     Michael and Beyer girls, till April.
         (late)Aug Belinsky to Prem: offends Père,   March Michael's letter to Tatiana.
                    falls for Alexandra: Tatiana fascinated by   April — moth over
                    him: Michael's reaction.   Nov Telescope suppressed.

                     Nov Belinsky leaves when Telescope suppressed,   Michael matchmakes Lyubov +
                     Michael leaves a few days later, with   Nicholas was gree to correspond.
                     Lyubov.   Nov — Nicholas turns to Hegel

         PUSHKIN   write schmittingly to Dyakov
1837   Jan: in Michael's absence, Varvara "weakens" on   1837   From Fichte to Hegel,   & in August
         Dyakov. Bakunin writes ("carnal").   April: Nicholas proposes, flees
         Spring: Dyakov at Prem Varvara turns again.   to Germany via family estate. April
         April: Lyubov receives Nicholas's proposal. (Varvara was   summer Belinsky to Caucasus. When
         └ June: Michael to Prem, till Autumn.   takes him to Germany)   he returns he studies Hegel with
                                                                     Katkov fell Michael anyway
         Letters from Nicholas to Lyubov in Germany   wrote to Michael in June (p.62)
Michael — summer   continue through winter from spas. Also
and autumn at Prem: letters from Belinsky, the first result. — Nov, M writes   1837 Deep: Moved about 1838, Belinsky back
plotting V. trip   Michael studies (Hegel)   * confession to Belinsky   from Caucasus, in frenzyments.
abroad.   Varvara backtracks, urges Dyakov, wants to   Feb — Nicholas writes to M, money short.
                     go abroad for summer. Lack of funds. Père   1838 Michael back to Moscow + Beyers
                     banishes Michael — December. (Letter to Moscow)   Feb. Michael + Belinsky study Hegel
                     Dec 31 month's letter to Père.   March: "Moscow Observer" —
                                                                     Belinsky and Michael rapture.
1838   Spring: Lyubov dying.   Jan: Michael near Prem, intriguing for Botkin values picture — Michael's
         Feb-March — Nicholas's letter to money, i.e. loans   Varvara   disciple. Belinsky declares
         to Michael for trip to Germany. Père rebels, to   independence.
Michael: to Prem   Varvara's going forced by husband's brother.
May (?)— closer to Lyubov (sc) June: Varvara leaves. Alexandra + Tatiana to Moscow, June
— the brothers.   July: Belinsky + Botkin to Prem.   Belinsky friendship continues he
                     Aug: Lyubov dies.   is invited back to Prem — but
                     Sept: the Belinsky letters to Michael from the bridges   back in Moscow he writes that M.
                                                                    has ruined his sisters' happiness.
1839   Michael in Prem till July   Dec. Michael briefly in Moscow
                                                                    annoys Belinsky

         Dec: Turgenev + Tatiana. Alexandra   July — Oct Michael in St P. —
                                                                    Maria Ogarev. Katkov.
1841   1840   ♠ March ♠♠ writes to Père for money. Aunt Hergon
                            1840 Michael to Berlin — July
                                 June — Nicholas died.

Graham Swift
1949–

Graham Swift was born in south London, an area that has provided the settings for many of his novels. Swift had already published *The Sweet Shop Owner* (1980) and *Shuttlecock* (1981) before the critical and popular success of *Waterland* (1983) brought his work to the attention of a wider audience.

Swift's narratives often take the form of a first-person interior monologue that moves back and forth across time, recalling events from the past that reach into the present with unforeseen but seemingly inevitable consequences. *The Sweet Shop Owner* is the story of the final twenty-four hours of a man who lives in the shadow of a past that is gradually revealed in flashbacks. In *Tomorrow* (2007), a woman spends the night thinking back over her life, preparing for the moment when a long-suppressed family secret will be revealed to her twin children. In *Waterland*, Tom Crick, a history teacher facing enforced retirement for reasons that slowly unravel, re-animates his school subject – in this novel, the monologue is a classroom performance – by telling stories of the Fens, its landscape and its natural and supernatural history, and the troubled and intertwined generational history of the Cricks and the Atkinsons. In Swift's most recent novel, *Wish You Were Here* (2011), Jack Luxton waits ominously (for the duration of the novel) with a loaded shotgun and a headful of unresolved family history for his wife to return.

Like *The Sweet Shop Owner*, *Last Orders* (1996) is framed by a single day. A group of friends journey from Bermondsey, via Chatham and Canterbury, to Margate, to scatter the ashes of butcher Jack Dodds. The novel is a mosaic of first-person memories spoken in a medley of east London voices, multiple perspectives on shared, and concealed, personal histories. The novel touches upon the larger currents of history and human affairs within the smaller turns of ordinary lives, and within the bounds of a colloquial eloquence. *Last Orders* begins with the observation 'It aint like your regular sort of day'. The author subsequently remarked: 'With *Last Orders* something happened which made the language different. I think it was to do with trusting, more than I ever had done, so-called ordinary language – the language of people who you could say, wrongly, aren't so articulate'.

A photograph of Graham Swift by Ekko von Schwichow.

'About the Fens', a draft page from the manuscript of *Waterland*: 'The Fens were formed by silt [...] a slow, sly, insinuating agency'.

[Needs thinning & condensing to avoid
repetitions & complexity — the thematic elements
need clarifying — 'the "how", why']

// About the Fens
??? (and a lot else)

which are a low-lying region of eastern England, over 1,000
square miles in area, bounded to the North and West by
the limestone hills of the Midlands and to the south and east
by the chalk hills of Cambridgeshire, Suffolk and Norfolk. To the
North the Fens advance, on a twelve mile front, to meet the North
Sea at the Wash; or perhaps it is fair to say that the Wash
recaptures the North Sea in a perpetual bid to recapture
its former territory. For the chief point about the Fens is that they
are reclaimed land, land that once was sea. And even today
the (new) dry land of the Fens still threatens to revert to its
former state.

Once the shallow, fickle waters of the Wash had out-stripped
of Boston and King's Lynn — but licked southwards as far as
Cambridge and Bedford. What caused them to retreat? The answer
can be given in one word: silt. The Fens were formed by silt. Silt:
a word which, as you utter it, like the mud itself, seems to linger between
your teeth, slow, tedious and insinuating — a word which (are you listening, S.?) marks and disputes
history. For long before the Egyptians built the pyramids or the
Greeks besieged the Persians at Marathon, silt was imperceptibly
changing the shape of coastlines and the course of rivers and
making dry land where no land was before. And what is all the
noble play-acting of history compared to the slow, muddy reality
of silt, to the silent shifting and forming of particle
after particle, by which continents are remodelled? Silt which
is neither progress nor decay; which
meant simultaneous erosion and accumulation. A sobering
subject for any man; but one which — since the house in
which he was born owed its solid foundations to silt — occupies a
special place in your history — no this mental landscape(s). which is
even synonymous, in his private vocabulary, with Time.

It came first from the coast of Yorkshire and Lincolnshire,
borne on the sea-currents which flowed southwards into the ancient
Wash. In the Blue-Black clay which lies under the soil between
Ely and Cambridge are deposits of silt containing shells similar

Wendy Cope
1945–

From the immediate success of her debut collection *Making Cocoa for Kingsley Amis* (1986), Wendy Cope has established herself as one of Britain's best-loved and bestselling poets. The emotional integrity of Cope's writing and her unflinching eye for the absurdities, as well as the intensity, of quotidian experience – particularly in the arena of romantic relationships – have allowed her to connect with an extremely wide and diverse readership. In 1998 many people believed she would succeed Ted Hughes as Poet Laureate (Andrew Motion was eventually appointed). Although she has at times divided critical opinion – and her relationship with the poetry world has not always been a happy one – she is widely recognised as an original and significant voice, and has been described as the rightful heir to Philip Larkin. Alongside an unparalleled formal mastery, there is an important feminist dynamic at play in her work, particularly apparent in her well-known parodies of established male literary figures such as T.S. Eliot, Ted Hughes and Seamus Heaney.

Born in Kent in 1945, Cope read History at Oxford University and worked for nearly twenty years as a primary school teacher in London before deciding to become a full-time writer. Her subsequent poetry collections include *Serious Concerns* (1992), *If I Don't Know* (2001), *Two Cures for Love* (2008) and *Family Values* (2011). She has also published numerous works for children including *The River Girl* (1991), a long narrative poem commissioned by a marionette company and originally performed on a theatre barge. Cope is a staunch defender of authors' rights and a vociferous contributor to the debate on copyright. She was awarded an OBE in 2010.

Cope's wit and her gift of connecting with others on a profound level through the use of humour distinguish her writing. Keen to emphasise that comic writing can be complex and nuanced, and also to reject what she regards as a tendency towards ostentatious expression in some modern poets, Cope has stated: 'I believe that a humorous poem can also be "serious" – i.e. deeply felt and saying something that matters'. Such striving towards authenticity of emotion and expression, which she regards as the primary business of poetry, is everywhere evident in her oeuvre.

A photographic portrait of Wendy Cope by Adrian Harvey.

Opposite: This is a page from a 1984 poetry notebook of Wendy Cope. It shows drafts of parodies of two of the most famous poems of the Romantic period, Wordsworth's 'Immortality Ode' and Shelley's 'To a Skylark'. The British Library acquired her archive in 2011.

Wordsworth: Ode on Intimations of Immortality

From recollections of early childhood.

To a mite
Things look bright.
Later on
Glory gone.
Still, must say
I'm OK —
Wise old sort,
Into thought.

Shelley: To a Skylark.   17/3/84

~~Is it a bird?~~
~~I~~ Art thou a bird?
Art thou a spirit?

In vain
Like a poet   Art thou a bird?
a maiden   Whither a spirit?
a stream   So Unseen but heard
more

Is it a bird?
Is it a spirite?
This is absurd —
Cut out it anyway.

Further Reading

M. H. Abrams and Stephen Greenblatt, eds, *The Norton Anthology of English Literature* (New York and London, 2001)

Alexandra Barratt, ed., *Women's Writing in Middle English* (London and New York, 1992)

Michelle P. Brown, *Anglo-Saxon Manuscripts* (London, 1991)

Sally Brown and Hilton Kelliher, *English Literary Manuscripts* (London, 1986)

John Burrow, ed., *English Verse 1300–1500* (London and New York, 1977)

John Burrow and Thorlac Turville-Petre, eds, *A Book of Middle English Verse* (Oxford, 1992)

P. J. Croft, *Autograph Poetry in the English Language*, two volumes (London, 1973)

Margaret Drabble, ed., *The Oxford Companion to English Literature* (Oxford, 1985)

Philip. R. Harris, *A History of the British Museum Library 1753–1973* (London, 1998)

The Index of English Literary Manuscripts 1450–1900, volumes 1–4 (London and New York, 1980–)

Location Register of Twentieth-Century English Literary Manuscripts and Letters, two volumes (London, 1988)

Location Register of Eighteenth- and Nineteenth-Century English Literary Manuscripts and Letters, two volumes (London, 1995)

Arthur F. Marotti, *Manuscript, Print and The English Renaissance Lyric* (Ithaca, 1995)

Ian Ousby, ed., *Cambridge Guide to Literature in English* (Cambridge, 1988)

Rodney Phillips, *The Hand of the Poet* (New York, 1997)

Andrew Prescott and Elizabeth Hallam, eds, *The British Inheritance: A Treasury of Historic Documents* (London, 1999)

Michael Swanton, *English Poetry before Chaucer* (Exeter, 2002)

'What Will Survive of us are Manuscripts: Collecting the Literary Papers of Living British Writers', *Oxford Journal of the History of Collections*, 20:2 (2008), pp. 250-272

Robert Woof, Stephen Hebron and Pamela Woof, *English Poetry 850–1850: The First Thousand Years, with some Romantic Perspectives* (Grasmere, 2000)

Acknowledgements

This book would not have been possible without the help of numerous friends and colleagues. Of those closely involved in bringing it to light I must offer particular thanks to David Way, Peter Way, Lara Speicher, Kathleen Houghton, Charlotte Lochhead, Belinda Wilkinson, Andrew Shoolbred, Natasha Kornilof and Laurence Pordes. For their encouragement and advice, I thank my colleagues Hilton Kelliher, Claire Breay, John Rhatigan, Andrew Prescott, Ann Payne, Hugh Cobbe, John Tuck, Christopher Wright, Michelle Brown, Rachel Stockdale, Jacqui Hunt, Greg Buzwell, Alixe Bovey and Jennie Patrice. The greatest debt of gratitude goes to my excellent contributors Sally Brown and, in particular, Roger Evans, who not only contributed many of the articles but also made special trips to take photographs for the book and undertook valuable picture research and careful reading of the text.

Jamie Andrews wishes to thank his colleagues in the English and Drama department at the British Library for their contributions: Chris Beckett, Steve Cleary, Rachel Foss, Duncan Heyes, Kathryn Johnson, Helen Melody, Tanya Kirk and Zoe Wilcox.

Picture Credits

All pictures are copyright the British Library except where noted otherwise. Pictures are listed in order of use from left-hand to right-hand page and from top to bottom. All effort has been made to contact copyright holders. We apologise for any omissions.

'BEOWULF': Cotton MS Vitellius A XV ff. 175v and 132; WULFSTAN: Stowe MS 944 f. 6: translation courtesy of The Electronic Sermo Lupi ad Anglos, Melissa J Bernstein, University of Rochester, Cotton MS Nero A I f. 110; 'HARLEY LYRICS': British Museum, Harley MS 2253 ff. 71v; 'SIR ORFEO': Yates Thompson MS 13 f. 62, Harley MS 3810 f. 4; LANGLAND: C99.f. 10 p. 6, Cotton MS Vespasian B XVI f. 9; 'THE GAWAIN POET': Cotton MS Nero A X ff. 42, and 43; GOWER: Roger Evans (portrait by kind permission of the Dean and Chapter of Southwark Cathedral), Harley MS 7184 f. 59v; CHAUCER: Lansdowne MS 851 f. 2 detail and f. 2, Harley MS 4866 f. 88 detail, C43h.19 prologue; THE 'SLOANE LYRICS': British Museum, Sloane MS 2593 f. 10v; KEMPE: Additional MS 29704 f. 192, Additional MS 61823 f. 3v; D'ORLEANS: Royal MS 16 F II f. 73, Harley MS 682 f. 88v; MALORY: G10510, Additional MS 59678 f. 35; HENRYSON: Harley MS 3865 f. 4, Harley MS 3865 f. 3v; WYATT: C117.aa.3, Egerton MS 2711 f. 69v; ANDREWES: British Museum, Harley MS 6994 f. 179; HARRINGTON: C70.g.1, Additional MS 18920 f. 46; PEELE: 840.i.33, Additional MS 21432 f. 7; SHAKESPEARE: C39.k.15, Harley MS 7368 f. 9, Egerton MS 1787, Sloane MS 2596 f. 52; RALEGH: 9005.h.2, Additional MS 57555 f. 172v; JONSON: G11630, Royal MS 18 A. XLV f. 2v; GREVILLE: 1765.c.17 Vol. 1, Additional MS 54570 f. 56; HERRICK: 11630.ee.38, Harley MS 367 f. 154; MASSINGER: 628.b.18 Vol. 1, Egerton MS 2428 f. 20; MILTON: Additional MS 34816 f. 353, Additional MS 36354 f. 55v; BROWNE: C118.g.1, Sloane MS 1862 f. 48; DRYDEN: 11771.aaa.4, Lansdowne MS 1045 f. 101; PHILIPS: 83.l.3, Additional MS 78234;

TRAHERNE: Chris Fletcher, Additional MS 63054 f. 164v; BUTLER: 12270.a.10, Additional MS 32625 f. 79; SWIFT: 1509/1192 frontispiece, Additional MS 39839 f. 35; POPE: 11630.aa.46, Additional MS 4808 f. 16; RAMSAY: Hirsch III 1003, Egerton MS 2023 f. 66v; DEFOE: G13274 Vol. 1, Additional MS 32555 f. 10; MONTAGU: 1568/5378, Additional MS 61479 f. 127; RICHARDSON: 12614.h.13, Additional MS 28097 f. 15; STERNE: 1180.a.34 Vol. 1, Egerton MS 1610 f. 60; GRAY: Additional MS 38511 f. 1v, Additional MS 38511 f. 7; JOHNSON: 1568/4058, Additional MS 12070 f. 8; BURNS: 991.b.1 Vol. 1, Egerton MS 1656 f. 30; COWPER: National Portrait Gallery, Additional MS 37059 f. 51; BLAKE: 2290b, Additional MS 49460 f. 56; COLERIDGE: C126.c.10, Additional MS 50847r, Additional MS 47497 f. 4; WORDSWORTH: 1162.l.8, Additional MS 47864 ff. 80; AUSTEN: 10855.e.8 frontispiece, Egerton MS 3038 ff. 9v; KEATS: National Portrait Gallery, Additional MS 37000 f. 1; SHELLEY (Percy): Ashley MS 5249 f. ii, Ashley MS 4086 f. 1; CLARE: 993.b.8 Vol. 1, Additional MS 54224 f. 144; SCOTT: 1765.c.17 Vol. 4, Egerton MS 1661 f. 68; SHELLEY (Mary): 2408.d.3 Vol. 1, Ashley MS A 4023 f. 114; BYRON: British Museum, Ashley MS 4754r; BROWNINGS: 10604.g.10, Additional MS 43487 f. 49, 1203.g.3, Additional MS 43485 f. 1; BRONTE (Emily): National Portrait Gallery, Additional MS 43483 f. 1; BRONTE (Charlotte): 12602.k.8 vol.1, Additional MS 43475 f. 179; BRONTE (Anne): National Portrait Gallery, Ashley MS 154 f. 9; DICKENS: 012612i.8, Additional MS 57493 f. 1, Dexter Collection Vol.3 part 2 129, Additional MS 56083 f. 1; TENNYSON: PP.1931.pcg, Additional MS 45741 f. 279; CARROLL: portrait by permission of the Governing Body of Christ Church, Oxford, Additional MS 46700 f. 19v; LEAR: 01092ff opp. 232, Additional MS 61891 f. 110; ELIOT (George): Ashley MS 712, Additional MS 34034 f. 5; ROSSETTI: 010920 f. 20, Roger Evans, Ashley MS 1376 f. 16; HARDY: 012618.h.27, Additional MS 38182 f. 107; WILDE:

Chariots on Chariots rowl
~~Fly diverse~~ ~~and~~
~~Tost~~ it Shock, while ye madding Ste
In vain they labour ~~up~~ the s
~~for~~ ~~Field~~
& Kings o'erturnd ~~lies~~ fou
Fierce on ~~their~~ ~~heat~~ Rear with
~~The~~ Plains ~~are~~ fill'd ~~innu~~
Thick Drifts of Dust invo
~~The Plains are~~ ^lost^ and
Clouds roll on clouds ~~their~~
Th' affrighted ~~Coursers~~ Chose
~~Fill all the~~ pways, and ^
~~Increase~~ ^ger^ the ~~Rout~~ and the
Loud ~~sounds~~ ^t^ the ~~Tumult~~ ~~rose~~ was hear
Where ye War bleeds, & w
Where ~~Horse~~ & ~~Steed~~ arms,
& bleeding Heroes under ste
No stop, no check, the ~~brid~~ Ste
From ~~Bank~~ ^to Bank^ ~~of~~ ~~Bank~~ ~~Pass~~ th' Imm
High-bounding ^^ oer ye ~~Banks~~
Smoaks ^thro'^ ^the^ ye Plain ~~overy~~ o
& thunders after Victory